THE AUSTRALIAN AIR CAMPAIGN SERIES – 9

CHANGING ALTITUDES

Stories of Australian Air Force Women

The publishing of this book has been funded and managed by History and Heritage – Air Force, Royal Australian Air Force. All enquiries should be made to HH-AF.engagement@defence.gov.au

All inquiries should be made to the publishers.
Big Sky Publishing Pty Ltd
PO Box 303, Newport, NSW 2106, Australia
Phone: 1300 364 611
Email: info@bigskypublishing.com.au
Web: www.bigskypublishing.com.au

Cover design and typesetting by Think Productions, Melbourne

Series: Australian Air Campaign Series; 9

A catalogue record for this book is available from the National Library of Australia

Front cover image: Sergeants Hilary Josephine Benn and Glennie Goodwin Morton, Women's Auxiliary Australian Air Force cinema operators, climbing into an aircraft, 1943 (State Library of Victoria, Argus Collection)

Sergeants Hilary Benn and Glennie Morton were among the first few Women's Auxiliary Australian Air Force servicewomen mustered as cinema operators, which was a diverse role.[1] One day they may have created filmstrips to instruct aircraft recognition, and the next recorded instructional films. Film topics ranged from completing 'the daily inspection of a bomber', to reconditioning spark plugs, to the importance of dental hygiene.[2] Indeed, the RAAF found that moving images were very effective teaching tools because details could be magnified and slow motion used to show even the 'smallest movement'.[3]

As pictured, Hilary and Glennie also frequently worked while airborne, filming bombing experiments or cargo drops, or paratroopers leaping from an adjacent aircraft. Reportedly, Glennie's 'most exciting aerial task was to photograph a fighter attack on a bomber … from the rear gunner's turret of … [the] bomber while a fighter "attacked" it.'[4] Their wartime experiences saw Hilary and Glennie both develop 'a love of the air'.

CONTENTS

ABBREVIATIONS

1BAGS	No 1 Bombing and Gunnery School
1RTU	No 1 Recruit Training Unit
2MRS	No 2 Medical Receiving Station
2TG	No 2 Training Group Headquarters
3CRU	No 3 Control and Reporting Unit
3SQN	No 3 Squadron
33SQN	No 33 Squadron
37SQN	No 37 Squadron
383CRS	No 383 Contingency Response Squadron
5SFTS	No 5 Service Flying Training School
6SQN	No 6 Squadron
76SQN	No 76 Squadron
77SQN	No 77 Squadron
8EFTS	No 8 Elementary Flying Training School
902nd AMES	902nd Aeromedical Evacuation Squadron
AC	Companion of the Order of Australia
ACO	Air Combat Officer
ACSC	Australian Command and Staff Course
ADF	Australian Defence Force
ADFA	Australian Defence Force Academy
ADG	Airfield Defence Guard
AFHQ	Air Force Headquarters
AFL	Australian Football League
AFLW	Australian Football League Women's
AM	Member of the Order of Australia
AMAB	Al Minhad Air Base
AMO	Air Mobility Officer
ANU	Australian National University
AO	Officer of the Order of Australia
ASD	Australian Signals Directorate
ATA	Air Transport Auxiliary

AWLA	Australian Women's Land Army
BBJ	Boeing Business Jet
CAC	Commonwealth Aircraft Corporation
CAF	Chief of Air Force
CAOC	Combined Air Operations Center (US)
CO	Commanding Officer
CREWATT	Crew Attendant
CSC	Conspicuous Service Cross
CWD	Combined Working Dress
CWGC	Commonwealth War Graves Commission
DFC	Distinguished Flying Cross
DFR	Defence Force Recruiting
DI	Drill Instructor
DMT	Driver Motor Transport
DPCU	Disruptive Pattern Camouflage Uniform
DWAAAF	Director of the Women's Auxiliary Australian Air Force
EATS	Empire Air Training Scheme
EDDH	Explosive Detection Dog Handler
EW	Electronic Warfare
GCI	Ground Controlled Interception
GPU	General Purpose Uniform
HADR	Humanitarian Aid and Disaster Relief
HIV	Human Immunodeficiency Virus
HMAS	His/Her Majesty's Australian Ship
HSW	Health Services Wing
IDP	Internally Displaced Persons
IET	Initial Employment Training
LGBTQ+	Lesbian, gay, bisexual, transgender, queer, plus others
MASH	Mobile Army Surgical Hospital
medevac	Medical Evacuation
MO	Medical Officer
MRTF	Mentoring and Reconstruction Task Force
MWD	Military Working Dog
MWDH	Military Working Dog Handler
NCO	Non-Commissioned Officer

NSW	New South Wales
NT	Northern Territory
OAM	Medal of the Order of Australia
OBE	Order of the British Empire
OC	Officer Commanding
OPCON	Operational Conversion
OTS	Officer Training School
PCS	Personnel Capability Specialist
PKF HQ	Peacekeeping Force Headquarters
PNG	Papua New Guinea
Qld	Queensland
RAAF	Royal Australian Air Force
RAAFNS	Royal Australian Air Force Nursing Service (1940–77)
RAF	Royal Air Force
RAN	Royal Australian Navy
RMAF	Royal Malaysian Air Force
RSL	Returned and Services League
SA	South Australia
SDA	Sex Discrimination Act
SFS	Security and Fire School
SPS	School of Post Graduate Studies
SSO	Specialist Services Officer
UAE	United Arab Emirates
UK	United Kingdom
UN	United Nations
US	United States
USAF	United States Air Force
VIP	Very Important Person
WA	Western Australia
WAAAF	Women's Auxiliary Australian Air Force (1941–47)
WATC	Women's Air Training Corps
WRAAF	Women's Royal Australian Air Force (1950–77)

RANKS OF THE AUSTRALIAN WOMEN'S AIR FORCE SERVICES

Star-rank officers

Air Chief Marshal (four-star)
Air Marshal (three-star)
Air Vice-Marshal (two-star)
Air Commodore (one-star)

Officers

Group Captain	(formerly Group Officer for women)
Wing Commander	(formerly Wing Officer for women)
Squadron Leader	(formerly Squadron Officer for women)
Flight Lieutenant	(formerly Flight Officer for women)
Flying Officer	(formerly Section Officer for women)
Pilot Officer	(formerly Assistant Section Officer for Royal Australian Air Force Nursing Service only)

General enlistment ranks

Warrant Officer	
Flight Sergeant	(formerly Senior Section Leader for women)
Sergeant	(formerly Section Leader for women)
Corporal	(formerly Assistant Section Leader for women)
Leading Aircraftwoman	(formerly Aircraftwoman 1st Class for women)
Aircraftwoman	(formerly Aircraftwoman 2nd Class for women)

ABOUT THE CONTRIBUTORS

Air Commodore Kirrily Dearing AM

Kirrily Dearing joined the Royal Australian Air Force (RAAF) as a supply officer (now logistics) through the Australian Defence Force Academy in 1988. Throughout her 34 years of permanent service, Kirrily served at Air Force and joint Defence establishments throughout eastern Australia in both logistics and other roles. She spent three years in Hawaii from 2014 to 2016 as the inaugural liaison officer to the US Pacific Air Forces. She deployed on numerous operational tasks overseas, including to Papua New Guinea, the Solomon Islands and the Middle East, including a deployment to Afghanistan. Kirrily retired from full-time service in March 2022, and now enjoys working on select Reserve opportunities and other work and hobby interests.

Squadron Leader Anna Williams PhD

Anna Williams is a museum curator, educator and social historian. She holds a Master of Arts – Museum Studies and a Doctorate of Philosophy from The University of Sydney. Her multidisciplinary thesis, awarded in 2022, sought to understand the disparities between the artefactual, archival, and written histories of Air Force training in Australia during the Second World War. Anna was appointed as a squadron leader (specialist capability officer) in the RAAF in December 2021. She currently works as a curator for the Royal Australian Navy and holds a reserve position with History and Heritage – Air Force. As an extracurricular activity, Anna enjoys singing for and with military veterans, transporting them to yesteryear with the sweet harmonies of the Second World War-era and beyond with her band Company B. She has a son with whom she shares her love of music, a pet rabbit called George, skiing and weekends kayaking on Sydney Harbour.

Flight Lieutenant Karyn Markwell MA MIntell

Karyn Markwell holds a Master of Publishing from The University of Queensland and a Master of Intelligence from Macquarie University. She joined the RAAF as a reservist in 2015 and has deployed on tasks and exercises to every state and territory of Australia (except Tasmania – but she lives in hope). A lifelong lover of history, she joined History and Heritage – Air Force in 2022. Her other passions include travelling, reading and cheesemaking, with triple-cream brie her specialty.

Flight Lieutenant Fiona Earl PhD

Fiona Earl joined the RAAF Reserves in May 2022, the same year she was awarded her PhD in aviation heritage. Fiona has long enjoyed researching and writing about aviation heritage, especially in Australia's Northern Territory. In 2018, she contributed the first definition of 'aviation archaeology' to the *Encyclopaedia of Global Archaeology*. Her role as a specialist capability officer in History and Heritage – Air Force provides her with a brilliant opportunity to combine her passions for aviation and heritage. Fiona's interest in aviation extends beyond her work and she enjoys flying ultralight aircraft.

Ms Rosalind Turner BHIP

Rosalind (Roz) Turner holds a Bachelor of Historical Inquiry and Practice from the University of New England. She also holds a Certificate IV in Museum Practice and a Diploma of Professional Writing (Editing and Proofreading). She joined Defence as an Australian Public Service trainee in 1989 and worked through various administrative positions before joining the Office of Air Force History in 2005. Having always had an interest in history, she was finally able to pursue her dream and in 2018 became the Deputy Air Force Historian. Roz was project lead on the publication *Then, Now, Always*, produced for the Air Force's Centenary in 2021. She finds leading others in their pursuit of historical research a very rewarding career and became the Executive Officer Historical Research and Reviews for History and Heritage – Air Force in 2023.

SERIES FOREWORD

The Australian Air Campaign Series produced by Air Force's History and Heritage Branch focusses on four themed sub-series:

- Campaigns, operations and battles
- Capability and technology
- Bases and airfields
- People.

These themed titles explore specific facets of the Air Force from its inception in 1921. What they reveal are unique insights, providing the reader with a greater appreciation and deeper understanding of those aspects that have shaped the Air Force's history and heritage.

Importantly, these publications are sourced from official records and research, often including first-hand accounts. While endorsed for studies in military history, the range of topics in these publications provides an ideal conduit for the broadest of audiences to pursue and learn more about the many aspects that have contributed to the development of Australia's Air Force.

Apart from being a significant point of reference, these publications ultimately acknowledge bravery, ingenuity and resilience – in essence, the service and sacrifice which is the hallmark of those who have served and continue to serve in the Air Force.

Robert Lawson OAM
Air Commodore
Director-General History and Heritage – Air Force

PREFACE

Changing Altitudes: Stories of Australian Air Force Women is a collaborative writing effort by a small team of women who proudly represent the Royal Australian Air Force and the Department of Defence. Each of us brought our own skills to the project – writing, communication and research – or lived experience of more than three decades in service and the Department.

The story of each woman has been developed using interviews and transcripts and is therefore a recollection in her own words. Significant research into each decade of service and relevant vignettes provide context around the social and political landscape of the time.

This book captures the unique experiences of women from all backgrounds who joined the Air Force for many reasons, including to serve their nation, to follow in the footsteps of a loved one, to seek a life outside of a small country town, or to pursue adventure. It is merely a snapshot of the stories of thousands of women who have dedicated themselves to the profession of arms. As a result, we pay homage to all women who have served over the decades.

FOREWORD

Over many years, I have had the privilege of meeting Australian women who have proudly worn the uniform of the Air Force and committed to serve their nation in times of peace and war. When I received a request from the Chief of Air Force to play a small role in the development of *Changing Altitudes: Stories of Australian Air Force Women*, of course I accepted. The Air Force has been a constant in the lives of Michael, my late husband, and me. Michael was an Air Force Reserve officer with the Queensland University Squadron when he was a university student and later with No 23 Squadron, and I am also a proud Patron of No 23 Squadron Association.

In my roles as Governor of Queensland and as Governor-General of Australia, I enjoyed many engagements with the incredible women of the 'Triple As' and 'Double As': the Women's Auxiliary Australian Air Force and the Women's Royal Australian Air Force. These extraordinary women were the trailblazers of our Air Force's development: joining at a time when Australia was still a maturing Commonwealth nation, and supporting the war effort in whatever field was available to them. During the Second World War, when a woman's role was traditionally a wife, mother and homemaker, thousands queued at recruitment centres to join trades as diverse as meteorological assistants, electricians, flight mechanics and instrument makers. Their emerging working role in the Australian war effort signified the vast, untapped potential of women in the workforce, going into a 'man's world' and excelling.

I have also met many talented and capable women of the contemporary Royal Australian Air Force on bases here in Australia, and on overseas deployments, including Afghanistan and East Timor. What has always impressed me deeply is their professionalism, work ethic, confidence and sense of humour. They all embody the strength and power of our Air Force capability.

Changing Altitudes: Stories of Australian Air Force Women captures a selection of the experiences of women of all generations and backgrounds: those of mothers, daughters, wives and friends. They are women who consider themselves ordinary everyday Australians, however their stories are filled with inspiration, adventure, humour and are at times poignant. In their own way, they are simply extraordinary.

Dame Quentin Bryce
AD CVO

Governor-General Dame Quentin Bryce and Wing Commander Kirrily Dearing, Commanding Officer No 1 Airfield Operations Support Squadron, at RAAF Base Townsville, Queensland, August 2013 (Kirrily Dearing)

INTRODUCTION

Changing Altitudes: Stories of Australian Air Force Women is a book capturing the unique experiences of women who have proudly served their nation in different elements of the Royal Australian Air Force (RAAF) since the 1940s. While not an official history, this publication incorporates significant historical events, the social norms of the day, and policies and government decisions that influenced the professional opportunities afforded to women. These all provide context to the featured stories of our women as they recount their own experiences of their time in service.

When Australian women first joined the ranks of the Air Force in an auxiliary capacity in the early 1940s, their contributions were considered as a temporary necessity due to the ongoing effort in support of the Second World War. Despite the woman's traditional role of the time as one of homemaker and mother, more than 600 joined the Royal Australian Air Force Nursing Service, and women joined the Women's Auxiliary Australian Air Force in their thousands. By the end of the war, more than 27,000 women were making significant contributions to Air Force capability. However, within two years of the war concluding, the auxiliary arm of the service was disbanded, having been deemed surplus to requirements, and many of these women returned to their family kitchens.

As the social norms have changed over the decades, so has the employment of women in the RAAF. Women now serve in every employment category: they are loadmasters, aircraft technicians, logistics specialists, personnel capability specialists, military working dog handlers and pilots. They all enable the RAAF to contribute to a broader defence capability in support of the Australian Government's requirements to ensure domestic and global security. Thousands have deployed on operations around the globe and domestically, often in dangerous environments in unfamiliar territory. They do so unreservedly, frequently leaving loved ones behind and, in many cases, having their partners looking after children – quite the role reversal from decades ago.

All of the women featured in this book recount their own unique journey as a serving member. Some stories cover only a handful of years, while others span careers over several decades. Some women joined as teenagers and others not until later in life, after having other careers and perhaps raising a family. All stories have either been drawn from the Oral History archives of the Air Force and other historical agencies, or from contemporary interviews conducted specifically for this book. Their stories highlight the challenges they have faced, and the opportunities they have created, as they recall their time in uniform, many breaking the stereotypical view of a woman's capacity in the profession of arms. Their recollections serve to inspire the reader, and perhaps even lead them to consider the world of opportunity that could await them as a member of the RAAF.

TIMELINE OF KEY EVENTS FOR AIR FORCE SERVICEWOMEN

1940 **The Royal Australian Air Force Nursing Service is established.**

Royal Australian Air Force Nursing Service 1940–77

Modelled on Princess Mary's Royal Air Force Nursing Service in the United Kingdom, the Royal Australian Air Force Nursing Service (RAAFNS) was established in July 1940 with 36 nursing sisters. Between 1940 and 1955, more than 600 women joined the RAAFNS, serving overseas during the Second World War, the Korean War and the Malayan Emergency, where they lived and worked in the same conditions as the men whom they served alongside. One of the key duties of RAAFNS nursing sisters – especially during the Vietnam War – was caring for patients during the long and demanding medical evacuation flights back to Australia.[1]

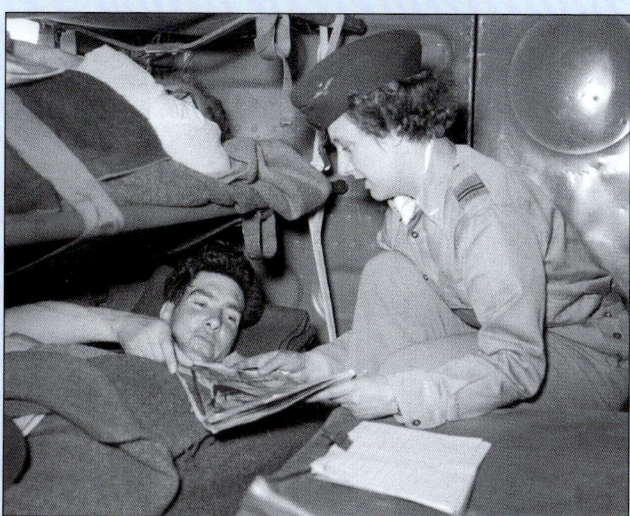

Royal Australian Air Force Nursing Service nursing sister Helen Blair gives a magazine to released prisoner Private John Mackay during a medical evacuation flight from Korea to Japan (Department of Defence)

1941 **The Women's Auxiliary Australian Air Force is formed.**

Women's Auxiliary Australian Air Force 1941–47

The overseas deployment of RAAF personnel (all men) during the Second World War created critical shortages within the RAAF back home in Australia. The Women's Auxiliary Australian Air Force (WAAAF) was approved by the Advisory War Council in February 1941, and formed as a temporary service in March, following lobbying by women who were eager to contribute to Australia's wartime effort. Initially working as wireless telegraphists (who were urgently needed for the war effort), as well as clerks and cooks, WAAAF servicewomen took on an increasing number and variety of duties, ultimately working in 77 per cent of the available RAAF roles.[2]

Women's Auxiliary Australian Air Force engine mechanics working on a Spitfire aircraft (RAAF Museum)

1947 **The WAAAF disbands and its members return to civilian life, with approximately 27,000 having served.**

1950 **The Women's Royal Australian Air Force is formed.**

Women's Royal Australian Air Force

1950–77

When the Korean War and Malayan Emergency once again required the overseas deployment of RAAF personnel, reinstating a women's Air Force was regarded as a solution to the resulting shortages within RAAF ranks. This was approved, in principle, by Cabinet in July 1950, with the first recruits to the Women's Royal Australian Air Force (WRAAF) commencing in January 1951.[3]

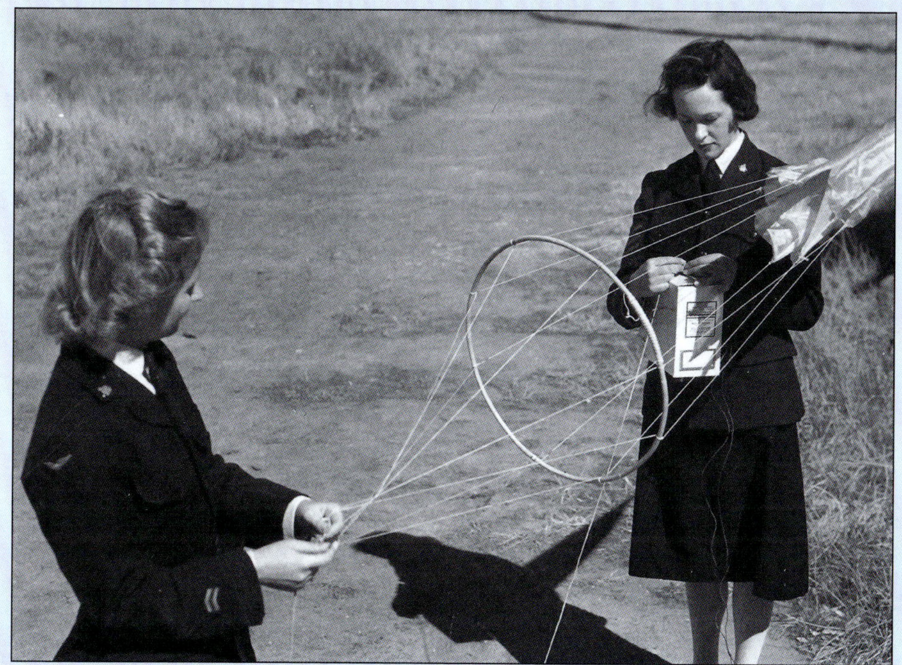

Women's Royal Australian Air Force meteorological assistants (RAAF Museum)

1957 **Her Majesty Queen Elizabeth the Queen Mother is appointed as the Air Chief Commandant of the WRAAF.**

1965 **WRAAF officers are offered permanent commissions.**

1967 **WRAAF servicewomen are permitted to serve overseas. Some deploy on Exercise *Southern Cross* to New Zealand.**

1969 **Servicewomen are permitted to remain in the WRAAF if they choose to marry. Already-married women are also able to join.**

1975 **Pregnant servicewomen are permitted to remain in the WRAAF.**

1977 **With the growing recognition that separate services for men and women are no longer required, the RAAFNS and WRAAF are integrated into the RAAF.**

1978 **RAAF servicewomen receive the same pay as their male counterparts.**

1987 **Women are eligible to join the RAAF as a pilot or aircrew on non-combat aircraft.**

1992 **Women are eligible to join the RAAF as aircrew on combat aircraft.**

2011 **The government of Prime Minister Julia Gillard removes gender restrictions from Australian Defence Force combat roles. Women are now able to serve in every specialisation of the RAAF, including as Airfield Defence Guard and Ground Defence Officer.**

Royal Australian Air Force

Present day

Women in the RAAF are on par with their male counterparts, earning the same wage and receiving the same rights. They can marry and have children while in service, reach star rank, deploy overseas on combat-support and humanitarian aid and disaster relief missions, and have long-term, rewarding careers in service to Australia.[4]

The first all-female C-27J Spartan aircrew from No 35 Squadron, 2022. Left to right: Flight Lieutenant Thea Margalit, Flight Lieutenant Katherine Mitchell, Flying Officer Lauren Townsend and Flight Lieutenant Emily Renshaw (Department of Defence)

THE 1940s

INTRODUCTION

When Australians first learned about the government's commitment to the war in Europe in September 1939, it is unlikely they foresaw the impact it would have on the nation. Unlike previous conflicts waged on distant shores, the effect of the Second World War was felt on the home front, and attacks were carried out on Australian soil. Australians experienced rationing, and there were sandbags in the streets and blackout regulations. Voluntary organisations were established, such as the Air Raid Precautions, Voluntary Aid Detachment and Volunteer Air Observers. Previously considered unfathomable, bombs were dropped on Darwin in the Northern Territory and Japanese submarines entered Sydney and Newcastle harbours in New South Wales. For the first time, Australia was involved in a state of total war.[1]

The Second World War was a technologically advanced war, with the developments in air power playing the most significant part. Within four weeks of the declaration of war, the Australian Government was in negotiation with the governments of the United Kingdom (UK), Canada and New Zealand to participate in the Empire Air Training Scheme (EATS), enabling each country to adopt the same system of training, thus allowing personnel to work cooperatively in a multinational air force. EATS saw our Air Force expand from 3489 to nearly 184,000 men and women at its peak in November 1944.[2] It also brought aviation to Australia in a way never experienced before. The buzz of aircraft overhead – a previously awe-inspiring event – became a familiar occurrence as Royal Australian Air Force (RAAF) airfields were constructed and occupied for operations and training. Roles included pilots, air observers, wireless operator/air gunners, engineers, fitters, armourers, clerks, cooks, instructors, motor transport drivers, butchers, accountants, radar operators, stores people and more. Raising, training and sustaining what would become the world's fourth-largest air force at the conclusion of the war was a monumental and unprecedented task, the likes of which has never been repeated.

War-related roles for women during the First World War had been restricted to nursing. Those who remained at home had to be content with domestic tasks and creating care packages: knitting and baking goods, packaged up with words of support from home.

The years between the wars sowed the seeds of social change. Peace was at the forefront of the minds of many following the horrors of the First World War. The economic Depression of 1929–34 brought with it widespread unemployment. Women were staying longer in education and finding work to supplement the family income. Families were getting smaller and labour-saving devices were freeing up time. Several women were also becoming involved in Australia's burgeoning aviation industry.

The growing instability in Europe in the late 1930s also manifested in Australia in the form of the establishment of voluntary paramilitary organisations such as the Women's

Voluntary National Register, Women's Emergency Signalling Corps and Women's Air Training Corps.

The Second World War was different to the First World War. Despite the continued and ingrained expectations of a woman's role in society, women pushed to mobilise in support of military service like never before.

Women's Air Training Corps

Mary Bell – pilot, licensed aircraft ground engineer, mother, and wife to Group Captain John Bell – established the Women's Air Training Corps (WATC) in Brisbane, Queensland, in April 1939.[3] The organisation conducted courses in wireless telegraphy, motor transport, cooking, stores, draughting, clerical work, aircraft maintenance, and photography.

Divisions were later formed in Victoria, Tasmania, South Australia, New South Wales and Western Australia. The women provided voluntary labour to the RAAF in the form of drivers and clerks.[4]

The women of the WATC formed the nucleus of the Women's Auxiliary Australian Air Force.

Women's Auxiliary Australian Air Force

By 1940, just 12 months into hostilities, the RAAF realised it did not have the manpower to sustain its rapid expansion. Its only solution was to recruit women into its ranks. Within a matter of months, the Women's Auxiliary Australian Air Force (WAAAF) went from a concept on paper to a force in blue. In December 1940, the 'formation of a Women's Auxiliary to the Royal Australian Air Force' was approved by the War Cabinet and, in January 1941, the Advisory War Council approved its official formation.[5] In February, the WAAAF was assigned an acting Director, Mary Bell, and general recruitment began in March.[6]

Women's Auxiliary Australian Air Force recruits with their enlistment paperwork (Australian War Memorial, VIC0498)

In May 1941, the Minister for Air, John McEwen, announced that Clare Stevenson, a university graduate and executive at Berlei Pty Ltd, had been appointed as Director of the WAAAF (DWAAAF).[7] 'The appointment is not only an hono[u]r conferred on me. It is a compliment to business women,' she said.[8] Rising to wing officer and then to group officer, Clare stayed in the role until March 1946.[9]

There was considerable resistance to women joining the military, from the idea that it was 'a man's job', and that service life would put women in moral danger, to concerns that men would be passed over in favour of cost savings.[10] Although service conditions for women were the same as for men, the women's rate of pay was generally two-thirds of that which men in similar musterings received.[11] DWAAAF 'was always fighting to get the money equal … [she] was determined that women should get equal pay'.[12]

The WAAAF was the first military organisation established in Australia to recruit women outside of the medical professions. Its establishment set the precedent for the formation of similar services in the Royal Australian Navy and Australian Army. One recruit said:

> There was a great camaraderie between us and it still exists today. You've only got to come up against a girl [who has] been in one of the services; it doesn't have to be the Air Force, it could be the Army or the Navy, and you immediately click. There is that feeling.[13]

The objective of the WAAAF was to allow women to join the ranks of 'Air Force blue'. Their role was not to work in traditional feminine roles but instead to work alongside men, as their equals, doing the same job and contributing equally to capability.[14]

A Women's Auxiliary Australian Air Force recruiting van (RAAF Museum)

The WAAAF offered adventure. Signing up at their local recruiting centres, in a recruitment van or on the RAAF recruiting train, women left their family homes to form lifelong friendships and learn new skills, which they put into practice in service of their country.

> [They] … came from all kinds of social status and economic status. They came from suburban homes and country homes. They came from the home of, say, [an Outback sheep or cattle] station owner. They came from the local pub. They came from offices in the cities and they came from little country towns.[15]

On joining the WAAAF, members attended an initial training course or 'rookies', where they were introduced to service life and kitted out (provided with their uniform and other items). Service life would have been 'a real shock to the system and to the way of living' for the thousands of young women, two-thirds of whom were under the age of 21.[16]

Morning parade at the Women's Auxiliary Australian Air Force Training Section, No 1 School Technical Training, West Melbourne, Victoria, November 1941 (RAAF Museum)

Their reasons for joining were unique. While some cited patriotism, others wanted to 'help the boys', and all were ready for new adventures. They chose the Air Force over the other services because of family links, an interest in aviation, or simply a preference for the uniform!

For the first two years of its existence, political and legislative delays saw the WAAAF operate as an auxiliary service. It was raised and administered under the Air Board with no legal constitution or employment contracts for its members. However, the women's commitment to serve was such that uniforms were worn, titles learned and orders followed regardless. The unprecedented expansion of the Air Force demanded the need for the WAAAF to be constituted as 'an integral part of the Royal Australian Air Force'. From 23 March 1943, the WAAAF was gazetted and women were subsequently appointed or enlisted as serving members as determined by their rank and were subject to the same statutory codes and regulations as the men.[17]

More than 27,000 women joined the Air Force for service in the Second World War.[18] Eventually, there were around 70 different roles or musterings available to women in the WAAAF and two of those were solely available to women: tracer (who made copies of plans created by draughtsmen or engineers) and accounting machine operator.[19]

Women's Auxiliary Australian Air Force engine mechanics servicing an Avro Anson aircraft (RAAF Museum)

Women's Auxiliary Australian Air Force fabric workers high up on the tail of a Catalina flying boat (RAAF Museum)

Women's Auxiliary Australian Air Force personnel marching in Melbourne, Victoria, during the Second World War (Department of Defence)

As with many RAAF units, the WAAAF progressively disbanded following what is now known as 'Victory in the Pacific'. The roles filled by women were intended to be returned to men after the end of the war. The WAAAF was completely disbanded in July 1947.

Victory parade in Melbourne, Victoria, 1945 (Australians at War Film Archive, 417)

Group Officer Clare Stevenson OBE AM

Director of the Women's Auxiliary Australian Air Force

Service number: 351001

Thirty-seven years old, smartly dressed and with a keen sense of humour.[20]

Group Officer Clare Stevenson (centre) with her nieces Sergeants Warnock and Grant-Stevenson, Victoria, circa 1944 (Australian War Memorial, VIC0822)

Establishing an arm of the Royal Australian Air Force must have been an overwhelming project for a woman with no military exposure, but Clare Stevenson had a wealth of civilian experience and leadership qualities. She considered herself a businesswoman in a man's world. She enjoyed a cigarette, thought women looked better with lipstick and cosmetics but considered lacquered nails 'a matter of taste … [and] out of place with a uniform'.[21] Her role was to provide advice to the Service Directors on matters affecting the wellbeing of the Women's Auxiliary Australian Air Force servicewomen.[22]

In interviews, she described the experience as 'difficult and lonely', but DWAAAF pushed through:[23]

> I didn't do a rookie's course and I didn't do an officer's course; I thought, well, I'm going to learn the rules of the game. And so I burnt the midnight oil reading Air Board orders, indexing and cross-indexing until I really knew them, or knew where to find the subject matter. And this, I can assure you, stood me in very great stead when I had to talk to some of the people who were perhaps, say, permanent Air Force officers who didn't really want us in the service or other people who didn't want us in the service, or who were trying to make difficulties about things. And I was able to … play the game according to the rules that they knew so well.

Acutely aware of what her servicewomen were up against, DWAAAF fostered a culture of moral courage among her officers.

> In times of administrative crises in units [a WAAAF administrative officer] had to be strong enough to stand up for her airwomen against unreasonable male authority. She must be strong enough to stand up to a threat of an adverse report on her attitude to a commanding officer.[24]

Clare Stevenson saw the service life as an opportunity for women to improve their lot in life post-war. She encouraged the members of the WAAAF to make the best of the educational opportunities available to them. She also continuously campaigned for equal pay and equal access to service healthcare.

On demobilisation in 1946, Clare returned to her role at Berlei. After retiring in 1960, she continued to campaign for veterans, their families, war widows and other disadvantaged people. Clare was appointed a Member of the Order of the British Empire in 1960 and a Member of the Order of Australia in 1988. She died in Mona Vale in Sydney, New South Wales, on 22 October 1988.[25]

Grounded WAAAFs with wings

Women were not permitted to become pilots in the RAAF during the Second World War. Corporal Pamela Penglase stated that:

> There was no calling for us to do that … the boys were there to do it and you didn't worry about the differentiation between you, the males and females. It didn't worry you. You just accepted that the boys were flying and the girls were doing things on the ground.[26]

Aircraftwomen Leila Gorey (standing) and Joan Morley (State Library of Victoria, Argus Collection)

However, there were a few savvy lasses who tried to find a workaround. Aircraftwomen Leila Gorey and Joan Morley, both country girls before the war, joined the WAAAF and were mustered as drivers. On hearing that the mustering of Link Trainer instructor had opened up to the WAAAF, the girls paid for, trained for, and obtained their pilot's licences. Newspapers and *PIX* magazine reported on their success of 'going solo' and their aspirations to become 'the first women to do this work'.[27]

Unfortunately, their dream of becoming Link Trainer instructors for the RAAF was never realised as, despite holding the qualifications, they were not mustered into the role.[28]

Smashing the glass cockpit

Margaret 'Mardi' Helen Gething (née Gepp) broke all of the 'rules for women' prescribed for her generation. Born in Melbourne, Victoria, in 1920, to Sir Herbert and Lady Jessie Gepp, Mardi obtained her pilot's licence in 1939, married in 1940, and became the first and only Australian female pilot to join the Air Transport Auxiliary (ATA), in 1942. She was finally accepted after her initial application had been rejected because she was considered to be too short![29] The ATA played a crucial wartime role in delivering aircraft from factories to the Royal Air Force. During her service with the ATA, Mardi ferried 42 different types of aircraft, including Spitfires and Mustangs, and Wellington and Blenheim bombers, clocking up more than 740 hours in the air.[30]

Left to right: Acting Squadron Leader Edward Arthur Hudson DFC and Bar, First Officer Mardi Gething and Flying Officer Wilfred Cyril Gordon DFC while on the Third Victory Loan Appeal tour of Australia, raising money for the war effort (Australian War Memorial, P03100.018)

In early 1945, Mardi returned to Australia to join the crew of 'G for George' on its tour of Australia to raise money for the Third Victory Loan Appeal. Mardi was the publicity and press liaison for the *Melbourne Age* newspaper on the tour and proudly wore her ATA wings throughout.[31]

Royal Australian Air Force Nursing Service

'We liked all our patients. It didn't matter what they were or anything. They were still patients.'[32]

Eight Royal Australian Air Force Nursing Service nursing sisters during their 'rookies' course at No 2 RAAF Hospital. Left to right: Kay Budd, Shirley Wynne, Joan White, unidentified, Nancy Johnson, Molly McDowell, Freda Zeunert and AM Hamilton (Australian War Memorial, P02720.003)

In July 1940, the Royal Australian Air Force Nursing Service (RAAFNS) was formed. Prior to this, RAAF personnel were cared for in sick quarters by RAAF orderlies (men) and civilian nurses.[33] With the rapid expansion of the Air Force following the outbreak of the Second World War, it was deemed necessary for the RAAF to employ a female nursing service to allow them to adequately care for the ill and injured. The RAAFNS was based on the Princess Mary's Royal Air Force Nursing Service in the UK and adapted for local conditions, similarly to the Australian Army Nursing Service.[34] The nursing sisters of the RAAFNS were the first women to join the Air Force and, as with the WAAAF, there was resistance to their joining.

The first Matron-in-Chief was Margaret Irene Lang. Margaret had served in the Army Nursing Service during the First World War. As Matron-in-Chief, her role was to provide advice on, direct and supervise the service. She was also responsible for the appointment, posting and promotion of all nursing sisters within the service.[35]

Nursing sisters joined the RAAFNS as appointed officers for unconditional service within and outside of Australia. Their duties were set in hospitals, sick quarters and on medical evacuation flights.[36] To be appointed, a nursing sister had to be a British subject (as all Australian citizens were considered prior to 1984), aged between 21 and 40 (although exceptions could be made up to the age of 50), a registered general nurse or masseuse, and they had to have passed examinations determined by the Air Board.[37]

Nursing sisters attended a 'rookies' where, similarly to the WAAAF, they learned the fundamental aspects of service life and parade drill. The latter was quickly abandoned, however, and nursing sisters were taught to simply accept a salute with a smile and a nod.[38]

Two unique sections of the RAAFNS included the Medical Air Evacuation Transport Unit, which was responsible for caring for patients in the air, and the Medical Training Section. The RAAFNS was responsible for establishing courses to train nurses, nursing assistants, WAAAF sick quarters attendants, nursing orderlies and male medical orderlies.[39]

The total appointments to the RAAFNS between July 1940 and 31 August 1945 was 632, an elite selection from more than 5000 applicants.[40]

Group Officer Margaret Lang OBE

Matron-in-Chief of the Royal Australian Air Force Nursing Service

Service number: 500001
Date of birth: 23 May 1893
Place of birth: Oxley, Victoria
Date of enlistment: 29 July 1940
Date of discharge: 15 November 1946

Margaret Lang, circa 1945 (Australian War Memorial, P00553.002)

Margaret Irene Lang was born in Oxley, Victoria, in May 1893, to John Douglas Lang (a miner) and his wife Annie. She trained as a nurse at Wangaratta Hospital, graduating in 1915. During the First World War, Margaret served in the Australian Army Nursing Service, including a posting to Salonika, Greece. After her return to Australia in 1919, she became Matron of District Hospitals St Arnaud and Stawell, then the Victorian Police Hospital.[41]

Margaret was appointed Matron-in-Chief of the RAAFNS on 29 July 1940.[42] Her nursing sisters held her in the highest regard, considering her:

> Strict, naturally, and efficient but one to whom you could chat and tell your problems – and we had a few one way or another – but often she could sort them out wisely, and so quietly, you hardly realised it was happening.[43]

On the fifth birthday of the RAAFNS, Margaret commented:

> For me these five years have been intensely interesting. The history of the service has been one of solid work, with no slack periods, [and] no let-up, which has been done quietly and efficiently. The results achieved would not have been possible without the co-operation of every member.[44]

Margaret was placed on the retired list in November 1946, returning to her role as Matron of the Victorian Police Hospital.[45] In August 1950, she was awarded an Order of the British Empire for her service with the RAAF. She passed away in February 1983.[46]

Sister Alma Skeers (née Pearse)

Nursing Sister

Service number: 501101
Date of birth: 8 January 1911
Place of birth: Wagga Wagga, New South Wales
Date of enlistment: 19 May 1941
Date of discharge: 4 December 1945

Alma Pearse (Australians at War Film Archive, 826)

Alma Sarah Jane Pearse was born on 8 January 1911 in Wagga Wagga, New South Wales (NSW), to father George James Dodds Pearse and mother Grace.[1] Alma grew up on the family farm at Brucedale, located between Junee and Wagga, on which they grew crops and raised dairy cattle. Her childhood was spent playing on the farm, helping to milk the cows, and running around the paddocks with her two sisters and two brothers. Her mother taught her how to cook and sew, and all of the kids pitched in to keep the house running. Alma's family was very religious; her father was Presbyterian and her mother attended a Uniting Church:

> We had to go to church every Sunday and … we used to go a mile and a half to school one way. [On] Sunday, we had to go four mile[s] to church the other way, and if Mum and Dad were running late, we'd have to go in the sulky with our old school pony to Sunday school, then Mum and Dad would follow in the buggy.[2]

Alma did not have any plans for when she finished school. Instead, she 'was quite happy to be at home and help with the home duties'. Her days were busy, with her afternoons spent playing tennis or down at the river. Her family held 'dances about once a month at our place … one neighbour used to come with a violin. Another with an accordion' and the neighbourhood would dance the night away.[3]

One year, her sister was hospitalised for five months with rheumatic fever. This experience inspired Alma to go into nursing. Because occupations for women were limited at the time, nursing was very competitive. To be accepted, candidates were interviewed by the matron of their local hospital and had to pass a nurses' entrance exam. The matron later sent successful candidates a letter notifying them of their acceptance, with a date to report to the hospital for training.

Alma started 'nursing in 1930 and I knew nothing else till 1973'.[4] She trained at the Royal Canberra Hospital, where she studied 'anatomy and physiology … medical and surgical; ear, nose and throat … [and] infectious diseases', graduating in 1938.[5]

Her nursing days were long; they 'started at six o'clock in the morning and we finished at half-past five of an afternoon and … you got one day off a week'.[6] The nurses had to provide their own uniforms: '16 of those long, white aprons … caps and collars and cuffs and we wore long sleeves. We had to have black shoes and stockings.'

When war broke out, Alma was working in Canberra:

> An Air Force doctor was doing rounds and he said, 'Have you ever thought of joining the services?' I had thought of joining the Army, but my uncle had been in the First World War and he said, 'No way.' He'd seen the nurses and what they'd gone through … then this doctor said, 'We're wanting nurses for the Air Force.' So anyhow, I wrote away and then when I was accepted, I told my uncle. He said, 'I told you not to.' I said, 'Yes I know, but … I'm not going to the Army. I'm going to the Air Force.'[7]

The application process simply involved writing a letter of interest to the Matron of NSW, Miss Doherty, who then sent 'back a form and I had to fill it in. That's all and that was … halfway through 1940, and in May 1941, I was called up.'[8]

The appointment of RAAFNS nursing sisters saw them 'liable to render continuous service either within or beyond the limits of the Commonwealth of Australia on the same principles as the male officers of the RAAF'.[9] Alma received short notice to report to RAAF Hospital Richmond, NSW, on 19 May 1941.

Alma took '[e]nough uniform [items] until you got your official uniform, and a few dresses ... You didn't have many clothes in those days anyhow, [be]cause no-one could afford them.'

Life at Richmond was a bit of a shock: 'Everything was so different, and you had to learn the ranks of everybody and military conditions':[10]

> We lived in tin huts ... They had little windows ... that tipped out. No curtains, no nothing. Everyone brought a piece of material and put a curtain up ... we were all in single rooms. I think there were five or six rooms to a hut and one hut was only where our dining room was ... we didn't go to the male officers' mess and we had our own chef and everything; [he] was a Dutchman. He spoilt us ... the hospital was weatherboard.[11]

The uniforms were initially:

> A white linen ... with the black Air Force buttons down the front. Long sleeves: short sleeves to the elbow, then there was an extension that buttoned on and went down to the cuff, but when you were working, that had to come off ... we always wore our capes ... round our collars ... we had white shoes and stockings when I first started and the big white veils.[12]

But after Japan entered the war in 1941, their uniforms were dyed a pale brown:

> We still had our white veils and our navy [blue] capes but we had drab uniforms and ... black shoes and coloured stockings ... [We also had] our coats: beautiful coats. We were never cold with them on ... they were straight coats [with] a big lapel and a big collar ... They had double-breasted buttons and a belt ... They were navy-blue ... [and] we had to wear black kid [leather] gloves in the wintertime and black cotton gloves in the summertime.[13]

The RAAFNS nursing sisters noticed two key differences between military and civilian hospitals. The first was that tasking was determined by seniority (firstly by rank, and then by who had served in the RAAFNS the longest). The nurses' uniforms were marked by chevrons on their sleeve, one for each year they had served in the RAAFNS. The second difference was that they had male nurses who were not Registered Nurses. These male nurses attended to dressings 'and things that were personal to a male ... [but] as the war went on, it didn't matter. We did it.' A typical day would involve taking temperatures, giving injections and replacing dressings – 'there was nothing to it'. It was much 'lighter than general hospital work' as there were fewer patients, with simple injuries or illnesses.[14]

While she was posted to Richmond, Alma also worked at No 2 Recruiting Centre in Woolloomooloo, NSW, where she conducted preliminary examinations of WAAAF applicants: 'Eye colouring, hearing, weights, urine testing and height … the practical part to start with, and then they went on for a medical to the doctor.'[15]

In June 1942, Alma was posted to the newly formed No 2 Medical Receiving Station (2MRS) at a property called 'Clydesdale' in Riverstone, located 10 miles from Richmond:[16]

> We had nothing; we had no beds or anything … camp stretchers … and blankets; they were in bundles … we had to make the dressings … wool swabs and things … and get everything organised and packed in boxes … everything had to be autoclaved [sterilised] … so when we got [to our next location], we just opened it up, because we were a mobile unit.

In September, Alma moved with the unit to Townsville in Queensland, setting up at Aitkenvale Road, just outside of the city. Because the climate was tropical, the nursing sisters were issued with a summer uniform consisting of WAAAF skirts, short-sleeve shirts, black ties and hats. They were accommodated in four-bedroom tents with hanging wardrobes, wire camp stretchers covered with a mosquito net, and 'a box with an Aladdin lamp'. 'The Red Cross gave us a pair of sheets each and a pillowslip' and a pillow. To keep cool, they put the sides of the tent up 'to get a breeze through … we had no air-conditioning'. One night, Alma's tent was knocked down by a tropical storm and she and her roommates had to venture out into the rain in their pyjamas, in search of help.

The unit was set up similarly to a bricks-and-mortar hospital with wards – except that each ward was a different tent. It also had an operating theatre complete with a sterilisation room, an x-ray and a dispensary. Apart from the operating theatre, which was lined with rubber so that surgical trolleys could be moved, the floors were compressed earth. The men would sprinkle water to keep the dust down, and the constant foot traffic led to the surface turning as hard as cement.

The most important task for the nurses in the tropical conditions was maintaining 'cleanliness'. Running water was piped from the town's water mains and sterilised in big 'coppers' (large cauldron-like pots usually heated over a wood fire) which the men never let go out. Water from the copper was used for everything from making a cup of tea to warming a tepid bath. 'Pre-surgical scrubbing was done in the sterilisation room.' There were also sterilisers heated by Primus stoves which would 'bring it up to a certain … temperature. We'd pack everything in, then close them up, and they'd bring the temperature right up to sterilise.' Scalpel blades and scissors were sterilised in pure Lysol. 'We never had any dirty wounds or infections.'

Unfortunately, while in Townsville, Alma was injured in a fire originating in the sterilisation room. Her burns saw her hospitalised for a month in the WAAAF ward. Alma spent her days in bed reading and writing letters, which worked well unless the river flooded over the train line and stopped the mail from getting through. Alma's mum sent her fruitcakes wrapped in layers of paper then finished off with 'a big piece of unbleached calico and stitched in'. Her name and service number were scrawled on the top so there would be no mistaking who the tasty treat belonged to.

Patients of the hospital comprised mainly those with dengue fever or injuries. One night, two men from No 7 Squadron were brought in by ambulance:

> They were screaming … One was a sergeant and one was an officer and … one said, 'What happened?' and the other one said, 'We ditched in' and that's the last [thing] they said to one another … the boy was … about 22 and he had the most beautiful black wavy hair and it was just charred … his fingers were so burnt that the skin was just split and … hanging off his fingers, and the officer was almost the same. I think they came in about one o'clock and they were dead [by] … about four or five o'clock. It's a shame they weren't dead before, [because of] what they went through. It didn't matter what [pain medication] you gave them; it didn't give them any relief. There was no hope for them. It was very sad.

For serious injuries with little chance of survival, the only thing the nurses could do was make the patients comfortable, usually by administering morphine. Use of the drug was strictly monitored; vials were kept in a locked cupboard and every use was recorded.

The nurses spent their downtime going to dances or the picture theatre. On Sundays during summer, two truckloads of personnel would head through Townsville to Ross River 'and we'd sing all the way … it didn't matter if you had a voice or not; everyone sang at the top of their voices', songs such as *Roll Out the Barrel* and *Kiss Me Goodnight, Sergeant Major*. Those who could not swim, such as Alma, got 'up to mischief' by filling the pockets of the swimmers' clothes (which they had left in the trucks) with baby powder.

In December 1942, 2MRS moved to Milne Bay in New Guinea and Alma was posted to No 5 Medical Receiving Station, which had recently relocated to Townsville. In July 1943, she was posted back south to Bradfield Park in NSW, followed by No 1 RAAF Hospital in Wagga Wagga in August 1943. She was very glad to be back home. Alma initially worked on the ward at Wagga until:

> They found out I could do X-rays so when the X-ray technician went off duty, I used to do the X-rays … I'd use a mobile plant … [I'd] wheel it around to a ward and X-ray a patient in the ward and take it back again.

Later, she worked at the RAAF Hospital in town in the operating theatre:

> Two of us worked in the theatre all the time and once a month, the specialist used to come up from Melbourne and operate at the weekend, so we'd be working with the specialist, a physician and a surgeon over the weekends … [The patients would] come in with all sorts of things. We took the Army [personnel] too. We had one poor man [who had dived into a river] … the water was only shallow [so his friends] were sitting. He thought they were standing and he dived in and got a broken neck.

In August 1944, Alma was posted to No 101 Fighter Control Unit in Bankstown, NSW, 'where people … traced the planes, where they were coming from and going to'. Alma was the sole medical member in the unit and was put in charge of the sick-quarters clinic, with two WAAAF assistants. The clinic was set up with a kitchenette and store on one side and an outpatient ward on the other, with a dispensary, dressing room, office, and three beds for WAAAFs and four for men. It was 'a real little community … five WAAAF officers and myself … lived in the one cottage, tent or hut together and we got on well together. We had a lot of fun.'

Alma was still at Bankstown when the war in Europe ended. Her commanding officer was a pilot who had returned from the Middle East; his wife was English:

> You can imagine how they felt about the war being ended over there, and they decided to have a party … All the messes were open … and we went from one mess to the other and it was a great havoc … we went on nearly all night … [the] next day everyone was very sick, sad and sore.

Alma was posted briefly to No 3 RAAF Hospital in Concord although she 'hated every minute of it' as it was a very large and impersonal place. There, Alma worked in the ear, nose and throat, surgical, medical and WAAAF wards. Despite her short tenure at Concord, Alma experienced two notable events. The first was the Japanese attack on Sydney Harbour:

> From Concord we heard everything, and the [patients] kept saying, 'There [are] bombs, bombs, bombs' … and I said, 'No, it's the trains going through the point'. They said, 'Don't give us that, Sister, that's bombs going off', and that was when the Jap[anese] came into the harbour; I'll never forget that night. [The patients] nearly drove us mad, screaming and going on, but of course they couldn't help it. It just brought [the war] back to them.[17]

The second was a visit from English actress and singer Gracie Fields:

> She sang 'The Lord's Prayer' … And we had a boy that was very seriously injured in a plane and he'd been brought down … to die and they pulled his bed right across from … the other ward, so as he could see her, and she went across and spoke to him and shook hands with him.[18]

Alma was discharged from the RAAFNS at Concord. After the war, she returned to nursing in civilian hospitals, serving as duty matron at Wagga Wagga, Junee, and Lockhart hospitals. In 1982, Alma married Jake Skeers, who owned and operated a Honda motorcycle dealership in Wagga. Jake was also an alderman on the Wagga Wagga City Council, stood for state parliament in 1957, and was a long-serving president of the Wagga Wagga Returned and Services League Sub-Branch.[19]

Alma believed that her service in the RAAFNS made her:

> a more responsible person … more able to stand up and think for myself … when I went [in]to the Air Force I was out on my own at times and I had to think for myself and … that's where I got more experience … that's what made me more practical and down to earth.[20]

In 1995, Alma donated her summer uniform, identification discs and pay book to the RAAF Wagga Aviation Heritage Centre. After the centre closed in 2005, her artefacts were moved to RAAF Base Point Cook, Vic. Alma campaigned heavily for the heritage centre to be reopened, which it was in 2010.[21]

Alma Pearse's Royal Australian Air Force Nursing Service summer tunic, 'dog tags' and pay book. Note the red chevrons on the tunic sleeve; an additional one was awarded each year (Peter Wyatt, RAAF Wagga Aviation Heritage Centre)

Alma passed away on 28 December 2010.

Flight Officer Norah Penglase (née Cooke)

Clerk General

Service number: 91544
Date of birth: 22 July 1920
Place of birth: Prospect, South Australia
Date of enlistment: 23 October 1941
Date of discharge: 15 February 1946

Pamela Cooke, 1942 (Australians at War Film Archive, 1737)

Norah Pamela ('Pam') Cooke was born to Percival (Percy) Bennett Cooke and Freda Johanna Minna Thiel on 22 July 1920 in Prospect, South Australia (SA).[1] Her mother had been born in Germany and her father in England.[2] During the First World War, Percy served in the Royal Navy, after which the couple moved to Australia with their first-born child, a son. Percy worked as an armourer at Keswick Barracks and the couple had two more children, Pam and her younger brother Gordon.[3]

Pam grew up in a brick bungalow with flowers out the front and chickens and a vegetable garden out the back. 'We had plenty of playing space and had dogs and cats and ducks and … chickens and what have you, so it was very happy.' Pam attended Colonel Light Gardens Primary School. At 13-and-a-half years old, Pam began to study at Scott's Business College where she learned shorthand, bookkeeping and typewriting. She left after two years when she reached the Intermediate Certificate standard.[4]

After school, Pam 'just wanted to work in an office and I hadn't thought much further than that … you didn't aspire to go to university in those days.' She got a job working in the Seymour Building, the tallest building in Adelaide.[5]

When war broke out:

> We were at home in the evening [sitting] around the radio and I can just remember Mother cried because she thought she had to go through another war … I don't think anyone ever realised that Mother was of German descent. Not that she ever hid it, but … most people thought she was English … I don't think her parents were alive so she didn't have that to worry about. But apparently there were cousins of mine – her sister had two boys – that were killed on the Russian Front.[6]

The first group of Women's Auxiliary Australian Air Force recruits at Adelaide Station, South Australia, October 1941 (Australians at War Film Archive, 1737)

To assist in the war effort, Freda joined the Red Cross, while Percy, aged 57, found himself in uniform once again, working as an armourer at the rank of warrant officer.[7] Pam joined the WATC after she saw an advertisement in the newspaper. She was passionate about aviation and had been for a joy flight out at Parafield Airport. Aviation 'was reasonably new and it got quite a lot of interest and it was very glamorous too, in those days ... [the pilots] were handsome fellows and there was the excitement of these great planes'. The WATC courses taught the girls the:

> Rudiments of marching and drill ... [and] the ranks of the service ... wireless telegraphy, and Morse Code of course, and tele-printing. They had aircraft recognition courses that we had to do and principles of flight ... [It] was preparatory to getting people sorted out and used to service before they went into it.[8]

Pam enrolled in the WAAAF on 23 October 1941 at No 5 Recruiting Centre in Adelaide, aged 21. She was the 44th WAAAF to enrol in South Australia, with her service number consisting of 915, the state's code, and 44, her number. Both her parents were very supportive of Pam's decision to sign up, considering it as having the potential to 'be a great adventure'. Her younger brother Gordon joined the RAAF and served as a cook.[9]

Her civilian experience and training saw Pam mustered as clerk general; however, her expectation of her service role differed from reality. Pam imagined her days would be occupied with 'shorthand and typing in a big office complex for records', but in her five years of service, she neither touched a typewriter nor used shorthand. Instead, she kept track of personnel by looking after 'records and writing up ledgers as to where people had gone'.[10]

The first group of WAAAFs from Adelaide were sent to the WAAAF Training Depot in Malvern, Victoria, for their 'rookies' course, and they caught the train together from Adelaide to Melbourne. Their training was conducted at St Catherine's in Melbourne and the girls were 'barracked in a beautiful old home at Toorak called "Orrong" in Clendon Road'. The rooms were huge, with rows of iron beds topped with straw mattresses, alternating with little metal cupboards. 'Some of the girls were a bit shocked'; while they 'didn't expect to be treated like something precious', given that they 'had probably never left home ... [they] were not expecting all this'. There also was not much space for personal belongings so they 'didn't take much ... [just] the odd dress and civilian clothes and your underwear'.[11]

The course was taught by a group of WAAAF officers who had been recruited to form the nucleus of the organisation. Pam remembered Olympic hurdler Flight Officer Doris Carter:

> There were various women that had high positions ... We all had to get used to calling the officers 'Madam' ... the men were 'Sir' ... That was a bit tricky, but we soon got used to it ... You respected the officers and you did as you were told. You didn't answer back or anything; you'd be in trouble if you did ... [One day] we were getting our food ... we lined up with our plates ... and a corporal – she was a disciplinary girl – she was walking up and down and I said [to the server], 'Hi

> there, Cookie, what's for lunch?' And [the corporal] marched up to me and she said, 'What did you call her?' And she had eyes like a cold fish and her nose was just about touching mine. I said, 'I just called her Cookie.' She said, 'You don't speak to her like that. You leave here and you do a fatigue tonight and you can come back in and help in the kitchen doing washing up' … I saw her many times after and … every time I'd be scared stiff of her. Even when I was an officer … she [later] became a warrant officer disciplinary.[12]

'Orrong' in Clendon Road, Toorak, Victoria, circa 1934 (Stonnington Local History Archives)

There was little spare time in the evenings and what was left was spent 'letter writing and doing your laundry'.[13] On the day the girls were issued with their uniforms, they felt like they had 'finally made it', having gotten through all of the drill, lessons and exams. Their uniforms were standard sizes issued from the equipment store and later tailored to fit. The shirts in particular tended to be too long. They were also:

> Very stiff material. They were almost like a denim, but they were just a bit softer than denim … we were all having trouble learning how to tie a tie. Then, of course, we had our caps. Your hair was supposed to be two inches above your collar … We were [also] all issued with navy-blue bloomers … they were cotton knit, like your t-shirts are made of … They were always referred to as 'bloomers blue, air women for the use of' … We always used to laugh at that, these awful bloomers … [but] they were nice and warm in the winter and Melbourne was very cold. It would be no place for scanties [small underwear] underneath a uniform.[14]

Pam's first posting was to Air Force Headquarters (AFHQ) Department of Postings, in November 1941. She was one of the first four WAAAFs posted into the department, which at that time was located at Victoria Barracks in Melbourne. The men and women all worked together in a big room and the officers had separate offices off to the side. It must have been 'quite a novelty to have girls' but 'we weren't there for romance ... we were there to do a job. That was the idea: to release these boys to go out in the front line. That's what it was all about':[15]

> We had these big books and they were all lined up ... we were given signals and things, like a telegram, of where so and so was posted. And you'd open up the book ... and enter [the information] ... when people got promoted in rank ... It was mostly officers, as I remember, that we looked after. There was another big department there called Records and they dealt with everybody other than officers ... [details included where] they were posted around, and if they got killed or if they were a prisoner of war.[16]

While Pam was posted to AFHQ in Melbourne, Japan entered the war. Everyone was shocked:

> We began to think we'd have the Jap[anese] running around the streets before long ... we were all very anxious ... they dug some slit trenches in case of air raids and they were building shelters ... We used to have practice [sheltering for] air raids and we ... had to grab these great big books. I could hardly carry it off the desk, let alone run with it.[17]

Director of the Women's Auxiliary Australian Air Force (DWAAAF), Group Officer Clare Stevenson, explained that WAAAF officers were selected for being:

> A combination of an 'educated' person as defined by Gasking in *Examinations and the Aims of Education:* a well-adjusted woman with social poise, having an interest in other human beings and an experience in paid work.[18]

Potential officers also had to have 'the added qualities of leadership, humanity and tolerance'.[19] While she was posted to the Department of Postings, Pam was selected for officer training. 'I could take a lead. If I was asked to do something, I'd be away doing it. While others would be thinking about it, I would have got the job done.'[20]

From October 1942, Pam attended the School of Administration for the Officers Training Course, at The University of Melbourne, for about three months. Part of her training involved going on bivouac (military style camping). DWAAAF was of the opinion that 'if we were bombed or invaded, it would be part of the WAAAF officer's job not only to look after her own airwomen, but to take care of civilian women and children', so part of their training involved a 'few days of camping out'.[21] The girls slept in tents: 'We all got very wet when it rained. Anyway, it was just a test to tell the sheep from the lambs, I suppose':[22]

> We had a proper passing-out [graduation] ceremony with the CO [Commanding Officer] of the School of Administration and possibly some of the officers from Air Force Headquarters; senior men. Then we were all in squadrons and flights and there was a proper marching out and giving of salute to the senior officer there ... It was just like the men would have.[23]

After completing her training in December 1942, Pam was discharged from the WAAAF and re-enrolled with the rank of assistant section officer. She then had a few days of leave in Adelaide to visit her parents and get measured for her new tailor-made officer's uniform before reporting to her next posting. On 7 December 1942, Pam was posted to No 2 Training Group Headquarters (2TG) in Wagga Wagga:[24]

> [2TG] controlled all the unit groups and stations for training pilots and gunners and observers within a certain area … requests would come into our headquarters from those stations for various things they wanted. If they wanted people posted or people brought in … anything to do with personnel would come through us.[25]

Doris Carter preparing food during a four-day bivouac as part of a Women's Auxiliary Australian Air Force officer training course, circa September 1943 (Australian War Memorial, VIC1307)

Several buildings in Wagga were adopted for use by the RAAF. The officers mess was located in the Riverine Club on the banks of the Murrumbidgee River, while the headquarters of 2TG operated out of the Court House precinct. The WAAAF officers were accommodated in what they called the Sheriff's Cottage, where the girls had proper beds with real mattresses. The officer on duty was responsible for checking that the WAAAFs who were accommodated in the 'WAAAFery' (a hotel in town) were all 'in their beds [with the] lights out'.[26]

'Wagga was very hot in summer and cold in winter, and very foggy.'[27] For entertainment, the girls would play tennis and go to the picture theatre and, in summer, go swimming at Wagga Wagga Beach: a sandy spot on the banks of the Murrumbidgee. They also had a concert troop who put on concerts at the town hall involving ballet, tap dancing, elaborate costumes and choruses, which the girls enjoyed. With RAAF bases at nearby Forest Hill and

Uranquinty, and an Army camp at Kapooka, the town was awash with uniforms. The Army boys would drive into town to take the girls to mess dinners.

While posted to Wagga, Pam met the DWAAAF. Group Officer Stevenson interviewed her about the behaviour of two girls at the WAAAFery:

> I got called into the office where she was at that particular time. 'Cooke,' she said, 'What do you know about so and so and so and so?' 'Madam,' (of course, Madam) 'They are awfully nice. They are very friendly girls. They are often there together on the bed. They are very friendly and they're always holding hands.' I was completely innocent and I had no idea what she was on about.[28]

Harold Payne and Pam Cooke in Wagga Wagga, New South Wales, circa 1942 (Australians at War Film Archive, 1737)

Within about a week, the pair were separated, with one sent to Townsville in Queensland and the other to Perth in Western Australia – with the entire continent of Australia between them.

> She probably did a few other inspections and checked out a few other things while she was up there … She was slightly intimidating and she didn't mince matters. She was a bit gruff and told you [if you] were a fool and even used stronger language if need[ed] … She was well respected by everybody but we thought she was a bit of a hard nut. I suppose she had to be, because she had to get this service going in the beginning and she had all sorts of opposition from men, all the time. She fought them all the way … She was a wonderful leader … a very capable woman … She'd laugh and she'd let her guard down sometimes.[29]

On one occasion, Pam had an eventful trip to Tocumwal in New South Wales via Mildura in Victoria, while she was seeking clarification on a record. Her group of three departed by air, flown by flying instructor Bill Robertson:

> [W]e were getting near to Mildura and we were over the River Murray and a place called Robinvale … Bill said all of a sudden … 'The petrol is getting low and we've got this awful north wind and I don't think we're going to make it to Mildura. We're going to have to make a landing. I'll look down and see where I can put the plane down.' He said, 'Will you be all right?' I said, 'Yes.' He said, 'Are you sure?' I said, 'Well, you're the pilot.' And I crossed my fingers and I hoped it was going to be alright and the plane was getting buffeted around … just above tree-top height … The next thing, we came down a bit lower and saw this empty paddock and a farmhouse. So we came down in … a ploughed field and it was as rough as could be. How the plane didn't tilt over, I don't know.[30]

After landing, Bill stayed with the aircraft while Pam and the other passenger went in search of a phone. When they finally got through to Mildura, a truck was promptly sent out with fuel to fill up the aircraft and equipment to tie it down overnight. Unfortunately, news that Pam had not arrived in Mildura on time had reached Wagga, causing some concern.[31]

In April 1944, Pam was posted back to Melbourne because the squadron leader to whom she reported in Wagga had requested she accompany him on his next posting.[32] 'I think he knew he could rely on me and what I was capable of doing.' This time, Pam worked at AFHQ at Albert Park Lake – a large complex full of temporary buildings. Pam remembers it was cold and miserable in Melbourne: 'I used to take a little jar of Bonox [beef extract that can be made into a hot drink] to the office.' The habit caught on and soon Pam was making six or more cups of Bonox every morning for her colleagues. However, Melbourne did have some benefits, in the form of night-time entertainment: 'We used to go to the ballet and concerts that were on and musical comedies … or we'd go to the pictures. There was always something to do.'[33]

While working at AFHQ, Pam was approached by DWAAAF to work as the Personal Assistant to the Chief of the Air Staff (now known as Chief of Air Force):

> The head fellow for the Air Force, the RAAF, he always had a PA. That was like a personal assistant, a secretary, and it was always a woman. I don't know whether they had men in the earlier days, but once the WAAAF had grown experienced enough [and] they had a lot of people to choose from, he always had a girl. And DWAAAF called me in towards the end [of the war] and said, 'Cooke, what do you think about being PA to the [Chief] … So and so is being demobbed; would you like to take her place?' I said, 'Yes, that would be wonderful.' It would have been wonderful. Of course, the war ended and that was it. They had decided they would appoint men as the girls were going, so they would start off afresh with a man. I thought it was quite a compliment to be interviewed.[34]

When the war was over, it was a 'great relief'. While there was still work to be done at AFHQ, the girls knew they would be returning to their civilian lives:

> [The war] had been going on for so long. We thought we were going to be in there for a couple of years and it would all be over … I'd been in since October 1941 and I came out in February 1946. So it was five years, I guess. That was a long time … it was a great relief when it was all over. We went into town and celebrated in the streets of Melbourne.[35]

Pam retired from the WAAAF on demobilisation on 15 February 1946 at the rank of flight officer.[36] She returned to Adelaide to live with her parents. A few weeks later, she married her boyfriend, Lieutenant Ronald Clyde Penglase DSC (Distinguished Service Cross) from the Royal Australian Naval Volunteer Reserve. The pair had been friends throughout school and had started dating during the war.[37] Their wedding was a marriage of two services punctuated by military traditions, from a 'Guard of Honour with the swords crossed' as they exited the church, to cutting the wedding cake with a sword.[38] Pam and Ron later had three children: one daughter and two sons.[39]

Pam did not return to office work after she left the WAAAF as she struggled with asthma. Instead, she raised her children, ran the family home and did volunteer work with the Anglican Church, Meals on Wheels and the Red Cross.[40]

Looking back on her time in the WAAAF, Pam reflected on the reasons for its success:

> Mostly the people that were in it were keen to be in it and were all volunteers to join it in the first place. Like me, a lot of the girls would have thought it was a chance to get away from home … and experience new things and a different style of life altogether. I think that's what it's all about … you'll find when you get amongst girls that have been in the services – it doesn't matter which one, even nurses – there is this camaraderie amongst each other. You just click and you talk the same language because you know what you're talking about. It just brings you close to those people.[41]

Pam passed away on 9 August 2013. She is survived by her children, grandchildren and great-grandchildren.

Corporal Audrey Haughton-James (née Philp)

Driver Motor Transport

Service number: 94177
Date of birth: 20 January 1916
Place of birth: Beaudesert, Queensland
Date of enlistment: 14 January 1942
Date of discharge: 24 July 1945

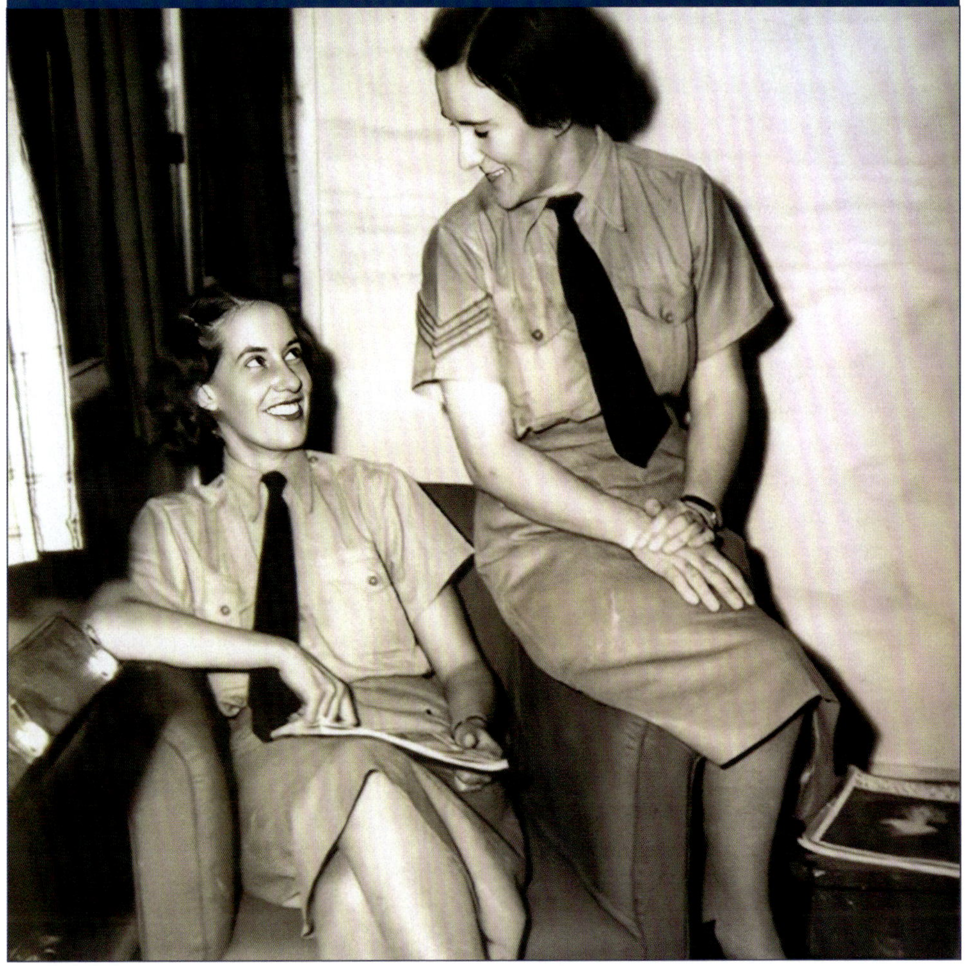

Jean Philp (left) and Sheila McGovern, circa 1942 (Australians at War Film Archive, 1535)

Audrey ('Jean') Campbell Philp was born at her family home 'Wyaralong', a cattle property located near Boonah in southeast Queensland (Qld).[1] Jean was an identical twin to sister Jessie.[2] The pair had three elder brothers and three sisters (one elder and two younger). Their days were spent swimming in a lagoon, riding horses, playing tennis, climbing trees, building treehouses and riding on the back of Harley Davidson motorbikes on the farm's 'speedway'.[3]

In their younger years they were educated by a governess, then at the age of 14, Jean and Jessie were sent to Somerville House, a boarding school for girls, in Brisbane. While Jean did not have particularly fond memories of the cold showers or being forced to 'eat everything that was put on your plate', she did enjoy the cultural offerings Brisbane provided. While there, Jean and her sister were taken under the wing of their Aunt May. Together they were treated to trips to the ballet and theatre and they became enthusiasts of Gilbert and Sullivan.[4]

After school, Jean moved to Sydney to study Tresillian 'mothercraft' nursing. Her training involved working with impoverished families in Woolloomooloo.[5] Nurses were taught how to support mothers and babies with better hygiene, feeding and nursing.[6] After graduating, Jean moved back to Queensland to work in the west of the state. She would pick up mothers and babies from hospitals in the regional centres and take them back to their homes, which were often very remote. 'It was interesting work, but you were on your own. No doctors or anybody else for miles and miles.'[7]

When the Second World War broke out, Jean returned to Wyaralong. While Jean had not yet joined up, she was immediately involved with the war in the air. Due to its proximity to RAAF Amberley and Archerfield Airport, the RAAF was using a few hundred acres of Wyaralong for bombing and gunnery practice:[8]

> Amberley would use it one week. And Archerfield [the next] … the groundcrew used to camp beside the big lagoon we had beside the house. The boys would just come over and do their bombing and gunnery and go back without landing … with five girls in the house the boys used to have … fun. They'd come up and we had big wide verandas and gramophones and we had a big dining-room table. We used to play progressive ping pong … They used to have a whale of a time coming up there.[9]

Before too long, the aircrew cottoned on to what the ground crew were up to and, as is aircrew custom, they came up with innovative ways to announce their pending arrival. While stationed at Archerfield Airport with No 23 Squadron, the Jackson brothers – John Francis and Leslie Douglas (twins, graziers, businessmen, air racers and, later, Distinguished Flying Cross recipients) – used to drop streamers from their aircraft which would float down, landing softly on the lawn.[10] The streamers contained messages detailing when the aircraft would likely have 'engine trouble' and would be landing:

> They used to throw the paper over … first thing in the morning – the first detail [group of aircraft] that came up. Then anything they wanted during the day, this message streamer would flutter down. One day, John Jackson dropped a message down to say he'd be having engine trouble at about 11 o'clock, so any chance of a

> swim? Then another plane would come over and say, well, when John Jackson has his engine trouble, I'll be coming up with the spare parts in what they used to call the Meinerschmidt – the Moth Minor … So this became quite a polished business, this having engine trouble.[11]

Jean enrolled in the WAAAF at No 3 Recruiting Centre at RAAF Amberley on 14 January 1942.[12] Living on the farm meant she had learned to drive at an early age so the role of driver motor transport (DMT) appealed to her. During her recruitment interview, Jean was taken out to Archerfield for her DMT trade test. Although the idea of the WAAAF was to allow women to join so they could 'release the men who were very badly needed, especially in New Guinea and places like that', there was still resistance:[13]

> There was quite a bit of opposition to girls being in transport because in those days … they thought, being girls, we wouldn't be able to handle the machinery that was required. Anyway, we were all bundled into this tender [transport vehicle] … [and] taken out to Archerfield for a trade test. The warrant officer there was very anti girls joining up, so he sacked several of the girls who had come in high-heeled shoes … he thought they were so impractical. But you drove in high-heeled shoes in those days too. It didn't matter. Things weren't quite so fast.[14]

That afternoon, the successful girls were 'bundled' onto the train and sent down to the RAAF station in Bankstown, New South Wales (NSW), to begin their initial training, or 'rookies':

> [We] had our inoculations as soon as we arrived. We were given hessian bags and pointed in the direction of the hayshed and told to fill them ourselves; those were our mattresses. Then we had two grey blankets each. And a pillow. No sheets, no pillow slips and so on.[15]

They took classes in administration and gas training:

> We had lots of lectures on different types of gases … we were all issued with gas masks … [and] never went anywhere without them because I think early in the war they were expecting somebody to use gas because every country had supplies of gas. But because of the horrendous stories of the last war with people being gassed and having suffered for years afterwards, I don't think any country was in a hurry to be the first to use it.[16]

There was also hours and hours of marching, which Jean considered as 'one way of knocking us into shape a bit or just getting us used to taking orders'.[17]

The girls were issued with men's uniforms 'with the cr[o]tch down to about our knees and miles of winding up on the sleeves … [and] two pairs of pink pyjamas. They were quite nice pyjamas, actually.' They were also issued with 'bloomers': 'voluminous affairs … I can remember one of the girls getting out in the hut and parading these things up and down to show us the beautiful cut':[18]

> We were issued with our fur hats, our digger hats, and our little navy-blue caps for [wearing] with our winter uniform. At first it was haphazard, in that we got a bit [of]

> winter uniform and a bit of summer uniform and part of this and part of that. But that became more organised as the war went on … Some of the girls were terribly homesick. A lot had never been away from home before. Some of them sat and cried on their beds half the night when the day was over: just wanting to go home to Mother. They were long days … by the time you scrubbed a few floors and did all the marching and you had a few injections … it was a completely different way of life for all of us.[19]

Just under a month later, on 10 February, Jean graduated from No 14 Recruit Drill and Gas Course.[20] She was posted to No 1 Bombing and Gunnery School (1BAGS) in Evans Head, NSW, two days later. She had never heard of Evans Head 'and nobody knew what we were in for'; indeed, similarly to many of the Empire Air Training Scheme (EATS) schools, they were not quite ready to accommodate the WAAAF. As such, the girls were accommodated in town at Mandalay Flats, affectionately known as 'Menace Mansions'.[21] The little seaside cottage had four rooms, each with two iron beds and a small kitchen for when they felt like a break from eating at the mess:[22]

> [Evans Head] was a lovely spot … a little fishing village … [with] beautiful wildflowers all over the place and acres and acres of Christmas Bells [flowers] as far as you could see … the whole place was very pretty because you had the Evans River flowing into it there and you had ocean beaches.[23]

The first eight Women's Auxiliary Australian Air Force servicewomen to arrive at Evans Head, New South Wales, circa 1942. Left to right, back: Maise Frood, Doris Mickan, Lorna Jennings and Lois Shaw. Front: Venus Starr, Barbara Porter, Jean Philp and Sheila McGovern (Australians at War Film Archive, 1535)

Initially, there were only eight WAAAFs at Evans Head and no officers or non-commissioned officers. Consequently, the girls instituted their own rules. One such rule was that no male visitors were allowed to Mandalay except for the commanding officer, chaplain and one warrant officer. In their free time, the girls attended the picture theatre and open-air dances. When they were granted weekend leave, they would catch the train from Evans Head to Brisbane. Because there were so few passenger trains on the lines during the war, they departed from Evans Head at midnight aboard a troop and goods train known as the 'midnight horror'.[24]

Jean and her fellow transport drivers once again encountered opposition to women working in transport. While the warrant officer in charge of transport approved of girls joining up to work in the mess or in an office, he did not consider transport as a suitable role for girls. As such, for a considerable stretch 'we had an undue amount of work on the sewage trucks and the garbage trucks … But we took it all in our stride.'[25]

The role of the DMT was to provide transportation for people and supplies. The women would pick up trainees from the train station and bring them to the school; they would take men to and from the bombing range. They would meet boats at the docks or trains at the station, unload and load boxes, then do it all again at the other end. '[We would keep] our trucks beautifully clean, [and] we were always on time. We were terribly conscientious.'[26]

The trucks (or tenders) were nearly all Bedfords:

> Bedford Bombers, as we called them … The ambulances were also Bedfords. The fire engine was a Daimler and it was a brute of a thing to drive … But we mastered them all, in the end. We'd just be told to take the tractor out and tow an aircraft in or push it out. So we had the tip trucks for the rubbish … With the various size tenders, we'd take the crews out to the bombing ranges. We'd pick up all the goods from Lismore [and] Casino from the railway station … [and] other produce from around the district.[27]

They would transport practice bombs and groceries; everything had to be brought in by truck because 1BAGS was located 12 miles out of town:

> I can remember the huge cartons of chocolates coming in … with [only] two blocks of chocolate left … [the remainder had] been rattled by the railway gang on the way up, but at least you only had to sign for what you got. And they were frequently dug into, because you couldn't buy confectionary in the shops at all and the only way you got it was if you knew somebody in the services. But the railway boys knew how to get it.[28]

A childhood spent on the farm with three older brothers went some way to prepare Jean for the antics she encountered with the men in the RAAF. The pranks were numerous but relatively benign. They ranged from the boys diverting the hot water from the girls' showers into theirs; to the boys demobilising the trucks by jacking the rear wheels, short circuiting the spark plugs with a lead pencil, or placing a potato in the exhaust pipe:[29]

> On the very first day I went out [to the bombing range], I'd taken about 15 fellows in the back of this truck and they went through all their antics going out.

> They all hammered on the sides of the truck … as we went over the bridge, so you thought you'd fallen through … [Another] trick was to all get right at the back of the tender and jump in unison, so your front wheels bobbed up and down … [Then] on the bombing range roads … they'd all stand with their legs apart and they'd sway in unison and that'd sway your truck, [making it] almost impossible to steer the jolly thing.[30]

For air-to-air and ground-to-air gunnery practice, the trainees shot at a drogue: 'a big long … silk sausage' towed by Fairey Battle aircraft. 'Four pupils at a time – one after the other – would fire at this thing … each had different coloured bullets.' When the activity ended, the drogue was dropped to the ground. A local farmer would drag it up the hill to the drogue hut with his horse. The drogue was then 'spread out on the table and all the different coloured bullet holes were marked so that each trainee knew how many shots he'd got in with his round of shooting'.[31] On Jean's first day out on the range, she was invited into the hut. The boys promptly grabbed her by the ankles, bundled her into the drogue and strung her up from the rafters:

> So I was in this long hut in this sausage-like thing … and I couldn't do anything about it … but they released me after a while … I think having had three brothers who were fairly good at this type of thing … probably prepared [me] for it … I got caught a few times.[32]

With the exception of the initiation pranks (and pranks for the sake of pranks), the boys and the girls had a good working relationship. 'We'd just all be part of the gang [and] work together. There was no "them and us" sort of thing about it at all. It was good.' The lads also made an effort to modify their behaviour and refrain from swearing around the girls: 'very seldom did any of them swear in front of us'.[33]

The girls did return fire on occasion as well. Growing up on the farm, Jean and her siblings had learned to shoot. While her brothers went fox and hare hunting, Jean and Jessie would hunt snakes and collect snakeskins. There were many snakes on the bombing range:

> I killed one out there one day because none of the boys seemed to want to get near it. It was a brown snake and they can be quite nasty … This big, tall boy was standing beside me and after I'd killed it, the snake's tongue was sticking out. This fellow was saying, 'Don't go near it. Look at its fangs, it's got its fangs out'. I said, 'They're not its fangs; that's its tongue. I'll show you his fangs.' I just got a little twig and lifted his fangs out … [the snakes] lower them back against the roof of their mouth and you can lift them forwards, and there was a dull thud behind me and this fellow [had] passed out cold.[34]

There was hard work among the shenanigans:

> At one stage, we were doing 36-hour shifts which meant we'd work all day, we'd have a couple of hours off for tea at night and then work through the night and have a couple of hours off for breakfast and then go straight on the next day. That was very

> hard to take, [be]cause you got awfully weary at the end of it. But all the shifts were quite long because there really weren't enough drivers … In a station like Evans Head where you had night flying going on, we had to be on the tarmac, somebody had to be in the ambulance every night and somebody in the fire engine. We had to start the engines up about every 20 minutes, [e]specially in wintertime. So that you were never [caught] out with a cold engine if you were needed in a hurry.[35]

Jean's second posting was to RAAF Base Maryborough, Qld, from August 1943.[36] Her memory of this period of service was not as fond, owing to the misbehaviour of a senior officer.[37] For Jean, Maryborough's greatest virtue was a dog that had attached itself to the transport section:

> He was Corporal Somebody-Or-Other. He had his dead meat tickets [identity tags] and everything. He'd love hitching a ride in the tenders to take a trip into town and knew all the stops, so he'd jump off [and] 'tootle round' and never missed the last tender back.[38]

Jean and the driver motor transport companion, RAAF Base Maryborough, Queensland, circa 1944 (Australians at War Film Archive, 1535)

Another fond memory of her time at Maryborough was when her boyfriend Douglas Todd Haughton-James – whom she had met before the war during a cruise to Fiji with her sister – proposed. Doug was a radar operator in the Army. He was stationed in Darwin and the letters the pair exchanged were heavily censored, with the dates scrubbed out. While censorship was necessary so as not to reveal the movement of troops, it did make discussing a date for the wedding very difficult!

Doug proposed in the gardens at Maryborough with his signet ring because engagement rings were impossible to obtain during the war. Jean purchased her wedding dress from a shop in Brisbane Arcade and the pair married on 1 April 1944 at her aunt's house in Mallow, Brisbane.

Jean and Doug on their wedding day, 1 April 1944 (Australians at War Film Archive, 1535)

In February 1944, Jean was posted to No 8 Service Flying Training School in Bundaberg, Qld.[39] While in Bundaberg, Jean was invited to put her complaints regarding her former senior officer in writing to the Air Board. He was subsequently charged with 'Behaving in a scandalous manner unbecoming the character of an officer and a gentleman', 'Conduct to the prejudice of good order and Air Force discipline', and 'Committing a civil offence that is to say common assault'. Jean was later flown to Melbourne for a court of inquiry and called to testify again at his court martial on 3 October 1944. He was found guilty of the first and third charges and not guilty of the second charge, and was subsequently 'cashiered from the service … the ultimate disgrace … you're lined up in front of a full parade and you have your buttons chopped off with a sword and your stripes [badges of rank] removed. And your hat taken off and you're drummed off the parade ground.'[40]

Regrettably, Jean and the other girls who had testified were not kept informed and, in 2004, she was still under the impression that this officer had resigned with his service record untarnished.[41] But his service record in fact states that he was 'Cashiered by sentence of GCM [General Court Martial]' on 23 October 1944, after his resignation had been accepted earlier that month.[42]

Jean was discharged at the rank of corporal on 24 July 1945 on compassionate grounds as she was pregnant with her first child. The esprit de corps she experienced survived the test of time and indeed traversed generations. As Jean recalled in the early 2000s, the Evans Head bombing range 'is now used by [RAAF] Amberley for their F-111s. And the range boys always invite all the oldies up for a barbecue on the bombing range and the F-111s come past.'[43] Jean returned to Evans Head every few years to catch up with friends, attend reunions and see how things had changed.

With her friend and fellow WAAAF Sheila Irene Manley, Jean wrote two books about their wartime experiences and those of others. Their first, *"As We Knew It" - Transport Section R.A.A.F. Base Evans Head, N.S.W 1942–43*, chronicled the story of the eight WAAAF DMTs at Evans Head. Their second, *Wings and War: RAAF at Evans Head, 1939–1945*, covered the EATS at Evans Head. After Sheila's death, Jean gave the rights of their book to the Evans Head Museum.[44]

Jean passed away on 28 September 2012.[45] She is survived by her two daughters, Christine and Catherine, and her grandchildren.[46]

Jean Haughton-James and Dame Quentin Bryce (Quentin Bryce)

The White Australia Policy

The *Immigration Restriction Act 1901*, known as the White Australia Policy, aimed to limit non-European, or 'non-white', immigration into Australia in an effort to keep Australia 'British'. However, the discriminatory law manifested in the form of racial prejudice, inciting fear of 'the other'. While the Act ended in 1958, other parts of the policy continued into the early 1970s until the *Racial Discrimination Act* was introduced in 1975.

One night, Jean and a male DMT colleague were waiting to catch the 'midnight horror' from Evans Head to Brisbane when an American troop train pulled in. 'You always jumped on whatever the train was. If it was a goods train, you got on some of the stuff at the back and if it was carrying vehicles, sometimes we sat up in the open air in a jeep or something'.[47] The passengers aboard this train were all African American and Jean and her colleague were uncertain about boarding, owing to:

> The hair-raising stories going around about … how dangerous they were … [This huge gent] came bearing down on us … he was enormous. He said, 'Were you wishing to travel on this train?' So we said, 'Er, um, sort of.' We didn't want to say 'yes'. We didn't quite know whether we wanted to be on the train or not … So he said, 'I'm (whatever he was, his rank and name) Yarra; I'm in charge of this train. I give you my personal guarantee you'll be safe if you'd care to travel on this train.' Very polite, very nice fellow.

For the duration of the trip, Jean and her colleague travelled in Yarra's compartment. The trip eroded preconceptions on both sides. 'It was a jolly cold night' and Jean was shivering. One of the gents climbed out of the train window and returned with a greatcoat for her to cover her knees. They heard 'Yarra calling me Jean, so they were singing "I Dream of Jeanie With the Light Brown Hair" … all making time with their … hand on their knees [and] singing beautifully for us.'

> I'd only ever heard how awful [African Americans] were. This fellow was telling us how they didn't want to come out here because we had our White Australia Policy … He said, 'In a case like this, I'm in charge of this train. There won't be any bother at all … I've got solicitors, doctors, barristers; all sorts of people on this train. But if a white American … in charge of this train … decided any of these men were being insubordinate, he was entitled to shoot them on the spot' … This fellow talked and talked the whole night, right the way up here to Brisbane. Most interesting. [He] couldn't have been more courteous or caring … It was really an eye-opening night. As far as I was concerned, I had a different feeling about the[m from then on] … because I got it from their perspective.[48]

By way of contrast, Jean and her colleagues were once refused passage on a white American troop train and were thrown off by the officer, with their passage to Brisbane permitted only by the guard who allowed them to travel in his compartment.[49]

Aircraftwoman Rena Pascoe (née Porter)

Fabric Worker/Telephone Operator

Service number: 91859
Date of birth: 12 May 1921
Place of birth: Yorketown, South Australia
Date of enlistment: 25 March 1942
Date of discharge: 5 November 1945

Rena Porter, circa 1942 (Department of Defence)

Rena June Porter was born to Christina and Wilfred Pascoe in Yorketown, South Australia (SA), a small country town known for its pink salt lakes. She had two brothers, one older (Wilfred James) and one younger (Leslie William). Her father was a Methodist lay preacher who had served as a stretcher bearer with the 32nd Battalion during the First World War. He was a farmer, a 'hard worker … [and] very strong man' but he had been wounded in France and suffered from his injury for the rest of his life. Rena remembered her upbringing as being rather strict. There was 'no dancing; [I was told] don't get too close to men; no cards in the house. No alcohol.'[1]

Rena went to school in Edithburgh on the Yorke Peninsula, SA, for her first two years of schooling, then continued her education by correspondence. Her lesson packets were delivered by post fortnightly, then she posted them back for marking. Postal delays would cause disruptions to the learning process, making it tricky at times. Because Rena had to move away and board for high school, she ceased her schooling at the end of Year 7.[2] She attended:

> Muirden College [in Adelaide, SA] for a little while and I came … to live with my grandma … I just had English and Maths to try and catch up … [But] my father's idea was you grow up and marry a farmer, so you don't need an education. [But] it didn't work that way.[3]

When the war broke out, Rena was living in Adelaide. Prior to the WAAAF forming, she signed up with the Women's Air Training Corps, which met one night a week. Rena volunteered as a fabric worker:

> Because I like sewing. And we had a man that used to come down from Parafield [in Adelaide] with an aileron [section of an aircraft wing] to teach us how to stitch and [to tell us] a bit of [the] history of what we [were doing] … I went to Parafield as a volunteer and taught the Dutch Indonesians how to mend a plane.[4]

In March 1942, Rena received the call to report for service with the WAAAF. She was among the first group of girls to undertake WAAAF training at No 4 Initial Training School at Mount Breckan in Victor Harbor, SA. The girls would catch the train to Breckan House and 'were marched down to the train and marched from there up the hill to Mount Breckan'.[5]

Women who were mustered to all trades undertook the course together, attending classes in gas education and military protocol:

> We had to learn to march in gas masks and … move from this chair to that chair. We had to move with our gas mask. They were very strict … and in March, I was pretty hot marching with [a] gas mask … We had little planes of all [the] countries … and we had to learn to recognise them. And we had to learn who you saluted and who you didn't – Army, Navy and Air Force … It was sort of the making of my adult life … it was a nice experience. I think because my dad was strict, that made me keep on the straight and narrow.[6]

The boys and girls were kept separate:

> The only time we actually met was at line up for our jabs [vaccinations]. At least the women waited until after they had the injection before they fainted. The men fainted before they got in there.

Rena's first posting was to No 6 Service Flying Training School in Mallala, SA. On their arrival, they were each handed a palliasse (mattress cover) and told to go and fill it with straw, but not 'too full because it's got to be folded in three every day'.[7]

Several of the girls were posted in from Mount Breckan – fabric workers, signals and cooks:

> I remember one … [of the cooks who,] when she did an about turn, she always swung her arms out. And our male sergeant drilling us said, 'If you swing those arms out again, I'll pull them off and slap you over the face with them.'[8]

Dust storms were common in Mallala. When they woke up in the morning, 'you could see your face on the pillow' – the imprint made 'by fine red dust. And then you'd have to be cleaning the hut out.'[9]

Women's Auxiliary Australian Air Force servicewomen wearing working gear in their recreation hut in Mallala, South Australia, 1944 (Australian War Memorial, P02221.001)

The girls took turns folding parachutes and eventually Rena started working in the camouflage section. It was located in a hangar shared with the maintenance crew for Avro Anson aircraft:

> I did that for about 12 months and I was training one young man and I was telling him to … [paint] the nose of the plane, and he was standing on a 44-gallon drum

> … his can gave way and hit the 44-gallon drum [and] sprayed [acetone] … into my mouth. And so I had a couple of weeks in hospital on malt extract and nothing else … After that, they sent me on to get some decent food [and you] couldn't get any decent food unless you went up to the officers mess … [The] Sergeant's mess they say was [al]right too, but ours was cabbage, and cabbage every day, and [on] Fridays we had 'goldfish' … I think it was shark.[10]

After Rena returned to work, they discovered that she had developed an acetone allergy and so she was transferred to the armoury section. The base flew Avro Ansons in a 'morning patrol and a night patrol'. The underside of the morning-patrol Ansons were painted a pale blue and the night-patrol aircraft were painted black.[11]

> While I was there, we had some unidentified planes, so [many] that we all shot down [for cover] in the trench … a couple of days after that, there was a[n enemy] submarine sighted that was heading up the gulf … I helped load the bombs [onto the aircraft]. They put the planes all over the place, all round the field … But apparently the sub[marine] decided that if they got up there they'd be trapped, so it turned around and went – so our planes were de-bombed and [the enemy attack] never happened. But I was proud of the fact that the plane that sighted it out there was one that I had camouflaged.[12]

Corporal Margaret Deal and Aircraftwoman Rosemary Kemp installing a Vickers machine gun into an aircraft, circa 1943 (State Library of Victoria, Argus Collection)

An Avro Anson in camouflage livery (RAAF Museum)

In February 1943, Rena was posted to No 4 School of Technical Training in Adelaide and trained in signals. In October, she remustered as a telephone operator and was posted to No 14 Stores Unit:[13]

> Every time anybody rang outside the building, it went through the exchange. And I was given … the number to ring if [there was an] invasion. I can still remember it: XY550 … never used, thank goodness … [but] there was a feeling here, because we were so close … to the sea, that we could be the same as Darwin and Sydney [as an enemy target].[14]

In June 1945, Rena was posted to Headquarters Southern Area in Toorak, Victoria.[15] She caught the troop train from Adelaide to Melbourne, with eight girls squeezed into compartments that would normally seat four. The trains travelled overnight; 'some of the girls slept on the floor', some on the luggage racks above and others 'sitting up all night leaning against something'. While in Toorak, Rena was billeted at the Japanese embassy because 'the Japanese weren't there. They still had straw-filled palliasses but they were supported by nice beds.'[16]

The Commanding Officer at Toorak was an earl and 'he would not let me salute him. Every time, he'd say, "Thank you, thank you" … I thought I'd arrived in Italy because there [were] so many accents which I wasn't used to.'[17]

Rena was discharged from the WAAAF in November 1945, but afterwards '[I felt] lost … I could not apply for a job for about six months. I'd think about it, look at the paper, and just could not.'[18] After some encouragement from her mother, she got a job as a telephone operator 'until I got sick of it'. After four years of life in the WAAAF, it was difficult for Rena to adjust to the pace of a civilian job:

> They were people just asking how much pastries were, and butchers ringing up [and asking] how much meat do they want? And to me, it just seemed a waste of a life.

Troop train artwork by Women's Auxiliary Australian Air Force servicewoman and artist Elsa Russell, 1944 (Australian War Memorial, ART29015)

Eventually, Rena was accepted into a nursing course in Mount Gambier, SA. 'I was given a month to get down there. And then [I] decided, I wouldn't go.'

In 1951, Rena met and married a former soldier who was later found to be suffering from 'war neurosis'. He had served in the 50th Field Battery, 13th Allied Regiment, Australian Imperial Force but 'they didn't get help in those days. And it got beyond us; as he got older, it got too bad.' Together they had one son, Ian, but the marriage ended and Rena went back to using her maiden name:

> I'm never sorry [about not working] because in those days, women didn't go out to work if they were married, so I was able to bring Ian up and also do a lot of voluntary work ... 82 years of voluntary work.[19]

Rena later remarried and volunteered with the Adelaide Hospital, Prison Aid (where she taught women how to sew) and the Returned and Services League.

Rena passed away on 20 September 2020, aged 99. She is survived by her children, grandchildren and great-grandchildren.[20]

Corporal Olive Jardine (née McNeil)

Clerk Stores/Clerk Accounts

Service number: 93766
Date of birth: 23 January 1921
Place of birth: Gladesville, New South Wales
Date of enlistment: 15 April 1942
Date of discharge: 17 June 1946

Olive McNeil, circa 1943 (Australians at War Film Archive, 225)

Olive Winifred McNeil was born on 23 January 1921 to father Hector and mother Olive Beatrice in Gladesville, Sydney.[1] She had a younger brother, Harry, with whom she enjoyed playing in the backyard. Their garden was full of fruit trees, vegetables, and chickens, whose heads you 'could lop … off [at] any time' to put dinner on the table.

Hector had served in the Army during the First World War:

> He went away fit and he came home unfit, and was medically discharged [as] unfit. He was shell shocked. He got pneumonia in the trenches [and] bronchitis. He was invalided to England and he came home. He was a very independent person, and when he came back, they offered him a full pension and he knocked it back. He said he was quite able to work and support himself … [but] he always suffered from bronchitis afterwards.[2]

Olive attended Gladesville Public School, then Riverside Girls Domestic Science School, completing her intermediate and leaving certificate examinations.[3] Her first job was teaching piano at the age of 16. After school, Olive trained as an accountant and worked for a local farmer, before getting a job as a bookkeeper at the Wentworth Laundry, 'doing all the accounts, reconciliations and things like that'.[4]

Olive enrolled in the WAAAF on 15 April 1942, aged 21, and began her initial training at Bradfield Park:

> Because you didn't have a uniform straight [a]way, we were in civvies [civilian clothing], and the DI [drill instructor] used to sing out, 'Pick them up, brown shoes!' And everyone used to get a fit of giggles. There were two girls to a room in the huts … You had needles in your arm for all the different things; the men used to drop before they even got the needle. We were very stoic; we survived … You had to go to lectures and you had to identify planes … It was very encompassing, all the things you had to do, but it was enjoyable at the same time. You had lights out at ten o'clock … and [were] up about six o'clock.[5]

At 'rookies', the girls were issued with:

> A kit bag, navy [blue], your number on the outside and 'WAAAF' … you had a 'housewife' [sewing kit], which was to mend your clothes with needle and thread; that was important. You had clothes that you were given [and] underclothes … I never got a nightdress, or pyjamas … We didn't have sheets on our beds, unless you brought them from home. You were issued with your blankets.

A month later, Olive was posted to No 5 Service Flying Training School (5SFTS) in Uranquinty, located near Wagga Wagga in the Riverina region of southern New South Wales, which she would call home for the next three years. During the Second World War, the region was abuzz with military personnel, with RAAF schools at Wagga, Temora, Parkes, Deniliquin, and Narrandera, and the Army at Kapooka. However, 5SFTS was unique in that its aerodrome had been built by the RAAF specifically for flying training in 1941. The land was resumed by the Air Force for Defence purposes from the Lewington and Tabner families, who found out the fate of their farms from the local newspaper:[6]

> It was a new station and … everything was [still] being built … it was very primitive. But it was a happy station … We came from rich, middle-class and lowly class [families], and we all got on together. And do you know what made us get on together? We all dressed alike; there was an equality. We ate the same food, we went to the same places; we perhaps did not make the same friends with each other, but we all got on … We were all the same … Our huts were wooden, unlined … No partitions, floorboards uncovered, wire stretchers, hessian palliasses, no sheets, unless you brought them from home … no curtains, but we did get some hessian ones later. We had a lot of rain the first winter; there was mud and slush everywhere. It was cold; there was no heating. We had to go outside to go to the toilet … We had no doors on our toilets [and] we had showers with no partitions; it was jolly awful. But then … We started a garden going, and had roses growing and things improved. In the summer, we had the heat, we had the dust … At one time, we had three days of dust storms and the planes couldn't fly. And all the dust used to get into the engines of the Wirraways … we had locusts, we had heat, we had moths, we had grasshoppers. It was awful, but we were happy.

The training school was 'run like a country estate', and Olive attributed its success to their Commanding Officer, Group Captain Thomas Curnow, who arrived in July 1943:[7]

> He was a fabulous fellow … he had a pig farm; he had vegetables grown with all the scraps and everything … He had girls and boys working on the estate. And our station was run very well … he set us on a good path and … he had lots of different enterprises going that set us apart.[8]

Olive was mustered as a clerk accounting:

> The flight sergeant in charge of Accounting [at 5SFTS], he welcomed us with open arms … But a lot of officer types, a lot of men in those days, didn't want the girls.

The Accounting section at a RAAF station was important because everything on the station had to be 'accounted for. I mean, all the nuts and bolts on a plane, for instance; the paint, people.' Indeed:

> Everyone who came on the station had to come through us, [to] be entered onto the station. And everyone that left had to come through us. People had to receive things, or leave things.

The role of the Accounting section was to count, tally the lists, and balance all of the items. The team worked a six-day week:

> We used to have Saturday off, because the Army had Sunday off, and they said there would be too many fights if they had both Services off on the one day … The Wagga people were wonderful. The hospitality those people gave us was incredible. They used to have us in their homes and we would stay overnight. Nothing was ever a bother to them.[9]

Once a month, Olive would have a four-day weekend and catch the troop train to either Sydney or Melbourne. 'We would travel all night and perhaps get to Sydney about six o'clock in the morning.'[10]

The 'Quinty crew', circa 1944 (Australians at War Film Archive, 225)

Olive had played the piano since she was a child and had graduated as an Associate of the London College of Music in the pianoforte.[11] Naturally, music became part of her life at 5SFTS. Olive initially played piano for church services and events. Later, she was invited to join both the Uranquinty and Forest Hill RAAF bands:

> I was the only girl in the two bands … [I played] the tenor horn. I used to play the organ and piano at the church services. But for VE [Victory in Europe] Day, I played the piano for the station, and then the band was down below.[12]

Learning to fly military aircraft in the Second World War was not without significant risk; hundreds of aircrew were killed or injured in flying accidents while training. At 5SFTS, this numbered almost 30 killed.[13] However, aircraft accidents were not the only cause of death for service personnel, with others suffering from illnesses and accidents. Olive recalls that funerals were intimate affairs and any talk of accidents was minimised:

> [I]t wasn't broadcast. You see, people didn't know all these fatalities had taken place, or a lot of them. Because, for the morale of the station, it wouldn't pay for people [to know], especially these trainees in these different courses. They have to

go up in the air knowing that one of their mates [had] just been killed … I went to one funeral; it wasn't a crash, it was one of our girls [Robina Kirk] … she got a bump and it turned cancerous. And I went to see her in the hospital in Wagga … but she died. She was a beautiful girl … she was married to an Army young man … We went to the funeral in Wagga Cemetery. It was the saddest funeral I've ever been to. We did the slow march. When they put the coffin down the grave, everyone went up and saluted.

Sister and brother, Olive and Harry McNeil, wearing their respective Air Force uniforms, circa 1944. Note the RAAF Band insignia on Olive's sleeve above her corporal chevrons (Australians at War Film Archive, 225)

In 1943, Olive's father, Harry, also died:

He'd gone down to Melbourne and he had taken sick down there … and he ended up in the Repat[riation Hospital], and he died. And my mother couldn't go down because of the [travel] restrictions on the border … [the WAAAF] wouldn't give me compassionate leave, at the time … so he was cremated down there. They sent his ashes home.[14]

In June 1945, Olive was posted to No 5 Aircraft Depot at Forest Hill. When it was announced that the war was over, there were incredible celebrations:

They had troop trains … to Sydney and to Melbourne. And when we got to Sydney, it was unbelievable. People were crying, and they were laughing … It was the most fantastic feeling. The war was over. And yet on the other side, you thought, 'Oh,

> there [are] people that are suffering' and you felt for them. And you felt for those who were missing, and the parents of those people; all these mixed emotions.

Olive discharged from the WAAAF in June 1946. On returning home after four-and-a-half years in the WAAAF:

> Everyone was exactly the same … I'd been writing to people all the time. We were still friends, but our interests were different; our outlook on life was different … we had a close bond in the Air Force, and you miss the companionship and that. It's hard to explain … I was the same person, and yet I had changed.

Olive was successful in finding work in clerical roles in both the public and private sectors because in 'those days, there [were] plenty of jobs for everyone'.[15] In November 1949, she married Gordon McNeil, who had served with the 23rd Field Company in Darwin.

Throughout her life, Olive remained active within the veteran community. She believed that their shared experience bonded them for a lifetime: 'I still see girls at meetings, at times, that slept in the same hut [as] I did at Uranquinty, fifty odd years ago.'[16] In 1999, she returned to Uranquinty for the unveiling of a memorial organised by a former 5SFTS trainee, Dr Peter Ilbery:

> Quinty was a station that was such a happy place that people have been in contact ever since. You see, [the] Lewington [family] used to own the property, before it became an Air Force [base], and through trial and tribulation they have regained it, and they opened their property … for us to go there. And people come at all times of the year just to think back on [the] times they had there … [F]ifty years later, when I went back to a memorial we had, all those trees [we'd planted] had grown and they were beautiful.

Olive passed away on 6 October 2022, aged 101. She is survived by her sons, grandchildren and great-grandchildren.[17]

Royal Australian Air Force bands

During the Second World War, Air Force bands were formed at almost every flying training school on the home front. From marching bands providing tunes for parades, to concert bands accompanying performances on stage, music provided a welcome addition to official events and was a much-loved after-hours pastime and entertainment.

No 10 Elementary Flying Training School's marching band, featuring members of the Women's Auxiliary Australian Air Force, September 1943 (Temora Rural Museum)

Because membership of unit bands was not recorded on service records, it is impossible to say exactly how many women were involved in Air Force bands during the war. However, from photographic records and testimonies such as Olive Jardine's, we know that women were certainly involved. Research has recently begun to shine a light on the role women have played in the RAAF bands' history. The results of these projects are beginning to be published.

The fife section of the Women's Auxiliary Australian Air Force band entertaining visitors during a fun fair in Toorak, Victoria, December 1942 (Australian War Memorial, 137428)

Today, the Air Force Band provides music for Australian Defence Force, commemorative and community events. There are specific bands for each type of occasion, including a ceremonial band, concert band, big band, wind quintet, brass quintet, jazz group, clarinet quartet and drum corps.

Corporal Laila Engle plays for a new recording of the Australian national anthem, St Kilda, Victoria, 2021 (Department of Defence)

Corporal Shirley Brettle (née Robinson)

Radar Operator/Radio Direction Finding Operator

Service number: 98395
Date of birth: 3 June 1921
Place of birth: Randwick, New South Wales
Date of enlistment: 27 June 1942
Date of discharge: 15 May 1944

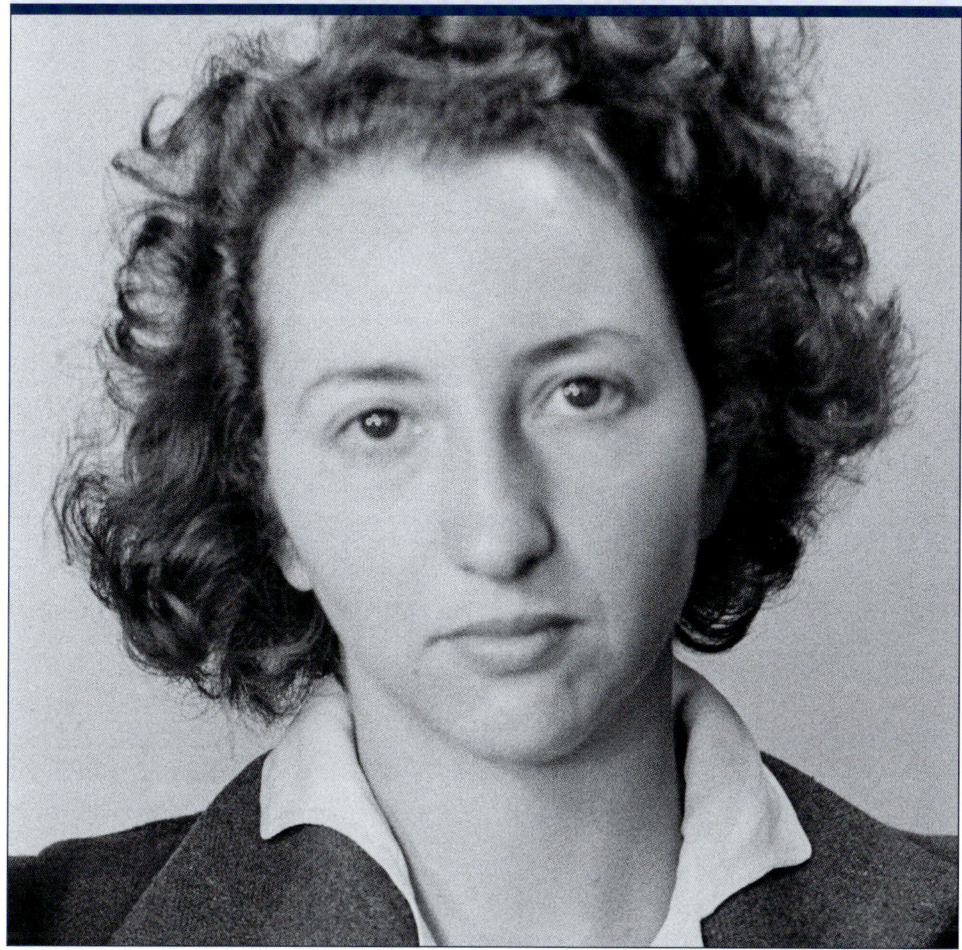

Shirley Robinson's Women's Auxiliary Australian Air Force enlistment photo, 1942 (National Archives of Australia, A9301, 98395; 4959436)

Shirley Joan Robinson was born on 3 June 1921 in Randwick, New South Wales (NSW), to Wilbert Eric and Freda Hope Robinson. Her parents were young but 'quite well-off'.[1] As such, Shirley was sent:

> To a good private school … and then the Depression came … we had three other children [in the family] and there was no money at all, so life was very different … the banks closed and you couldn't draw any money out of your bank account.

Shirley's family was lucky, though; her grandparents did not keep their money in the bank.[2]

After school, Shirley attended night school four nights a week. 'I'd got my leaving [certificate], so I could go to university but I had to get a job … I thought, well I liked mathematics and I was reasonable at it, so I became a Comptometer Operator' at David Jones department store in Surry Hills, NSW.[3]

After war broke out, Shirley saw a notice in the paper for the WAAAF and put her name down. She enrolled at No 2 WAAAF Depot in Bradfield Park, NSW, on 27 June 1942. Following her interview, Shirley was invited to go on the first course for WAAAF radar operators in NSW, at No 11 Operators Course Radio School in Richmond, from 2 August:[4]

> We had no idea what we were going to do. I had never done science and it was wonderful! … So we did this long course … about nine weeks learning about the brand-new cutting-edge technology.[5]

Shirley recalled that, 'The training was conducted under tight security, with everyone taking the Secrecy Act very seriously'.[6]

Women's Auxiliary Australian Air Force radar plotters (RAAF Museum)

After Japan's entry into the war, an extensive network of early-warning radar units and Ground Controlled Interception (GCI) units were established along the most vulnerable sections of the Australian coast. Their purpose was to detect enemy aircraft which were beyond the range of sight.[7] The stations transmitted bursts of radio energy. If there was an object in the sky, it appeared as a 'flicker of green light on a small square screen'.[8] Calculations could then be made to determine the object's height and bearing. The results were reported to each of the different services' Group Fighter Sections or Operations Rooms.

The role of the WAAAF radar operators was to detect the difference between a real echo and:

> [The] normal background mess of flickering green light, then fix its position accurately from a grid superimposed over the screen … no special skill was required, only dedication to a one hundred per cent watch, and integrity to keep radar a secret operation.[9]

After her training, Shirley was sent to Ash Island, a small island located in the Hunter River near Newcastle, NSW, which was home to No 131 Radar Station.[10] As with all Australian radar stations, it was originally equipped with a British GCI mounted on 4×4 Crossley trucks beneath darkened and weatherproof canopies, which Shirley referred to as a 'tent':[11]

> There was nothing on this island except mosquitos and cows. And here we are in the tent … we're getting close to the war and we really did work. You'd work six hours on, 18 hours off … and after about a week of that, you were nearly all off your head because you had to turn a handle to make the aerial go around, the aerial didn't even go around.[12]

Women's Auxiliary Australian Air Force quarters at No 131 Radar Station on Ash Island, New South Wales, 1943 (RAAF Museum)

By the time the station closed in 1946, it was equipped with the most modern Canadian GCI set within a concrete igloo and was staffed by an almost all-WAAAF contingent.[13]

While at Ash Island, Shirley was part of a team which was sent with urgency to set up a temporary radar station in Maroubra, NSW. Their role was to observe ships which were travelling up the coast. 'They had some knowledge of a date … [and] a lot of information, [but] you don't know what's going on; you haven't a clue and you're not told.' They did observe something that came from the south one night. Shirley later speculated that it may have been the transport of the Japanese midget submarines which entered Sydney Harbour.[14]

No 131 Radar Station personnel outside the orderly room, circa 1943 (RAAF Museum)

In May 1943, Shirley was posted to No 51 Radar Station in Coolangatta, Queensland. There, she was:

> In charge of my shift. We worked the same hours: six on, 18 off, six on, 18 off, and by the time we'd worked for two weeks, we were just about conked-out so then we'd have three days off.[15]

The RAAF radar stations were responsible for monitoring the skies and used a different technology to the Royal Australian Navy's sonar, which monitored the surface:

> It was only when we got abnormal conditions, or [if] something was happening with the equipment that we would get something on the surface … [people] think we used to see these things, but we didn't. All we saw was the blip. All day long it was ok, because we had IFF [Identification Friend or Foe]. We watched our Catalinas [aircraft] go up and down … but they changed their signal every day so you always knew it was one of ours … it would come down and the distance it came down shows you how big it was … you never took your eyes off the screen.[16]

Women's Auxiliary Australian Air Force radar plotters (RAAF Museum)

In November 1942, Shirley married her childhood friend, Horace Joseph Brettle. In May 1944, Shirley was discharged on compassionate grounds at the rank of corporal.[17]

After the war, Shirley became an interior designer, and Horace a civil engineer and then one of the first lecturers at the University of New South Wales. The couple combined their love of studying with their love of travelling and skiing. They also enjoyed designing and building houses. Shirley passed away on 15 September 2018, aged 97. She is survived by her sons James and Roger, and a 'large loving family'.[18]

Corporal Margaret Clarke (née Johnston)

Clerk Stores

Service number: 105705
Date of birth: 19 May 1924
Place of birth: Rockdale, New South Wales
Date of enlistment: 10 August 1942
Date of discharge: 14 August 1945

Mum took my photo but I did not particularly like it. At that stage, we were only issued with berets, as there were not any proper caps available and I would have liked to wait, until I had my cap.[1]

Margaret Johnston on a visit home halfway through her 'rookies' course, August 1942 (Jacqui Kennedy)

Margaret McIntosh Johnston was born in Rockdale, New South Wales (NSW), on 19 May 1924 to Charles and Ida Johnston. Her father had a farm at Rankins Springs, NSW, but unfortunately lost it during the Depression; 'after that, he was usually either on the dole or doing working jobs on [other] farms.'[2]

Margaret was the eldest of four children. She had two brothers, David and Charles, and one sister, Anne.[3] Her primary school years were spent at Erigolia and Rankins Springs, and through correspondence with Blackfriars School in Sydney. Margaret was an avid reader and would often rise at 4:30 am with her father to complete her homework.[4] Her family moved to Sydney so Margaret would not have to board and could attend William Street Junior High School to attain her leaving certificate.[5] After she finished school, Margaret attended Sydney Technical College and later got employment as a clerk.[6]

Margaret grew up listening to stories of service during the First World War. Her father had joined the Royal Australian Navy as a cadet in 1912 and served as an able seaman until 1919, while her uncles on her mother's side had served with the Australian Imperial Force. When women were called up to assist in the Second World War effort, Margaret was 'very excited to try to do something … I was patriotic'. She 'didn't like the uniform of the Army and … wasn't keen on the hats that the Navy [servicewomen] wore'; consequently, she decided to complete her family's service trifecta by adding Air Force blue. Her father refused to sign the permission papers, 'but after some pleading', her mother did. Her brother David also joined the Air Force and served as a wireless operator/air gunner.[7]

Women's Auxiliary Australian Air Force recruits during gas-mask training at Bradfield Park, Sydney, New South Wales (Mitchell Library, State Library of New South Wales)

Margaret enrolled at Bradfield Park, NSW, in August 1942 and was mustered as a clerk, in line with her civilian occupation. She remembers that her drill instructor (DI), Corporal Hunter Owen, 'had a voice like a foghorn and was very strict, but she was kind and she put up with our tripping over our legs when we first started'. During 'rookies', the girls also had to participate in a gas drill:

> We put on a mask, went into a hut and then it was filled with tear gas. We had to stay there for a short time, take the mask off and then we came running out, spluttering and coughing with tears running out of our eyes.[8]

Margaret also completed a training course at the Equipment Training School in Laverton, Victoria, graduating from No 23 Course in January 1943.[9] Her first posting was to Headquarters RAAF Station Nowra in September 1942, along with three other WAAAF servicewomen from her rookies course. However, as WAAAF personnel were only recent additions to the station's establishment, there were still some improvements required to best accommodate the girls:

> We shared an ablution [bathroom] block with the men, and there was a dividing thing for it [between the men's and women's sections]. And some of the men had bored holes in it so they could look at us showering in the nuddy, and it was one of the kind married men that told our DI about it. So the CO [Commanding Officer] immediately had a separate one [assigned to us]. But the men would hear our voices, [and] they [would] say, 'Oh, is that you, Margaret? Are you going to the dance tonight?' This was over the shower.[10]

The role of a clerk involved completing paperwork for orders of uniforms and supplies. Margaret ordered the tailored uniforms for the men when they were promoted, and the metal for the experimental torpedo section. She also completed reports on the serviceability of the station's aircraft: 'I had to do that every night. It was in code … and I thought, 'Geez, even a kid going to kindergarten could work this code out.'[11]

The food at Nowra was 'so-so' and then there were days when it was 'bad':[12]

> Herrings in tomato sauce, 'dog biscuits' and margarine … But the roast dinners were always very nice and breakfast was … toast and porridge and Weetbix and things. I didn't eat a lot at the unit. I've always been a fussy eater … and I used to have a lot of meals in town, because I used to go into the dances a lot … in the summertime, I ate a lot of pineapple and I ended up getting a very bad attack of hives from the toes to the waist, and I was in hospital for a week.[13]

After Margaret was promoted to corporal in December 1943, she attended payday parades where she:

> Had to issue clothing cards [and] coupons … it gave me the opportunity to look at people's files … [when] a chap would ask me out … [I could see from his file if] he was married or not and I wouldn't go out with them [if they were married] and they'd say, 'Why?' I'd say, 'Oh, I just have a feeling you're married', and they never knew how I found out. I was a bit sneaky sometimes.[14]

Margaret very much enjoyed the social aspect of service life. For a short time, she wrote for the station's gossip column: 'I was able to supply [the editor] with lots of short stories … I even wrote some about myself, so no one would guess I was the author.'[15] However, her favourite pastime was attending dances both on and off the base. On one occasion, she returned to base late at night after a dance in town and was exhausted:

> Something [was] happening off the coast … and the Air Force plane had gone out [to search. They'd raised the] air raid siren and I'd just come in from a dance at 11:30 at night, and [our DI] came rushing in; the hut was empty. She said, 'Margaret, you have to come out and get into the trenches.' I said, 'They're full of mud! … I'm not going out. I'm going to bed', and I got into bed. She didn't do anything about it … because I never caused her any trouble. I was always on morning parade; I was always in bed at night … anyway, when all the other girls came back in, they said, 'What are you doing here? You're supposed to be out [in] the trenches.' I said, 'I didn't know anything about it!'[16]

When the girls lost loved ones, the whole WAAAF contingent grieved. One of the girls lost her husband when his aircraft was shot down over the Middle East, and another lost her son in New Guinea: 'It was a bad time.' However, their 'D.I. was a "rock" for the two girls and I am sure her support/guidance for them and a lot of anxious WAAAFs was appreciated.'[17]

There were also terrible accidents. Margaret recalled one over Jervis Bay:

> I never knew the crew but I saw them going in and out of the operations room, and [on] the day that they were killed, I saw two of them walking down to the dispersal area and they were laughing and joking. And one of them was such a good-looking, tall blonde chap. I was smitten by him. I knew he was married … the whole eight of them were killed in that accident. Two planes [Beauforts A9-27 and A9-268 on 14 April 1943].[18]

Margaret and Leo in Martin Place in Sydney, New South Wales, on 'the day Leo bought the ring' (Jacqui Kennedy)

In August 1944, Margaret was posted to No 51 Radar Station in Coolangatta, Queensland (Qld). Owing to personality clashes with a WAAAF officer, she was not particularly fond of that posting. While there, Margaret was told about the sinking of the hospital ship AHS *Centaur*, which was attacked and sunk by a Japanese submarine on 14 May 1943.

In addition to her clerical duties, Margaret helped in the kitchen when the kitchen personnel had time off. This involved 'clearing table[s], getting rid of rubbish, washing and drying dishes … wiping down tables and chairs and mopping'. However, she enjoyed afternoon swims at the beach and she also met her future husband, Leo Clarke, who was in the 1st Armoured Regiment.[19] They met by chance at a bus stop while they were both on their way to Southport for a dance. The pair married in Sydney in April 1945 and had a daughter, Carol, and a son, Stephen. Leo and Margaret later divorced.[20]

In March 1945, Margaret was posted to No 8 Stores Depot in Macrossan, Qld. The three-day train trip there was made interesting, courtesy of the 7th Division Pipe Band:[21]

> They played the bagpipes a lot, and there were a lot of civilians on the train and they didn't dare complain … the soldiers were going from one end of the train to the other all day, saying hello to people, talking, [and] playing the bagpipes. It was an interesting time. There was dust … and Bindi-eyes [burrs] blowing through the windows … when we stopped at some station, the local Red Cross … came out and were giving us tea and biscuits and cake and things.

Again, Margaret's memories of Macrossan were not overly pleasant, owing to her not getting on well with the other WAAAFs, bouts of hives from eating too many oranges, 'boring work checking out things in a book nearly all day', being in the first trimester of pregnancy, and experiencing interrupted sleep owing to possums 'running through the huts at night'.[22]

Margaret Clarke being awarded a Chief of Air Force Gold Commendation by Group Captain Warren Bishop, 2019 (Department of Defence)

Margaret was discharged from the WAAAF on 6 June 1945 on compassionate grounds.[23] After the war, she worked part-time in a factory. In 1960, she got a job with the Repatriation Department (known as the Department of Veterans' Affairs from 1976), from which she retired in the 1980s.[24] In 2019, Margaret was awarded a Chief of Air Force Gold Commendation for her efforts to document the history of the WAAAF through social media and a website of her family's history.

Margaret passed away in June 2022. For the last three years of her life, she kept a 'Wendy the WAAAF' doll by her bedside. The doll was knitted by Margaret's friend Dorothy Kraft from an original 1940s pattern published by *The Australian Women's Weekly* magazine. Margaret's niece Jacqui Kennedy donated Wendy and the pattern book to the Air Force Heritage Collection in 2023. Margaret is survived by her children and grandchildren.[25]

'Wendy the WAAAF' doll with the original knitting pattern (Emily Constantine)

In 2022, the RAAF renamed its 'Warrant Officer of the Air Force Creative Writing Award' the 'Corporal Margaret Clarke Award'. The objective of the award is to encourage and inspire enlisted RAAF aviators to consume, contribute to, and contest contemporary air- and space-power issues, and to research, analyse and debate possibilities for air and space power beyond the future Air Force.[26]

Sister Lucy Lane (née MacKenzie)

Nursing Sister

Service number: 500358
Date of birth: 11 October 1918
Place of birth: Pusan, Korea
Date of enlistment: 15 February 1943
Date of discharge: 25 October 1946

Lucy MacKenzie (Australians at War Film Archive, 417)

Lucy Georgia MacKenzie was born in Pusan, Korea, on 11 October 1918 to father Reverend James Nobel MacKenzie and mother Mary Kelly. Her parents were Australian missionaries who lived in Korea with their four daughters (a son had died from diphtheria when he was two years old). The girls all spoke both Korean and English at home:

> There was a dormitory of the primary school next door to us and we made friends with the children there … We played all the usual children's games and we loved going to eat at their dormitory. We'd have to help them with their chores and so on. Washing the rice and carrying water up from the well … Mother used to get cross because she said it was taking food away from them … [We ate] Western-style meals always at home. We had porridge for breakfast and … a meat casserole or roast [for lunch] … and we had fish every evening … meat was a problem because there were no cows … mother always kept goats for milk for us … the lack of milk was a problem for mothers and babies. Because if mothers didn't have enough breast milk for one reason or another, they used to feed the babies on rice water … They didn't survive.[1]

Both of Lucy's parents did important work within the local community. Mary had lived and worked in Korea as a teacher before she married:

> She spoke Korean very well and had a rapport with all the Korean women … She mostly worked with women because … the men were [considered to be] much more important than the women and … wouldn't be taught by a woman.

Reverend MacKenzie worked in a leprosy hospital, which was always short of beds. The family would often:

> Have beggars at [the] gate of our compound house, pleading with Dad to be admitted, and there just wouldn't be room … it was an enormous problem … Because lepers were complete outcasts in Korea then. Any sign of leprosy and they were just [put] right out [of their communities] … They were just turned into beggars. There wasn't any real treatment.

For her first two years of school, Lucy attended the local Korean school. Her primary schooling then continued with correspondence lessons from England, which were overseen by her mother. At age nine, Lucy commenced boarding at an American school in Pyongyang.

Every seven years, Lucy's parents would return to Australia on a sabbatical:

> The second time I came [to Australia], I was twelve going on thirteen, and I went to PLC [Presbyterian Ladies College boarding school] for one year and then, when I finished American high school [in Korea] … I went back to PLC for the last term of the year to sit for my Leaving Certificate, because Australia didn't recognise my American certificate although our graduates went straight into Harvard and Yale and places without any problem.

Lucy's dream was to become a nurse. Her eldest sister worked in medicine, and her second sister had just finished her training at the Children's Hospital in Melbourne when Lucy started nursing, so she was able to show Lucy the ropes. When war was declared, Lucy was working at the Queen Victoria Hospital in Melbourne:

> This friend of mine … [came into] the sitting room one day [and] said, 'Women, let's join the Air Force.' So I said, 'Alright, let's.' And we did … we joined the Air Force rather than the Army because it was a nicer uniform.

Lucy wrote a letter to Margaret Lang, the Air Force's Matron-in-Chief, supplied the appropriate references and paperwork, had an interview, and was promptly offered a position in the RAAFNS. She was appointed on 15 February 1943 and reported to No 2 RAAF Hospital in Ascot Vale in the Melbourne showgrounds, which had been converted into a hospital:

> I first went to the cow pavilion which was a medical ward … we did the same sort of work as we would anywhere. We didn't have to do any drill … We didn't have to salute. We were saluted. We went in as officers … I had my first experience of the miracle of penicillin in that time at Ascot Vale. We had a patient admitted with osteomyelitis of the frontal bone … He was extremely ill and they managed to get some penicillin from the Americans, who had taken over the new Melbourne Hospital in Parkville … it was a miracle. He just was cured almost overnight. It was terrible treatment. You had to give enormous doses of this penicillin solution into their buttocks four hourly. But he was cured … within forty-eight hours.

In May 1943, Lucy was posted to the sick quarters at RAAF Station Point Cook, Victoria. It was 'a beautiful place' with well-established trees and permanent buildings. The sick quarters had 'about thirty-five beds … there were five sisters and WAAAF medical orderlies and male medical officers'. The nursing sisters lived in one of the married officer's quarters: 'We had our own bedrooms and very comfortable living [quarters] and we had our own WAAAF cook.' Because the main hospital was at nearby RAAF Base Laverton, the sick quarters at Point Cook only had to deal with illnesses and immunisations.

Life at Point Cook provided Lucy with new experiences. Growing up, 'drinking was taboo and so was smoking' and the only dancing that was done was 'around the maypole':

> When I first joined the Air Force, I hadn't ever been to a dance; would you believe? I was twenty-three … there was a shortage of women and there were five of us nurses – this was on the station at Point Cook and, of course, [as] soon as the music started … 'May I have this dance?' I said, 'Sorry, I can't dance.' 'Don't be absurd,' they said, 'of course you can.' I said, 'No, I've never danced.' 'Well, it's time you learned.' So off we went, [and] by the end of the evening, I could dance.[2]

On her days off, Lucy also enjoyed spearfishing for flounder (and cooking up the catch for supper), ice skating and playing tennis. 'We had pictures on picture nights on the station … [but as] we worked fairly hard, long hours … I didn't worry too much about [my] social life.'

In January 1944, Lucy was posted to No 5 Embarkation Depot in Perth in Western Australia, where she worked at Hollywood Hospital (110 Military Hospital) near Shenton Park. 'We had one Air Force ward attached to the Army hospital … there were only about eight or maybe 10 Air Force nurses there at the time.'

Three months into Lucy's time in Perth, there came a call for volunteers to join a new unit overseas:

> [T]he Medical Air Evacuation Transport Unit … was being formed to transport patients by air in New Guinea … they wanted volunteers for the unit because they thought it was going to be dangerous … So of course we were all keen and we all applied and there [were] certain restrictions … you had to be a certain height and only 130 pounds [58.9kg] weight … Years after, we were having a reunion of our unit … and the subject came up about … this restriction of height and weight, and I said something about my terrible problem of being overweight. And the two medical officers who had started this unit, they looked at each other and laughed. And I said, 'What are you laughing at?' And they said, 'Well, about the weight restrictions: when we decided that we could have our pick of fifteen nurses out of all the Air Force nurses … we thought we might as well have the best-looking ones.' And that's why they put this weight restriction in. I could've killed them.

Lucy was selected and posted to the Medical Training Unit in Laverton, Victoria, in April 1944. Training went for a few weeks:

> They put us into two-man tents … we had lectures about tropical diseases and finding our way out of the jungle if you[r aircraft] went down and how to nurse patients in the air and the problems that might arise and so on … they took us to a swimming pool so that we could all [learn to] swim … [and we went to a] pressure chamber at Point Cook and they took us up to [a high] altitude to make sure we could stand being at [high] altitudes and not collapse and so on.

The nursing sisters also undertook survival training, during which they learned which plants they could drink water from, and they were given silk maps (which wouldn't be destroyed if they got wet) so they could find their way to safety in the event their aircraft went down.

In May 1944, Lucy began her journey with No 1 Medical Air Evacuation Transport Unit and, from July, she was based in Nadzab in New Guinea. As she had expected, the camp was very basic. There were 15 nursing sisters in the unit and they were accommodated in tents:

> The senior sister had a tent to herself. The rest of us shared a tent … [we had] camp stretchers … [and] a little later, the Air Force provided us with mattresses, which made them more comfortable … We had mosquito nets … wooden floors … [and] little cupboards made to put things in. Which we painted … The Red Cross were very good. They used to give us materials and things to make curtains out of … [we made] a frill to go around the dressing table … we did a lot of sewing … we'd catch [damaged] supply parachutes … [and put them] under the roof of the tent [to catch insects gathering around the lights] … We made gardens around the entrance to the tent. Everything just grew like mad.

No 1 Medical Air Evacuation Transport Unit training at RAAF Base Laverton, Victoria, 1944 (Australians at War Film Archive, 417)

The mess had a thatched roof, bare tables and a dirt floor but the food was good, although they did miss salads:

> There weren't any lettuces around. But we were lucky because, periodically, we flew patients to Brisbane or Townsville … So anybody who went to Brisbane would come back with some lettuces and some fresh eggs and milk.

In the beginning, there was no electricity in the camp, so the laundry coppers were heated by wood and kerosene:

> The heat was always a problem. And you were always wringing wet and sweating. Keeping clean was a problem. Laundry and so on. But once we were in our established camp, we sort of worked things out fairly well.

To accommodate the tropical climate and its risks, the nursing sisters' uniform differed from the standard issue uniform. Skirts were replaced by trousers and after dark they 'had to wear long sleeves and gaiters' to reduce the amount of skin which was exposed to malaria-carrying mosquitos. They applied insect repellent to their faces and took Atebrin, '[an] anti-malarial [drug], so we all went yellow'. Safari jackets were added, along with a tie to transform it into a formal uniform, and forage caps were worn when flying, along with a fur-lined jacket to counteract the 'cold at altitude'. When they were off duty around the camp, they wore a casual dress, but as soon as they ventured out of the camp, they had to wear their uniform.

For their first few weeks, the nursing sisters flew with American crews and an American flight nurse. After about a month, the American nurses left and the RAAFNS operated as a 'crew of two. A sister and an orderly on every flight.' They flew in 'American transport planes [C-47s] and [with] mostly American patients too. Because they were the ones that were doing the fighting.'

Their days started at 4am with breakfast, then they would take off 'at first light when it was smoother. By late afternoon, you didn't fly in New Guinea at all. The weather always was bad':

> We'd fly forward with … cargo. Sometimes direct, sometimes [making] a few stops along the way. And [the crew] would radio ahead to the … casualty clearing stations as to the estimated time of arrival so [the stations] would load the patients into the ambulance and be at the airport [to] meet us, because you didn't ever want to have the plane on the ground very long. A) so they could[n't] be shot at and B) so that they didn't get too hot.

When they arrived at the airports, the patients were loaded 'onto the plane according to how sick they were'. Seriously injured patients' medical histories were handed over by the orderlies, while patients who were able to walk had their medical details attached to their shirts:

> Psychotic patients were the most difficult to cope with and there were a lot of them … they'd be sedated before they left the hospital, but often there was a delay [due to] weather or engine trouble … And the sedation would wear off before we got to the destination. They'd usually have to be strapped down and restrained if they were very bad. They weren't all violent. Some of them would just sit and stare into space.

On the aircraft:

> [We] didn't have much equipment … we had an oxygen cylinder. We did use oxygen quite often. And we had [a] gallon Thermos flask which we'd fill with water … The Red Cross would … usually put on a tin of biscuits … One of the most important things I always carried with me was a few packs of cards. Because if you could get the men playing cards … It's a wonderful way to pass time.

The walking wounded would sit in metal seats along the side of the aircraft and were given blankets to keep them warm. The seriously injured would be placed in the stretcher beds attached to the fuselage. 'It was pretty uncomfortable … But they were pleased to be being evacuated and there were very few complaints.' The nursing sisters had the equipment to administer intravenous fluids but these were not often required. They also had aspirin available for pain relief. At the end of their journey, ambulances would meet them at Lae, which had a base hospital:

> We'd unload them into the ambulances and that was the finish of our duty … [once there were] murmurings that the air evac nurses weren't working hard enough.

> Because we'd have days off … We'd fly one day and have the next day off … sometimes we flew two or three days running … the idea was that … we should go down and work in the Army hospital [between flights]. And they sent a matron up to have a look and she lived with us for a while … she went up on a flight on one trip and they lost an engine and they had to throw things overboard and things were a bit dicky and she came out in a … nervous rash for a long while. One way or another, she worked out the air evac nurses did work hard enough.

The nursing sisters also kept logbooks:

> We had to put the date [and] the hour of take off at each take off and landing. Type of aircraft. Pilot's name and … whether we were carrying patients … on posting or … leave or returning from the mainland … and the length of each leg of the flight … [A]t the end of the month, we tallied up the number of hours we'd flown and it was signed by the commanding officer … I finished up with eight hundred and three hours and five minutes.

Life in Nadzab 'was never dull':

> We played … a bit of tennis. We used to go for a lot of picnics on our days off. Cause the men were always keen and they'd come along with their jeeps and we'd supply the food. Mostly [from] tins.

Washing day at Nadzab, New Guinea, circa 1945 (Australians at War Film Archive, 417)

The nursing sisters were also well looked after by the Salvation Army and Red Cross, who supplied fabric and a sewing machine for them to make curtains or swimming costumes, and gave them cups of coffee or tea and notepaper so they could write letters home. The Americans also gave the nurses access to their post-exchange (commonly referred to as PX) stores:

> They had all sorts of wonderful luxuries in those stores. And we were able to buy their shirts … And things like boxes of Kleenex [tissues] … occasionally we'd be able to get nylon stockings … And a few of the girls were lucky enough to have trips. The Americans were short of flight crew[s] and [some of the Australian nurses] were able to escort a load of Americans [who were] being repatriated to America, and they flew to San Francisco. So they were very lucky. Three or four of our girls had those trips and they did some wonderful shopping … we all gave them shopping lists … Nice nighties and things like that they'd bring back. And they'd bring back stockings, of course.

In September 1945, Lucy was posted to No 2 Medical Air Evacuation Transport Unit on Morotai Island (now in Indonesia) to work with No 33 Squadron. However, she was back at Lae in New Guinea when the war ended:

> [The end of the war was] wonderful for everybody. I don't remember any wild celebrations … [there] weren't too many people to celebrate with, but we were all of course very pleased. Then the best part of the whole time up there started, when we brought out the prisoners of war … the camps were scattered all over the islands and Borneo and up to the Malaysian peninsula. And they brought them all back to Singapore where there were large hospitals and they were sorted out there and the very worst ones were built up a bit … before they sent them home … But they were getting them out and home as quickly as possible. And they used every plane available … half our unit was based at Morotai and they flew immediately to Singapore and from there they flew to the various islands and escorted the patients back … they were all in a pretty grim state … [I] did a few trips to Bangkok and back with prisoners of war who had been stranded in Bangkok … and then I was sent to Rangoon [now Yangon, Myanmar] to get … two Australians … who'd got left behind … I remember one was blind as a result of berri-berri [thiamine deficiency].

In December 1945, Lucy was grateful to be posted back to the sick quarters at Point Cook in Victoria:

> There was just one other sister … and a few medical orderlies and we weren't at all busy; we spent half our time making sponge cakes and scones and things for everybody who came for afternoon tea, and for the patients.

One of the guests who enjoyed afternoon tea was Lucy's future husband, John Lane, a doctor who was staying at the officers mess while working at Albert Park Barracks in the 'new science' of 'aviation medicine'. He had joined the RAAF after his residency at Sydney Hospital and had worked with a Catalina squadron in Cairns, Queensland.

Lucy was discharged from the RAAFNS at RAAF Station Laverton in October 1946.[3] She went on to complete her infant welfare certificate and thereby qualified as a triple-certificate nurse. Lucy and John married at Scots Church in Melbourne in 1947. She made her wedding dress:

> Out of a nylon parachute … I didn't have to worry about styling [it] too much because I just gathered it in at the waist and it was very full. And I used lace from my father's [court dress] – he had been a moderator of the Presbyterian Church and they wore court dresses … we had clothes rationing and it was very difficult to get materials and things to sew … my daughter wore [my wedding dress] again when she was married.

After Lucy married, she was no longer allowed to work as a nurse because 'no hospital would have [a married woman]'. When her children were a bit older, she did some casual work as a doctor's receptionist. Throughout her life, Lucy stayed in contact with many of her Air Force friends and colleagues.

Lucy passed away peacefully at home on 21 August 2014, aged 95 years. She is survived by her children, grandchildren and great-grandchildren.[4]

Aircraftwoman Sheila Van Emden (née Ferguson)

Flight Mechanic

Service number: 177348
Date of birth: 7 May 1926
Place of birth: Paddington, New South Wales
Date of enlistment: 3 August 1944
Date of discharge: 15 February 1946

Sheila Ferguson's Women's Auxiliary Australian Air Force portrait (Australians at War Film Archive, 369)

Sheila Catherine Ferguson was born on 7 May 1926 in Paddington in Sydney. Her family lived in Erigolia, a small close-knit town northeast of Griffith, in regional New South Wales (NSW).[1] Sheila came from a large family and was one of 12 children: 10 girls and two boys. The children learned to do everything on the farm, from milking cows, tending pigs and poultry, and riding horses, to growing vegetables, ploughing, harvesting, and cutting lucerne.[2] The girls also learned how to cook, which was especially important during the shearing season when it was 'all hands on deck' to keep the young men fed.[3]

Sheila's family had a strong history of military service. Her paternal grandfather, George Ross Ferguson, had served in the Sudan War.[4] Her paternal uncles, Eric Robert Ferguson and Charles Edwin Berry, had served in the First World War, with Eric killed in action in France in July 1918.[5] Sheila's maternal uncle, George Thomas Byron Dalzell, had been killed in action in France in July 1916.[6]

When the Second World War broke out, Sheila's father, William Henry Ferguson, and eldest brother, Ronald George Ferguson, enlisted to serve with the Australian Imperial Force.[7] Sheila's mother joined the Voluntary Aid Detachment and Sheila's older sister, Joan Mary (Beryl Ada), joined the Australian Women's Land Army (AWLA).[8] Although Sheila was too young, she followed suit, and was granted an exemption because of her family's farming background. Her service number was No 429.[9]

Sheila Ferguson's Australian Women's Land Army portrait (Australians at War Film Archive, 369)

Sheila recalled that the country girls in the AWLA helped the city girls and that everyone 'mixed very well':[10]

> [The city girls] were very, very nice and they really wanted to help in the war effort. Most of them had left very good jobs to go into the land army … they were educated girls and they knew what they were going in for … it was work that needed to be done.[11]

Sheila's first assignment in the AWLA was to a pig and citrus farm in Yanco, near Leeton, NSW. Having grown up on a farm, she had some experience with both pigs and citrus, a fact unknown by the pig farmer whose face betrayed him as the 'two kids' got off the bus. However, his opinion changed in next to no time because the girls learned fast. They cleaned the sties, separated the pig litters, neutered the males, and assisted in the orchard. They also irrigated, pruned and picked the fruit from the farm's trees at harvest time.[12]

The AWLA workers were sent where they were needed when they were needed. They would work on their knees in the dirt planting, weeding and harvesting row after row of carrots, spinach and onions that had been sown in paddocks converted from grazing land. They were up and down ladders spraying, pruning and harvesting the orchards of citrus, peaches and apricots. Occasionally, there would be 'a scream from somebody who grabbed an orange … [with] a great big spider on it … [the spiders] used to hang on the fruit, mostly on the sunny side'.[13]

In the mornings, they would prepare jam sandwiches, packed in Arnott's biscuit tins, to take to the paddocks for lunch. For fear of their lunch being invaded by ants, the girls were always selective of where they stored the tins. Sometimes the farmers' wives would bring them a billy of tea, accompanied by scones or cakes, for morning tea.[14]

On weekends, they picnicked and on occasion went to dances or dinners with the pilot trainees at No 8 Elementary Flying Training School (8EFTS) in Narrandera. Sheila had fond memories of the pilot trainees flying over the fields in their de Havilland Tiger Moths and dropping boxes of chocolates to the girls. Undoubtedly, these interactions influenced Sheila's decision to join the Air Force when she turned 18. She served in the AWLA for two-and-a-half years and then was discharged to join the WAAAF.[15]

Sheila enlisted as trainee technical at No 2 Recruiting Centre, Bradfield Park, on 3 August 1944. At the time, she was living in Marrickville, a suburb in the inner-west of Sydney, with a few of her sisters. Their father had purchased the house for them to live in and get jobs in Sydney as there was not enough work for them all on the farm. At her enlistment, Sheila expressed an interest in technical training and was mustered as a flight mechanic.[16]

She commenced initial training at No 5 WAAAF Depot in Penrith, NSW. There was a 'mixture of girls' from all walks of life, including two who had been Tivoli dancers. She recalled her 'rookies' training which went for approximately six weeks:

> In that time, you marched and marched and marched. You marched before breakfast and then you'd have breakfast and then more marching and then PT [physical

> training]. You'd have lessons because we had to learn all the Air Force rules and regulations; aircraft recognition and lots of different things like that. And learning to live together.[17]

The hygiene and sex education components also proved enlightening to many of the girls during rookies. Sheila recalled that a lot of 'the girls didn't know that they could wash their hair while they had their periods. That was an old grannies' tale … that had to be cleared out of their mind[s].'[18]

On 6 October, Sheila commenced training as a flight mechanic at No 1 Engineering School, located in the showground in Ascot Vale, Victoria.[19] There were about 40 girls on the course, including both flight mechanics and wireless telegraphers. The girls were accommodated in the 'Hall of Manufactures'. It was a cavernous space, partitioned with stretchers and small lockers. The lavatories were located at the back of the building and large coppers were provided for them to wash their clothes and linens:[20]

> We learned how to use all the different tools … different files and we were given a square block with a bit of metal and we had to make that into a proper square … then we had to do technical drawing, electricity and magnetism … and maths. And I hated maths … My best friend in the WAAAF and I used to sit together. And our sergeant used to say, 'What are you two working out?' And [together] we could work out the maths and we could pass. Anyway, when it came time for our exams, he said, 'You two can sit together', and we topped the class in our maths. He said, 'Two heads – even those two heads – two heads are better than one.'[21]

A Supermarine Spitfire model which Sheila Ferguson made from a penny during training at No 1 Engineering School. Exercises such as these were taught to fitters and mechanics during metalworking courses (National Museum of Australia; 1993.0075.0005)

A brass and chrome ashtray which Sheila Ferguson manufactured during her training at No 1 Engineering School. It forms part of the material legacy of the Second World War and Australia's involvement in the Empire Air Training Scheme (National Museum of Australia; 1993.0075.0002)

On 9 May 1945, Sheila was posted to No 5 Service Flying Training School (5SFTS) in Uranquinty, near Wagga Wagga in the Riverina region of NSW.[22] Fourteen people from her course at No 1 Engineering School were sent to 5SFTS, all of whom were posted to the Major Inspections Hangar.

Sheila mainly worked on the Commonwealth Aircraft Corporation (CAC) Boomerang and de Havilland Tiger Moth aircraft. She also worked on the two-seat CAC Wirraway trainer, the main aircraft type at 5SFTS. She recalled they 'were great … and nice to work on'. One of her first taskings was patching fuel tanks. Unfortunately, on one occasion she was severely burned by fuel while servicing an aircraft, which saw her struggle with eczema, dermatitis and skin cancers for years afterwards.

Major aircraft inspections were undertaken every 240 flight hours. Everyone had their own tools and, at the end of every day, each member checked that their tools were all there and that none had been 'left in the aircraft':

> We had a flight sergeant and a corporal who had … [recently returned from] the Middle East … They had never seen the [WAAAF] girls before and Flight Sergeant Row, he was fantastic. He got us all together and said, 'I know you've all just come out of the course … I don't want you to worry about anything; if you don't know anything, ask me. I don't want you to guess at anything. I'm here for you.' And everything just worked out fine.

If the girls noticed something different or out of the ordinary, they would call a colleague or the sergeant over to offer advice. '[We] were good at working as a team.' After each aircraft had been serviced, it had to pass a test flight:

> When the test pilots came into the hangar to take them up [for a flight] … they'd just pick out someone and say, 'I'm taking it out on a test flight, do you want to come with me?' And you had to go; if you said 'no', then they wouldn't take [the aircraft] … I don't remember that when the test pilot came in that I had anything to worry about, because I knew the other girls were as good as I was and that we had all done the right thing.

When the trainees were undertaking night flying or cross-country training, the WAAAFs were positioned on the satellite airfields to conduct minor inspections between flights:

> We'd take a bedroll and sleep out there … They'd bring us food for our meals … when the boys were doing their first night flights only with instruments. They had to have everything blacked out … the boys would all be nervous, hanging around waiting for their flight … it was good to be there and keep them talking, because it was a bit hair raising doing your first night flight.[23]

There were a lot of accidents at 5SFTS and the WAAAF girls were often tasked with cleaning out the aircraft, which was an unpleasant job.[24]

Uranquinty was relatively remote; Sheila described it as a 'lovely station'. The accommodation huts, although hot in the summer and cold in the winter, had the perk of a potbelly stove, allowing the WAAAFs to prepare their own dishes to supplement the food from the mess. The school also had its own piggery, a practice adopted from schools in the Royal Air Force:[25]

> We could have pork whenever we wanted … and the cooks used to throw out what they didn't want, so we'd go through it … We used to get buckets of mushrooms and cook [them] up … with tomato and onion and we'd have that in our huts at night-time.[26]

Owing to Uranquinty's remoteness, extracurricular activities were considered especially important. Sheila recalled they 'had dances in the hall once or twice a week. And we would put on concerts and all sorts of things like that to occupy us, and most of the boys joined in.' It was also 'lovely when … [the trainees] had their passing-out [graduation] parades and they got their [pilot's] wings. Their families came and we all had to go on parade and watch.'[27]

Sheila served at 5SFTS for the remainder of the war and was discharged on demobilisation from No 2 Personnel Depot on 15 February 1946.[28] After the war, she was planning to complete a course to become a dressmaker but ended up working at the David Jones department store in its mail-order department. A few of the girls who worked there thought Sheila was in too much of 'a rush', as she adjusted to the slower pace of civilian employment.

Sheila married Jack Louis Van Emden after the war. Jack was a watchmaker who had served as an instrument maker with the RAAF during the war.[29] They had met when Sheila was serving with the AWLA near Leeton and Jack was stationed at 8EFTS. Their relationship was 'on again, off again' until Sheila joined the WAAAF and they crossed paths in Ascot Vale. Their romance was helped along by Sheila's posting to 5SFTS as Jack was stationed at No 5 Aircraft Depot at Forest Hill in Wagga Wagga. They would rendezvous in Wagga and on the days when Sheila was unable to get transport into town, Jack would come and pick her up on his motorcycle, which was a sight in her 'tight skirts' and garters. On weeks off, they would catch the night train into Sydney or Melbourne, sleeping on the way in preparation for their 'wild weekend'.

In 2018, at the age of 91, Sheila Van Emden was among the ranks of women who led the Anzac Day march in Sydney on 25 April. That year was the first time female service personnel led Anzac Day marches in parades across Australia.[30] Sheila had been one of a passionate group of former serving personnel who had campaigned to the Returned and Services League to provide more recognition of servicewomen, particularly AWLA servicewomen, who had not been permitted to march in Anzac Day parades until the 1980s.[31]

Sheila passed away on 5 August 2018 at the age of 92. She had been married to Jack for 70 years and is survived by her children, Paulette, Cathy, John and Mandy, their children and her great-grandchildren.[32]

Second World War recruitment language and imagery

Recruitment advertisements and articles published during the Second World War depicted the valuable contribution of WAAAF servicewomen to Australia's war effort, including undertaking jobs which had previously been available only to men.

Support the men

One of the most urgent and compelling messages of WAAAF recruitment advertisements and articles was that women could (and should) support the RAAF to free up men to carry out other essential war work.

The article 'W.A.A.A.F's [*sic*] do vital war jobs' from 1942 features a photo of a WAAAF servicewoman serving a RAAF officer at a dining table.[1] The article reads:

> Among numerous duties which WAAAF's [*sic*] perform is serving at table on RAAF establishments. Aircraftwoman O'Brien ... gives smiling service to Flight-Lieutenant Gill. This work has released a number of men for other war work.[2]

PIX

Vol. 9, No. 18
Saturday, May 2, 1942

WIDESPREAD DUTIES

W.A.A.A.F's. DO VITAL WAR JOBS

MEMBERS of Women's Auxiliary Australian Air Force are doing a vital job in nation's war effort. Among numerous duties which WAAAF's perform is serving at table on RAAF establishments. Aircraftwoman O'Brien (above) gives smiling service to Flight-Lieutenant Gill. This work has released a number of men for other war work. While the neatly-uniformed WAAAF's are too often erroneously considered a glamorous wartime creation, it is to their credit that they retain their femininity while performing duties which are far from glamorous. Actually, hard but interesting work performed under army discipline, is the lot of the WAAAF's. They do it cheerfully, and like it. Members come from all walks of life. They include accountants, secretaries, artists, dressmakers, cooks, waitresses, beauty parlor specialists. Many have actually given up better-paid jobs to engage in this essential war service. This has resulted in the release of hundreds of physically fit young men for more active service in the RAAF. As further enrolments of women are made, the number of men released will obviously increase. WAAAF duties include wireless-telegraph operating, clerical work, store-keeping, large-scale cooking, nursing, laundry work, truck-driving and many other essential jobs. All members are physically fit. In photographs on this and following pages, PIX shows the service value of WAAAF's at RAAF stations.

PIX——Page Three

See Next Pages

'W.A.A.A.F's do vital war jobs' article in *PIX*, 2 May 1942 (National Library of Australia)

After describing the recent intake of women into the WAAAF, the article continues, 'This has resulted in the release of hundreds of physically fit young men for more active service in the RAAF.'[3] Or, as one of the most famous WAAAF posters succinctly puts it: 'Keep them flying!'[4]

'Keep them flying!' recruitment poster, circa 1942 (Australian War Memorial)

The language and imagery in this poster imply the WAAAF servicewoman at its centre is directly helping to keep aircraft operational and flying. These aircraft were crewed only by men.[5]

Referring to women as 'girls' is common throughout WAAAF recruitment advertisements and articles. A photograph taken in 1943 at Flinders Street train station in Melbourne shows a WAAAF recruitment billboard which reads, 'Girls! Help him!'[6] Even the recruitment advertisement with the respectful heading 'Airwoman we thank you' refers to women as 'girls' in the body of the text. However, we can accept this language as culturally appropriate for the time, and instead look at the broader messaging of the importance of women's contribution to the war effort.[7]

'Airwoman we thank you' recruitment advertisement, 1943 (Department of Defence)

Additional wording in this ad – seemingly delivered by the smiling pilot to the marching WAAAF servicewoman – reads, 'To-day, more than ever, the R.A.A.F. appreciates your co-operation and capacity for hard work.' The other imagery in the ad shows a group of servicewomen diligently working on various tasks, including in communications and folding parachutes.[8]

Similarly, the recruitment ad 'A tribute to the W.A.A.A.F.' from 1943 mentions the contribution of WAAAF servicewomen from a male perspective: 'Theirs is a comradeship of which the R.A.A.F. is mighty proud'.[9]

'A tribute to the W.A.A.A.F.' recruitment advertisement, 1943 (Department of Defence)

The key messaging of such recruitment advertisements and articles was that a woman – traditionally a man's 'helper' in a marriage, family and home – could support men in their wartime duty as well.

Serve your country

A second common message in Second World War recruitment advertisements and articles was that women who joined the WAAAF would thereby fulfil their patriotic duty.

The 1942 article 'W.A.A.A.F's do vital war jobs' states that:

> Members come from all walks of life. They include accountants, secretaries, artists, dressmakers, cooks, waitresses, beauty parlor specialists. Many have actually given up better-paid jobs to engage in this essential war service.[10]

Through this example, the article implies that women should be willing to make personal sacrifices to serve their country.

Similarly, the article 'Girls with sports ability volunteer for W.A.A.A.F.', published in *The Telegraph* in 1942, notes that:

> Miss Valma Simpson travelled from Cairns to volunteer as a store clerk. 'I've no brothers, so it's up to me [to join the war effort],' she says. Hazel Gardner, second of three sisters thinks the same.[11]

This sentiment is echoed in another iconic WAAAF recruitment poster, which urges, 'play *your* part in the big task ahead' (emphasis in original).[12]

'Doing a grand job!' recruitment poster, 1942 (Australian War Memorial)

The title of this poster, 'Doing a grand job!', was similarly used in other advertisements. The recruitment ad 'I wouldn't be out of it for anything, Dad!', published in *The Australian Women's Weekly* in 1944, states, 'You'll love the life, doing a grand job for Australia!' This ad continues to ask its readers, 'How, then, can you hesitate to join when your country is needing you? … Your country looks to YOU to enlist with pride in our Air Force.'[13]

The consistent messaging in these recruitment advertisements and articles is that it was every Australian woman's duty to contribute to the war effort, and that personal sacrifice was expected. In return, the country would extend its thanks. The 1943 poster 'A tribute to the W.A.A.A.F.' states that, 'Australia owes a debt of gratitude to members of the W.A.A.A.F. for the splendid service they are rendering.'[14]

Join for yourself

The 1944 recruitment ad 'I wouldn't be out of it for anything, Dad!' depicts a young woman justifying to her father (who was traditionally a woman's guardian until she married) her decision to join the WAAAF. The language attributed to her states that:

> It's a grand life and we all love it. I like the comradeship, the jolly girls of my own kind, and the feeling of pride we all have in the work we're doing.[15]

'I wouldn't be out of it for anything, Dad!' recruitment advertisement, *The Australian Women's Weekly*, 28 October 1944 (National Library of Australia)

This ad describes the many personal benefits of joining the WAAAF, including the 'good pay' and 'plentiful and wholesome' food (Australia was experiencing food rationing at the time). It emphasises: 'Here is your chance to do a fine war job under happy conditions, among companionable girls of your own kind.'[16]

Perhaps noteworthy for today's readers, this ad mentions that WAAAF servicewomen 'can obtain permission to wear "civvies" [civilian clothing, i.e., not their uniform] when attending Air Force dances'. WAAAF recruitment advertisements and articles frequently emphasised that women could both serve in the military *and* keep their femininity, thereby demonstrating that the latter was a societal expectation of women in the 1940s.[17] For example, the 1942 article 'W.A.A.A.F's do vital war jobs' includes the sentence:

> While the neatly-uniformed WAAAF's [*sic*] are too often erroneously considered a glamorous wartime creation, it is to their credit that they retain their femininity while performing duties which are far from glamorous.[18]

W.A.A.A.F.'s (Continued)

WHAT THEY DO – HOW THEY ARE PAID

WAAAF pay is two-thirds of RAAF pay. Members also shared in recent increase of RAAF pay. This meant an increase of eightpence a day to all WAAAF's. Some girls live in WAAAF quarters; others are boarded out. Latter are allowed living allowance of 3s 8d per day. A WAAAF Group Officer (equivalent in rank to RAAF Group Captain) gets 23s 2d per day; Wing Officer (rank equal to Wing Commander) gets 20s 8d per day; Squadron Officer (equal to Squadron Leader) gets 18s 2d; Flight Officer (equal to Flight-Lieut.) gets 15s 8d; Section Officer (equal to Flying Officer) 10s 8d; Assistant Section Officer (equal to Pilot Officer) 10s. Pay of an ACW, Corporal, Sergeant, Flight-Sergeant, or Under Officer varies according to the Group in which she works.

COWLING Handling Cowlings for aeroplanes is no easy job, but Aircraftwoman Blackman lifts one up into rack without any trouble. ACW Blackman works in aircraft component store.

ENGINE PARTS These WAAAF's Handle aeroplane engine components, do general storekeeping, check, record, store, issue and pack parts ready for despatch. Before joining WAAAF's, ACW McIntyre (front) worked in a beauty parlor. ACW Hasking (centre) was a voluntary worker, and ACW Parker (rear) acted as secretary to a doctor.

COLLAR In Charge of replacement store at RAAF Headquarters in ACI Cato. Picture shows her issuing collar to RAAF Corporal.

TWINS Before Enrolling, these twin sisters ran a dressmaking business together. They are ACW Falconer, M., and ACW Falconer, P. They look after clothing, etc., in RAAF stores. Pay rates for Group 4 (clerks, cooks, store-keepers, teleprinter operators) are:—Under Officer, 8s 4d per day; Flight-Sergeant, 7s 8d; Sergeant, 7s 4d; Corporal, 6s 8d; ACW, 5s. Last three ranks are equivalent of RAAF Sergeant, Corporal, Aircraftman.

COOK ACW George is no novice in cooking art. Before joining WAAAF's, she used to run her own cake and catering business. ACW George is in Group 4. Rates of pay for Group 2 (Wireless Operators) are:—Under Officer (rank equal to RAAF Wireless Telegraph Operator Under Officer) 8s 8d per day; Flight Sergeant (rank equal to RAAF Sergeant Major) 8s 2d per day; Sergeant, 7s 8d per day; Corporal, 7s; Aircraftwoman 6s 4d.

MAY 2, 1942 PIX——Page Four

LOADING ACW Stockdale checks loading of materials onto clothing contractor's lorry. These rolls weigh half-a-hundredweight, but ACW Nelson (foreground) and ACW McCaffrey make light work of them.

TELEPRINTER ACW Hill Works on teleprinter. Messages typed on this machine are received in type at other end. This used to be a man's job, but WAAAF's are doing it just as well. Before being accepted for training, applicants must be able to type at least 30 words a minute.

WIRELESS ACW Henry is keeping Wireless Watch — which means she's receiving and sending messages by morse. Training took six months. The trainees are passed out when they are able to do 20 words a minute. ACW Henry's husband is wireless operator with forces.

ARMAMENTS Work Of These WAAAF's consists of storage and checking of armaments prior to issue to RAAF units. ACW Page (left) was a lodge-keeper. ACW Pickering (right) was telephonist.

KNACK Lifting Aircraft Petrol tanks is no easy job—unless you know the knack. ACW Page has been taught how, and handles these heavy objects with ease and efficiency.

DRIVER ACW Russell drives an army truck. Here she receives instructions from Corporal John. Before joining WAAAF's, ACW Russell was a water-colorist.

CLEANLINESS Before Joining WAAAF's, ACW Whitehead was a waitress. Now she's a mess-woman, stewardess, helps keep headquarters clean. Rates of pay for Group 5 (Disciplinary Under Officer, drill instructors, mess stewards, mess-women, telephone operators, teleprinter operator trainees, wireless operator trainees) are:—Under Officer, 7s 8d; Flight Officer, 7s 4d; Sergeant, 6s 8d; Corporal, 6s; ACW, 5s 4d.

PIX——Page Five MAY 2, 1942 END

'W.A.A.A.F's do vital war jobs' article in *PIX*, 2 May 1942 (National Library of Australia)

However, the overall message of these advertisements and articles was that joining the WAAAF was a sensible decision (of which their fathers would approve!) which a woman could make to benefit herself, as well as Australia and her fellow Australians.

THE 1950s

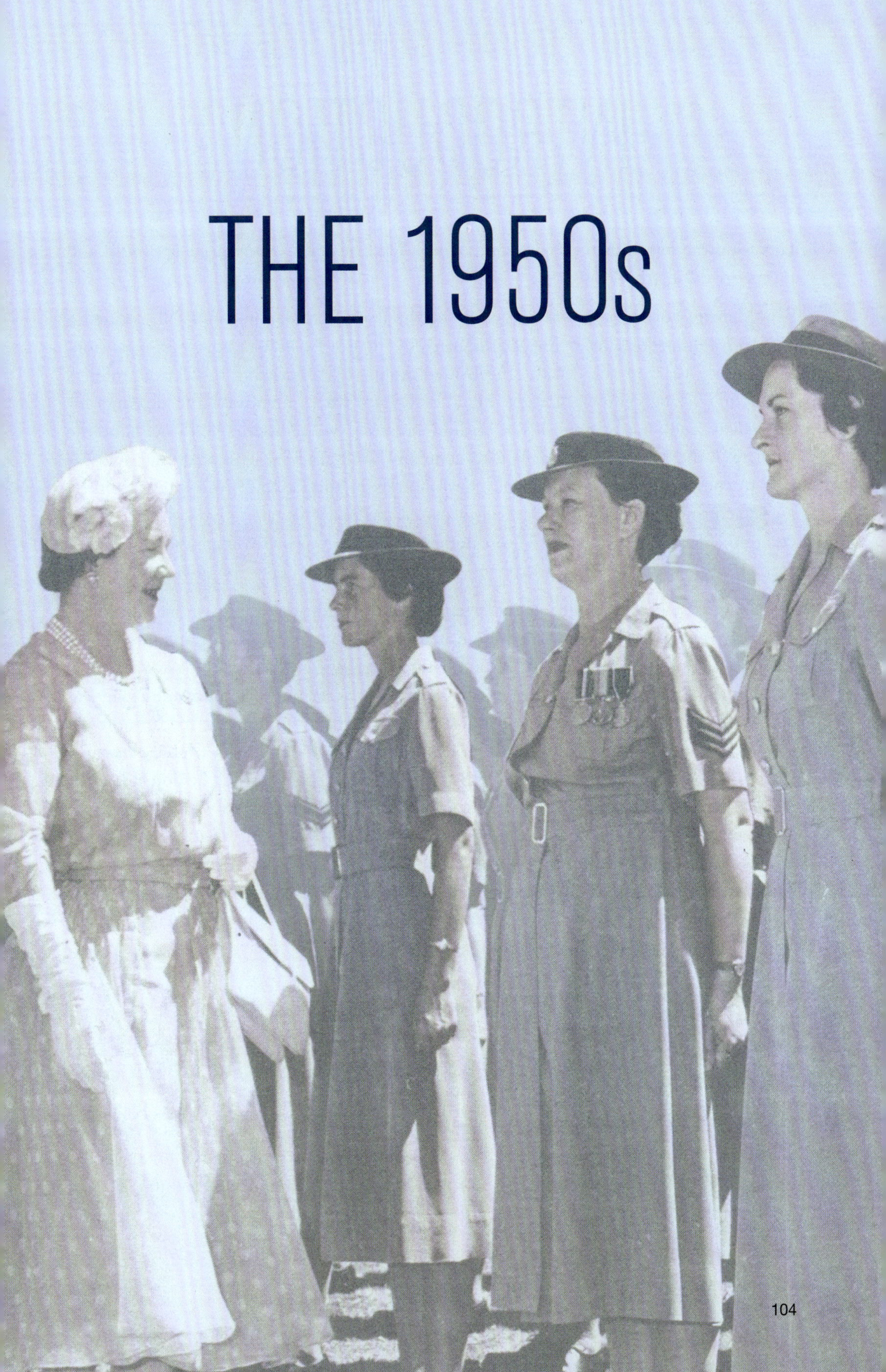

INTRODUCTION

Following the hardships of the Second World War, Australia experienced optimism and prosperity during the 1950s.

The Menzies government was in power for the entire decade and, in 1950, secured a US$100 million loan from the World Bank to finance Australia's post-war expansion. In the early years of the decade, the United States (US) – seeking to keep its soldiers warm in freezing temperatures during the Korean War – increased the demand for Australian wool. Large deposits of natural resources were discovered throughout the country in the 1950s, while the mining company BHP doubled its steel output and was able to compete on price with steel manufacturers in the US and Europe. Agriculture, manufacturing and property prices all increased in the 1950s, along with wages. By the end of the decade, Australia's real gross domestic product was increasing by seven per cent each year.[1]

This increased prosperity led to changes in living conditions for Australian families. Electricity and mains water reached more areas during the 1950s, leading to more houses having electrical appliances and indoor bathrooms. With the end of post-war petrol rationing in 1950, car sales increased dramatically which led to the outward expansion of cities as more families bought quarter-acre blocks in the suburbs. As roads improved and more people journeyed by car to work and for leisure, the number of service stations, drive-through services (such as drive-in movies) and motels increased. The home delivery of milk and other daily essentials declined as ice chests were replaced with refrigerators, and householders shopped at the new supermarkets and shopping centres which were increasingly popping up in the suburbs. Some food brands still familiar to us today were launched, including Twisties, Streets Paddle Pops, Bird's Eye fish fingers and Tip Top bread. The Vegemite advertisement was aired on radio for the first time in 1954 and soon became one of Australia's most recognised jingles.[2]

More than 400,000 immigrants who arrived in Australia between the end of the war and 1950 helped Australia transform into a multicultural society. Australian women followed the fashion trends of Europe and the US, favouring Christian Dior's 'New Look' of small waists and ballet-length skirts. Australia still valued its place in the Commonwealth, with one million people taking to the streets to welcome Queen Elizabeth II and Prince Philip when they visited in 1954, at a time when the country's population was only nine million. Television arrived in Australia in time for the 1956 Olympic Games in Melbourne, an event which helped to put the country on the world stage.[3]

Against this cultural backdrop, two Australian women's air forces coexisted in the 1950s.

Her Majesty Queen Elizabeth II during a ceremony in Canberra, Australian Capital Territory, 16 February 1954 (Department of Defence)

The flame for the Games of the XVI Olympiad was carried on board a Royal Australian Air Force Canberra bomber from Darwin in the Northern Territory to Cairns in Queensland, 1956. Cairns was the starting point for the torch relay down the eastern coast of Australia to Melbourne, Victoria (Department of Defence)

Royal Australian Air Force Nursing Service

Royal Australian Air Force Nursing Service (RAAFNS) personnel served during both of the international conflicts of the 1950s: the Malayan Emergency and the Korean War.

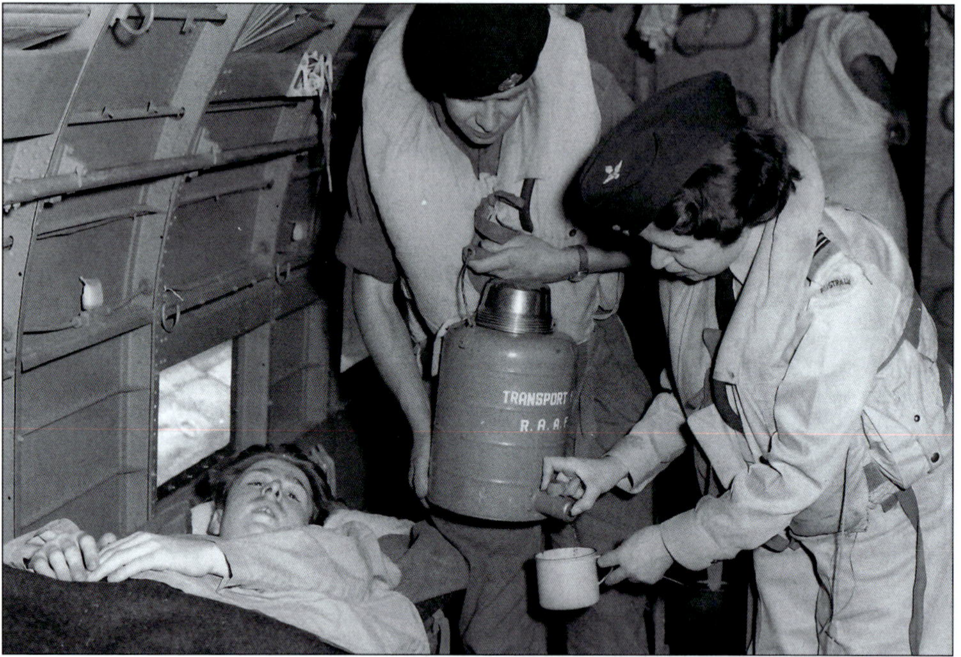

Royal Australian Air Force Nursing Service nursing sister, Flight Officer Betty Washington, prepares a cup of tea for a patient in a Royal Australian Air Force Dakota aircraft during a medical evacuation flight from Korea to Japan, circa 1951 (RAAF Museum)

The Malayan Emergency (1948–60)

The Malayan Emergency was fought in British Malaya (the present-day Malay Peninsula and Singapore). On one side was the communist pro-independence Malayan National Liberation Army; on the other were military forces from the Federation of Malaya, the British Empire and the Commonwealth, including Australia. The Malayan National Liberation Army fought for independence for Malaya from the British, while its opponents fought to combat communism and to protect Britain's interests in the region.

The Korean War (1950–53)

The Korean War was fought on the Korean Peninsula from 25 June 1950 when North Korea invaded South Korea. North Korea was supported by China and the Soviet Union, while South Korea was supported by the United States and its allied nations, including Australia.

Women's Royal Australian Air Force

The shortages in the RAAF workforce caused by men deploying to fight in the Malayan Emergency and Korean War emphasised the need to reinstate an Australian women's air force. Unlike the Second World War-era Women's Auxiliary Australian Air Force (WAAAF), the Women's Royal Australian Air Force (WRAAF) would be a permanent force and was granted the use of 'Royal' in its name. Acknowledging the contribution made by the wartime service of the WAAAF, by the time the WRAAF formed in July 1950, it had a waiting list of 2000 names.[4]

Initially, women could serve in one of 21 different roles, including cooks, drivers, clerks, medical orderlies and teleprinter operators. Over time, more roles were made available and, in 1959, the enlistment period for WRAAF personnel increased from two to six years, providing the opportunity for women to remain in the service for longer periods of time. However, just like the earlier WAAAF personnel, WRAAF servicewomen were paid only approximately two-thirds of the salary of their RAAF (male) counterparts and were required to leave the service if they married. However, the seeds of equality had been sown to be slowly and gradually reaped in later generations and, in the meantime, there were small compensations. Realising that fashion was important to many women in Australia's increasingly prosperous 1950s society, a director of Georges department store in Melbourne, Miss Rita Findlay, was consulted regarding the design of the new WRAAF uniform. The result was considered to be a much more fashionable and higher-quality uniform than the wartime WAAAF uniform. Just three years after the 1954 royal visit – which was a time of peak popularity for the royal family among Australians – Her Majesty Queen Elizabeth the Queen Mother was appointed as the Air Chief Commandant of the WRAAF in 1957, thereby lending a touch of royal glamour to the young service.[5]

The first Women's Royal Australian Air Force officers are congratulated on their commissions, 30 January 1951 (Department of Defence)

Her Royal Highness Queen Elizabeth the Queen Mother, who was appointed the Air Chief Commandant of the Women's Royal Australian Air Force, inspects a parade at RAAF Base Richmond, New South Wales, 1958 (Department of Defence)

Leading Aircraftwoman Chapman serving as a driver in the Women's Royal Australian Air Force (RAAF Museum)

Leading Aircraftwoman Cleary serving as a telephone operator in the Women's Royal Australian Air Force (RAAF Museum)

Sergeant Shirley McLaren AM (née Lemon)

Drill Instructor

Service number: W23838
Date of birth: 11 February 1932
Place of birth: Sydney, New South Wales
Date of enlistment: 29 January 1951
Date of discharge: June 1955

I hope future generations will honour the contribution of our service to the nation and commemorate those who gave their lives, and appreciate the sacrifice of all women, wives, sisters and mothers, and the incredible role that they played in the defence of this country.[1]

Corporal Shirley Lemon at RAAF Base Richmond, New South Wales, 1951 (Shirley McLaren)

Shirley Lemon grew up in Lakemba in Sydney's south which, at that time, was considered to be 'way out in the sticks'. With lots of vacant land, a farm at the top of the street and days spent riding her bike down Canterbury Road, 'it was a great place' to grow up. Shirley attended primary school at Wiley Park and then Canterbury Girls High School. After finishing school, by day she worked as a machinist and in the evening she was an instructor at the Physical Education Centre in Bent Street in Sydney, where she taught physical education to children aged 8–10 years.[2]

During her teenage years, Shirley had a close group of girlfriends with whom she went camping and played netball and softball. The girls were also members of the Australian Air League Youth Group: 'marching, drill, camps, sport'. When they saw an advertisement calling for expressions of interest for women to join the forces – Navy, Army and Air Force – while they were on holiday in Byron Bay, New South Wales (NSW), they each resolved to sign up. Because they all belonged to the Australian Air League, the WRAAF 'seemed to be the thing'. However, Shirley was the only one out of her group of friends who was selected to join:

> All my friends were rejected for various reasons … So, they crossed the road and joined the Women's Royal Australian Army Corps … I joined [the WRAAF] on 29 January 1951. There were 50 women – oh, the applications! – the Commonwealth Government at the time didn't think that women would be interested in joining the services after World War II, because it was a period of really high employment, and so they were surprised when all these thousands of applications rolled in from women all over Australia. Twenty-five went to RAAF Base Laverton [in Victoria] and 25 went to RAAF Base Richmond [in NSW]. We were co-joined as the first course. We came in [and] swore allegiance to King George VI on the same day; same date, same time.[3]

Shirley was one of the group of WRAAFs who were sent to Richmond, which:

> Wasn't really set up for ladies and we found there were no doors on the showers, there were no blinds on the windows, so there was no privacy at all. They did fix that within a very short time while we were still on recruit course.

The course went for four weeks, and the girls learned about Air Force law, hygiene, cleanliness and housekeeping, alongside plenty of 'beautiful' drill:

> We were trained by a RAAF DI [drill instructor] … Corporal James 'Jimmy' Carter … Very firm but very, very good and … [he] had the responsibility and continually told us that we were the cream of the bunch … [We were] hand-picked and we were there to set an example for future WRAAF[s] to come through the service … There were four WRAAF[s] on that course that had applied to be DIs and he did pick on us we felt, but we think that was … for our benefit … I [had] applied to be a transport driver but because of my background with physical education and [the] Australian Air League and all of the marches and parades that I had done, they said they needed [me as] a drill instructor. There were very limited musterings on the first course and they just wanted the basic ones to start the WRAAF off: clerks, clerk general, equipment stores, service police, one tailoress, four DIs.[4]

Shirley (middle, seated) with Women's Royal Australian Air Force Course No 1, 1951 (Shirley McLaren)

The first WRAAF course graduated on 26 February 1951. Shirley's mother, father and younger brother attended her graduation ceremony. Shirley's father was a clerk in the Army and she was very proud to have him at her graduation parade, wearing his uniform.

'The diagonal march' during the graduation parade for the first Women's Royal Australian Air Force course in New South Wales, held at RAAF Base Richmond, 26 February 1951 (Shirley McLaren)

Shirley spent the first two years of her WRAAF career at Richmond conducting recruit training:

> I was with [the recruits] seven days a week … [one] course would finish and I would do a run up … to Brisbane [in Queensland] to pick up a group of recruits and bring them back down. In that day and age, it was steam trains. It was very dirty and Richmond to Brisbane, it was a long, long trip … But it was a lovely way to bond with the future recruits that were coming in to be on my next course from interstate. And that happened for the two years … Till they moved recruit training from RAAF Base Richmond to RAAF Base Laverton [in November 1952] and all training for WRAAF recruits went to Victoria … I am told by ladies now that were … on [my] recruit training courses, they were terrified of me. And when they look at me now, they wonder why. But there was one thing that I did … as a DI. I did not swear at my recruits. At any time, I did not swear, and I have been told by those [whom] I had trained that they appreciated that, because there were others that did. And I also did not get drunk … I was always there and my door … was always open, seven days a week. And no matter where I would be on the base, they always felt that they could stop and say, 'Can I have a word?', or 'When you've got a moment', or 'Can we meet in the rec room?' et cetera. And they have said they have always appreciated that I had been there.[5]

In November 1952, Shirley was posted to RAAF Base Fairbairn in Canberra as an administrative non-commissioned officer. Her role was:

> Looking after the girls and I used to march them down to the parade ground and march them back [and] inspect the barracks and … [do] bed checks … 10:00 each night … and 12:00 on weekends. We were very cloistered; we were very cocooned … I think because we were the first … that was the reason that they were very, very protective of the first lot of WRAAF[s] that were recruited.[6]

At Fairbairn, they had 'dances and theatres and picnics and barbeques and trips'; there was also a RAAF tender which took them up into the snowfields. During her time at Fairbairn, Shirley met Roy McLaren, an airframe fitter and recent apprentice graduate from Wagga Wagga. They met at a dance at the Albert Hall and soon became engaged.

Following her promotion to sergeant, Shirley's next posting was to RAAF Base Williamtown, NSW. During this time, Roy was deployed to Korea so 'there was lots of letter writing'. At Williamtown, the WRAAFs were often invited by the married couples 'over for a meal, or just a drink or get together as a social occasion' but 'those invitations came from sergeants because there was no fraternisation with the officers':

> While I was at Williamtown, Roy was posted back … from Korea and he was posted to Williamtown … but that joy was short lived because I was then posted to Point Cook … because they could not have a WRAAF sergeant engaged to a corporal RAAF on the same base.[7]

Shirley was posted to WRAAF Training at Point Cook and later to Eastern Area Headquarters Command (now RAAF Base Glenbrook) in Lapstone, NSW:

> There was some trouble there and they needed my … expertise as a DI … to settle the trouble down. And it was [then that] Roy and I decided that we would marry, and then I was posted from there to Richmond for discharge … [O]ur recruitment was for four years … that was our term … [with] immediate discharge on marriage or pregnancy. And I was quite happy to accept that. They were the rules; they were the government regulations. But it didn't only happen to people in the Defence Force. [Married female] Teachers were not allowed to have full-time jobs in the 1950s. They could have part-time but they couldn't have full-time jobs. [Married female] Bank employees couldn't have full-time [jobs] – if they were female, they could only have part-time. [8]

Shirley and Roy married in 1955.[9] After her discharge, Shirley joined Roy in Newcastle, NSW, and trained girls in marching in Nelson Bay. When Roy was posted to Malaya, Shirley accompanied him and trained as an early childhood educator, a profession which served her well as Roy was posted from place to place. Together, they had three children: two sons and a daughter. Sadly, Roy died of a heart attack in December 1972.

Shirley and Roy at the winter dance at RAAF Base Fairbairn in Canberra, Australian Capital Territory, 1953 (Shirley McLaren)

Shirley has remained active within the Defence community as an ex-service member, from attending WRAAF reunions to becoming patron of the WRAAF Branch in Sydney. She has held leadership roles with the Northern Beaches War Widows Guild and her local Returned and Services League (RSL) Sub-Branch. She has also been involved in Legacy events for many years and, at the time of writing, is a resident at RSL ANZAC Village in Narrabeen in Sydney's northern beaches.

Shirley McLaren in the taxi cavalcade through Elizabeth Street in Sydney, New South Wales, Anzac Day 2021 (Shirley McLaren)

Left to right: Secretary of the WRAAF Association, Mrs Margaret Wells; President of the WRAAF Association, Mrs Betty Sutherland; and Patron of the WRAAF Association, Mrs Shirley McLaren, during a luncheon at RAAF Base Glenbrook, New South Wales, 2013 (Department of Defence)

In 2004, Shirley became an avid campaigner for women in the Women's Royal Australian Naval Service, Women's Royal Australian Army Corps and WRAAF to be eligible to receive the Australian Defence Medal. In 2006, her efforts were realised.

In 2020, Shirley was awarded a Chief of Air Force Gold Commendation for superior achievement, in recognition of her service in the WRAAF as well as her ongoing support to the ex-service community. In 2021, she was awarded the Medal of the Order of Australia for 'Services to Veterans and their families, and to the community'. She is very proud and humbled to have received these awards.

Her family's tradition of service in the ADF has continued, with one of Shirley's sons and her granddaughter both having joined the Royal Australian Navy.[10]

Australian Defence Medal

In 2004, the Australian Government announced the establishment of an Australian Defence Medal, eligible for all who had served in the Australian Defence Force for a period of six years.[11] This unfortunately disqualified personnel whose government-mandated service period had been less than six years, including members of the WRAAF who had signed on for four years and then were discharged if they married or became pregnant. As such, there was significant public outcry. Former service personnel and their supporters campaigned for eligibility criteria that would take into consideration former discriminatory Defence policies.[12]

In 2006, the Minister for Defence, the Hon Bruce Billson, announced the approval of the official regulations and design of the Australian Defence Medal. Eligible for personnel who have served since the conclusion of the Second World War, the award now recognises personnel who enlisted for an indefinite period and rendered four years of qualifying service, or who enlisted for a fixed period and completed the specified period of enlistment (whichever is the lesser).[13]

Former members who did not complete the qualifying period may also be eligible to receive the medal if they: died in service, were medically discharged, were discharged due to a discriminatory Defence policy of the time or were discharged as a consequence of mistreatment.[14]

In recent years, hundreds of Australian former servicewomen have come forward to claim their Australian Defence Medal.[15]

The Australian Defence Medal (Department of Defence)

Sister Grace Halstead (née Bury)

Nursing Sister

Service number: N35304
Date of birth: 21 March 1929
Place of birth: Bairnsdale, Victoria
Date of enlistment: 5 March 1951
Date of discharge: 13 April 1954

Gay Bury with mascot goat Marilyn Monroe at Kimpo K14 Air Base, South Korea, 1953 (Gay Halstead)

Grace ('Gay') Elizabeth Bury was born on 21 March 1929 in Bairnsdale, Victoria, to father Frank Chadwell Bury and mother EA Daley.[1] Gay was home schooled with her two brothers. When she was 11, Gay was sent to Corowa, New South Wales (NSW), to live with her aunt while her uncle 'was away at war':

> [My aunt] was a wonderful person. At one stage there was the fear of invasion and bombings, so my aunt decided we should build a trench. We dug and dug, it rained, the trench filled with water and that was that.'[2]

While living in Corowa, Gay attended the Church of England Girls Grammar School but, having grown up with brothers, she found the social aspect of an all-girls school 'challenging'.[3]

Gay trained to become a nurse at the Royal Melbourne Hospital and in March 1951 she was appointed to the RAAFNS, reporting to RAAF Station Laverton, Victoria. In May 1951, Gay undertook a Medical Air Evacuation course and was then posted to Air Force Headquarters. From March 1952, she was attached to RAAF Station Fairbairn, Canberra, and then in July was posted to RAAF Amberley, Queensland, where she remained for almost a year.[4]

Members of the 1951 medical evacuation course. Left to right, back: Sisters Patricia Tansy, Mavis Catchlove and Pam Scholtz, and Senior Sister Elizabeth Baldwin (tutor). Centre: Sister Joan Bengough, Senior Sister Margo Maloney, and Sisters Vivienne Boswell and Helen O'Mahony. Front: Sisters Betty Wallbank and Gay Bury (Gay Halstead)

In April 1953, Gay was posted to No 391 Squadron in Iwakuni, Japan.[5] Several RAAFNS nursing sisters had been based in Japan as part of the British Commonwealth Occupation Force since the end of the Second World War in 1945.[6] In 1950, together with No 77 Squadron (77SQN), the nursing sisters had been scheduled to return home; however, the outbreak of the Korean War had put a stop to that.

During the Korean War, the RAAF was responsible for the medical evacuation (medevac) of all Commonwealth wounded soldiers from Korea to Japan. Iwakuni is located about 40 kilometres south of Hiroshima and had been home to an American and Commonwealth air base since 1945. The RAAF hospital on the Commonwealth base at Iwakuni was a wooden building 'with well-equipped wards, an operating theatre, an outpatients [ward], three consulting rooms, staff and patients' dining rooms, store rooms, pharmacy and kitchen'.[7] The wounded soldiers were transported from Seoul to Iwakuni aboard a Douglas C-47B Dakota. The cargo compartment was fitted with a system to safely transport injured personnel in litters or stretchers. Each aircraft could carry four litters on either side, making a total of eight, plus walking wounded, including those who were suffering from psychological injury.[8]

The weather in Japan was extreme, and not at all like the stable Queensland climate Gay was familiar with, so it took some getting used to. The nursing sisters were initially advised to '"put on everything but the kitchen sink" under our flying suits [for warmth] … [but] by July, we had never experienced such heat.'[9]

In the early days, the Australian casualties were brought into Seoul in Korea by the Americans:

> [They were actually med[e]vacing] our boys as well as their own, and our boys came to the RAAF Station in Iwakuni in those early days … And there were no [nursing] sisters actually in Korea at the time … Japan was just across the Japanese Sea [from] Pusan [Busan] and the fighting was very, very intense and we had lots of casualties … RAAF 30 Squadron took over the airlifting of patients to Iwakuni and as the advance came, they went … further and eventually … they pushed back … the North Koreans to the 38th Parallel [the line of demarcation between North and South Korea] … Because they came straight from the front, the wounded then went to the advance dressing station, carried by stretcher, and then to the various MASHs [Mobile Army Surgical Hospitals] which incidentally were quite similar to [on] the TV series *M*A*S*H*.[10]

Shortly after her arrival in Iwakuni, Gay was:

> On a med[e]vac going to Korea to pick up patients … with another sister who was training me all the way. We had to learn on the job … and so we were up very early, about four a.m., and picking up all the paraphernalia which is highly organised. It was the most wonderful organisation, really, right from the front … to where they came in [at] Iwakuni.[11]

Gay's day started at 3:15 am when she dressed, breakfasted, gathered her equipment, and made her way to the aircraft. At 4am, the Dakota took off, loaded with mail and supplies for the troops in Korea. An hour later, they descended into Pusan on the southern tip of the Korean peninsula to deliver their supplies. Taking off again, they then made their way to Seoul to collect their patients:

> [We] would receive them into the plane in their litters … they had to go in according to [the severity of] their injuries … [those with] fractures were [put] on the upper

> litter so the fractured limb would be out of the way … The most seriously ill patients would be right on the bottom litter and right up near the bulkhead so that the sister would be, on take off and landing, sitting between the two [most] seriously ill patients … The pilot and the navigator and the whole crew were marvellous, because they would ask what sort of patients we had and how [we] wanted them to fly … [some patients] would have a colostomy bag that needed attention and [the pilots] needed to fly as low as they possibly could. If they had to go up really high, we had to have oxygen cylinders ready.[12]

Gay discussed other complexities of medevac flights:

> There were lots of things that we had to think of – tea and coffee and comics and books and things – to keep [the patients] quiet and keep them comfortable … when we flew into Iwakuni, the pilot would open the door and ask if there was anything special that they had to tell the hospital [so they could] be ready. And [the patients] were met by ambulances and taken into the hospital and sponged and looked after … The journey from Seoul, Kimpo [in Korea] to Iwakuni, Japan was three hours and it was the sisters' responsibility to assess whether the patients were fit to fly.[13]

On one occasion, one of Gay's colleagues discovered that one patient:

> Had third-degree burns and was not fit to fly and she had to send him back to one of the MASHs, which was a terribly hard thing to do, but it saved his life … those are the sort of decisions you had to make.[14]

Sisters Gay Bury (left) and Pamela Leahy, arriving at Iwakuni in Japan, being greeted by Sister Cathie Daniels, 1953 (Gay Halstead)

In April 1953, Gay was posted for temporary duty with 77SQN in Korea:

> I was picked up by the RAF [Royal Air Force] MO [Medical Officer] and taken through the streets of Seoul, which of course had had two battles through it and was rubble, really, more than anything else. Dreadful sights: little children without their legs and some of them shell-shocked and all the houses just, you know, rubble again. Little shelters they built out of kerosene tins or anything they could get … [The hospital was in a] very decrepit high school and we had [a] funny little wooden [classroom] … and every time you trod very heavily, you went through the floor. And we had Papasan [a term for an elderly Korean man] coming in with pieces of soapbox or any old piece of timber that he had, nailing it to the floor.[15]

Prior to leaving Australia for Korea, the nursing sisters had been given a list for the Myer department store of equipment they would need to take:

> Half the things I didn't buy, which was silly, and one [rule was that] you mustn't take any nightdresses or anything like that over. And of course I did, and when this air raid siren went, I grabbed my greatcoat and a lipstick in my pocket and a couple of letters and rushed downstairs … and of course, when the lights came on, here's my frill [hanging] right down the bottom of my greatcoat, which gave the boys a great laugh. I only did it once … I had no idea what I was going to when I flew off [to Korea]. But it was a wonderful experience … five thousand men to one woman in Korea … We were the first Commonwealth [nurses] and we flew out eleven-and-a-half thousand patients [and] casualties and we didn't lose one.[16]

During Gay's last medevac flight to Iwakuni, she was met by her matron, Senior Sister Betty Docker, who informed her she had been posted back to Australia for a 'special job':[17]

> I said, 'What sort of job?' And she said, 'You have been selected [to be] hostess to the Queen … with the Queen's flight and you have to go back … to join the flight at Richmond, New South Wales, to train.' And I said, 'Oh my goodness, oh all right.' And she said, 'But you're not getting off lightly.' I said, 'What do you mean?' And she said, 'You've got to take back a load of casualties to Australia with you, when you go.' So I said, 'Oh well, fair enough.' … [It was] very exciting and … it was the first time the Queen had come [to Australia], of course. And we actually celebrated her coronation in Korea, which was an amazing event.[18]

Gay was the first of a select few RAAFNS nursing sisters who would serve as air hostesses to Queen Elizabeth II during her first royal tour of Australia.[19] On 3 October, Gay flew on her last medevac flight back to Australia aboard a Qantas Skymaster:

> The Royal Tour was big news and, on arrival, I was besieged by the press – a taste of what was to come in the following months – and I became acutely aware of the tremendous honour and responsibility bestowed upon me.[20]

From 18 November 1953, Gay was attached to the NSW Squadron Air Training Corps. During this time, she learned how to be an air hostess with Qantas Empire Airways:[21]

> One of my initial tasks was to familiarise myself with the geography and any points of interest on any of the routes we would be flying ... Another task was to accompany VIP [Very Important Person] crews ... One of the features of the [RAAF] VIP planes in those days was its very basic galley equipment but, because of the presence of a hostess, passengers could not be blamed for treating [the] RAAF [aircrew] similarly to the civil variety. I was occupied in the galley ... when one of the staff arrived requesting glasses. I apologised and explained we only carry cups. 'What kind of an outfit is this?' he bellowed. 'A military aircraft, Sir', I replied. He leapt along the aisle to inform his master of the ghastly inadequacies. With nonchalance, the Viscount replied, 'And what is wrong with brandy out of a cup?'[22]

The crew of the Queen's aircraft, Dakota A65-123, 1953. Left to right: Squadron Leader John Cornish AFC, captain; Sister Gay Bury, air hostess; Squadron Leader Charles Brackenridge, navigator; Flight Lieutenant Tom McGrath, signaller; and Pilot Officer John Newson, co-pilot (RAAF Museum)

In contrast to the Dakota which Gay was accustomed to in Korea, the Queen's RAAF Dakota, A65-123, was known as the 'glamour puss'. The royal compartment was equipped with leather seats for the transit and a fully carpeted rose-coloured boudoir, with full-length mirror, wardrobe, vanity and toilet. The rear accommodation, which was separated by a green curtain, consisted of an anchored table and seating for the three royal tour officials.

Gay's 'little seat for take-off and landing was positioned just outside my galley'. The 80 hours of rehearsal flights included stand-ins for the royal couple:[23]

> We went round Australia three times. Chocks to chocks with a stopwatch … the Air Force is like that; everything has to be absolutely spot on. Near enough is not good enough … So I was the poor little thing who had to have all these stand-ins for Her Majesty before she actually arrived … It was exhausting but we were all on a 'high' … the royal hysteria was catching and all seemed to want to be involved … Streets in capital cities were being decorated and thousands of people were arriving every day … excitement was in the air as 3 February drew near. There was still so much to be done. I had to find out the Royal preference for toilet soaps, stockings and so on, and purchase the same, complete the first-aid kit, organise supply and delivery of flowers … I had a phone in my galley allowing communication with the crew, which was to be invaluable in the days to come … If we were running into any turbulence, a short, sharp ring enabled me to prevent any calamity.[24]

Sister Gay Bury wearing the specially designed air-hostess uniform for the 1954 royal tour (RAAF Museum)

The Queen arrived in Mascot, NSW, on 12 February 1954:

> The cavalcade of police escort with the Rolls Royce flying the Royal Standard [arrived] … The crowd went wild. Suddenly, there was a scurry of activity and the Royal Tour officials arrived to take their seats, then the Queen's Lady-in-Waiting, Lady Pamela Mountbatten, with the Duke's equerry, Wing Commander Mike Cowan. Then, finally, the Royal couple, Her Majesty Queen Elizabeth II and His Royal Highness the Duke of Edinburgh arrived. I curtsied, and the Queen and the Duke of Edinburgh chose their seats. The Royal Standard was now fluttering for the first time from [A]65-123. It was the first of the happy trips. Our final flight, from Perth to Busselton and Albany [all in Western Australia] and return, completed the Royal Tour of Australia on 30 March 1954.[25]

Gay recalled some 'funny little things' from the royal tour:

> From memory, they had eight aircraft following us. They had the VIPs, they had the press, they had the luggage, they had the security … I'd heard via the grapevine that [the Queen] liked Peace roses and, of course, this was February and Peace roses weren't out in February, so I had to have them air freighted from Queensland. And we also heard via the grapevine that the Duke liked tonic water and, of course, Australia didn't have tonic water in those days, so we had to have it sent over from New Zealand. All these funny little things, and also I found out what cosmetics she used and I had my little pannier … with all emergencies like stockings and cosmetics and all the rest of it … [I]t worked out to be a wonderful time. We had twenty wonderful trips and fun. It was fun and relaxed and the real thing was so much easier than the make-believe ones and it was just a very happy time.[26]

A little over a month later, on 3 May 1954, Gay married aeronautical engineer Harry Halstead at Toorak Presbyterian Church, Victoria. Her wedding gown 'of white organza had a high neckline, long sleeves, and a sweeping train'.[27] As was policy at the time for married women, Gay had resigned from the RAAFNS and been discharged on 13 April.[28]

Gay and Harry had two children, Michael and Louise. Passionate about history, Gay started her own publishing business, Nungurner Press, and authored five histories including *The story of Metung and its first inhabitants*, *The story of St Ives NSW and some of its neighbours*, *The story of Terrey Hills and Duffys Forest 1805–1988*, *The story of the RAAF Nursing Service: 1940–1990*, *Whispers over Wildwood 1066–2003*, and *Major General FK Simmonds, CBE, MVO, MC: A man among men*. In 1984, Gay received an Advance Australia Award for her contribution to Australian literature.[29]

Sergeant Yvonne Thompson (née Tebay)

Equipment Assistant/Clerk Equipment

Service number: W218404
Date of birth: 21 October 1938
Place of birth: Woy Woy, New South Wales
Date of enlistment: 7 March 1957
Date of discharge: 14 November 1963

Yvonne Tebay wearing her Women's Royal Australian Air Force uniform (Yvonne Thompson)

Yvonne Marie Tebay was born on 21 October 1938. She lived with her parents and two sisters in Wyalong St, Woy Woy, at the bottom of Blackwall Mountain on the New South Wales (NSW) Central Coast. Her days were spent running barefoot through the bush with her sisters, enjoying the wildflowers, and exploring:

> One day we burst into an area that was being cleared by Clydesdale horses and a few workmen. We struck up a conversation with them and were told that the area was being cleared for an emergency airfield. With nothing else to do, my sister and I would while away our time watching the work in progress, until the very last layer of red gravel had been laid. Within a day or so, we watched from our backyard a military aircraft coming in to land, and bolted through the bush and just stood there silently watching.[1]

After a while, one of the crew invited the sisters to see inside the aircraft:

> My sister didn't need a second invitation; she was already inside the aircraft. And after I had refused several times, he gently picked me up and carried me up the stairs and inside the aircraft [and] took me around … Showed me the different working parts of the aircraft … a day or two later, I watched as the aircraft … took off into the blue sky, never to be seen again. But the legacy, the encounter, was enduring.[2]

This experience was a formative memory for Yvonne. From 1943 onwards, 'while all the other girls were reading *Anne of Green Gables* and *Little Women* … I was reading *Worrals* and *Biggles* and all the flying novels.'[3]

When Yvonne was 18, she applied to join the WRAAF and was accepted. '[We] were timid little girls in those days … with no life experience' so catching the train from Woy Woy to Central Station in Sydney, then a bus to Rushcutters Bay, for her aptitude and medical tests, was quite an adventure. Yvonne enlisted in March 1957 and was posted to RAAF Base Point Cook, Victoria, for her training on No 77 WRAAF Recruit Training Course:[4]

> It was a shock to the system, I tell you. It really was, because we were just such a lot of little timid 18- and 19-year-old girls. And you get these drill instructors and [we] had to stand to attention … and we marched, we saluted … [we had] panic nights where everything had to be spotlessly clean. Our uniforms … we wore overalls when we were marching and saluting and … little black highly polished [shoes] … We didn't get a lot of sleep because we were up at some ungodly hour of the morning … before we left for parade, we would have to do what they called the 'bedroll' … you had to fold your blankets in a certain way, your sheets in a certain way, and put them like a sandwich and wrap your blanket … around it, and it had to be dead perfect, otherwise, when you came back off the drill … there it was on the floor: do it again … Most of us didn't get it right, even by the time we'd left; after a month, they were still throwing it on the floor.[5]

However, Yvonne recalled:

> An art learned from the 'oldies': smear your black polish on your shoes; you set a light to it with a match, burn it and then [add] a little bit of spit, a little bit of liquid, rub it in and you get that lovely mirror finish.[6]

Yvonne's graduation parade included a pleasant surprise. 'We were all so nervous, we didn't take much notice of what was going on.' While the girls were forming up to march, the RAAF Central Band was also forming up behind them and when the girls were given the order 'by the left, quick march', the band 'struck up "Eagle Squadron"'. The tune has held special significance for Yvonne ever since: evoking memories of a happy and proud moment.[7]

Yvonne's first posting was to RAAF Base Williamtown, NSW, and she 'was absolutely delighted' because it was the base closest to her mother's house in Woy Woy. 'Williamtown was just a leftover relic from the Second World War with the gravel roads, Nissen huts, and the one little [cream weatherboard] … headquarters building with a flagpole.' The girls lived in a large dormitory – the 'WRAAFery' – which accommodated around 50 girls, who each had their own room. Their supervising WRAAF officer, 'Madam WRAAF', lived in separate quarters at one end of the WRAAFery. The girls spent their downtime in the recreation room which had 'big leather lounges', a TV, and a 'highly polished' floor.[8]

Yvonne was mustered as an equipment assistant. At Williamtown, the equipment section was housed in a weatherboard building with the 'equipment section at one end and the accounting section' at the other. It was positioned close to the hangar where all of the equipment was stored. However, whether because she had taught herself how to type, or her warrant officers believed that WRAAFs were better suited to clerical duties, Yvonne was soon remustered to clerk – equipment.

Three Women's Royal Australian Air Force members standing in front of a Royal Australian Air Force Vampire aircraft (Department of Defence)

The flying activity at Williamtown was 'pretty intense' with its Sabre and Vampire aircraft:

> [One day] I walked into one of the hangars. The old warrant officer came up to me and he said, 'Deary me … Please do not do that again.' And I said, 'What do you mean?' He said, 'Never walk into the hangar when men are working, without whistling or making a noise so that the boys know not to swear in front of you.'[9]

With the backdrop of the Cold War, 'it was a dangerous time for the aircrew'. In 1959:

> We lost three Sabres within about three weeks … as soon as the crash alarm went, you'd have all the COs [Commanding Officers] in their Jeeps down on the strip, watching to see whose aircraft it was … I remember standing at the WRAAFery and looking out and seeing this Sabre just trawling out, like a feather, and hoping like mad to see a parachute. But he would have been too low anyway … it just went into the ground and exploded.[10]

In December 1959, Yvonne met Gordon Thompson, an instrument fitter, at a Christmas party and they became very good friends. However, in 1960, they were separated when Gordon was posted to RAAF Base Butterworth in Malaya (now Malaysia) and later attached to No 79 Squadron in Ubon in Thailand. At the same time, Yvonne was posted to Richmond, NSW, so to keep their friendship alive, they wrote many letters to each other, until Gordon returned to Williamtown at the end of 1962:

> Williamtown was kind of one big, happy family. And you avoided saluting as much as you could … [As a contrast] at Richmond you weren't allowed to amble to work. You had to march smartly in a group of girls with an NCO [non-commissioned officer] in charge, and you saluted everything that moved on the way.[11]

Yvonne's next posting was to Headquarters Operational Command in Glenbrook, NSW, for a short period where she was the 'NCO in charge of aircraft status'. However, towards the end of 1963, Gordon suggested they 'run off' and get married and, on 1 November, they did:

> [It] was mandatory in those days that you … request your discharge before you [got] married. But we did it surreptitiously and Gordon organised … the Air Force padre [chaplain] … two WRAAFs … two airmen … Oh, and Gordon's parents … I told absolutely no one. And yet, when we got home to Woy Woy after being married … underneath the door was this telegram. And I opened it up and there it said, 'Love and best wishes for your future happiness, Joan McPherson, Flight Officer' … I never got around to asking her how did she find out.[12]

Yvonne stayed in the WRAAF for another fortnight:

> Until 14 November, and then my discharge came through. And I was no longer a member of the WRAAF … It was a bittersweet moment, because in some way[s], I was looking forward to being just an ordinary housewife … [but] in other ways, I regretted it.[13]

Yvonne moved from Richmond to her childhood home in Woy Woy, which she had inherited after her mother had passed away in 1962. Gordon would come home from Williamtown on weekends and their first son, Scott, was born in 1966. However, life as a 'RAAFie's' wife and dependent was not without its challenges, mainly owing to the demands of service life. In 1969, Yvonne and Scott joined Gordon at Butterworth, where he was posted with No 3 Squadron. The family was allocated married quarters and an amah (servant), who was responsible for taking care of the house: 'It was a bit awkward. I'd never had servants before.'[14]

While they were in Malaysia, there were riots in Pataling Jayah in Kuala Lumpur on 13 May 1969:

> And in no time at all, we were advised that we were under … curfew, because they weren't certain whether all those killings and rioting would spread to Penang Island [where we lived] … we were allocated times for us to go and replenish our bread and milk and groceries … it was a bit scary, because it was my first time out of Australia … And all the men, most of the RAAFies, were in Singapore. So they were flown back straight away to be with their families … they still went to work, but they were escorted [by armed guards] … We were told not to even go into our yards, because we could be shot too by the security forces … and if there was an emergency, we should … hang a white towel in front of our porch … and [at night] switch the light on, so the patrolling security forces … could realise that we needed assistance.[15]

Things did settle down and Yvonne made friends and learned to speak Malay. Their second son, Blake, was born at No 4 RAAF Hospital.

Yvonne Thompson's family's private beach in Malaysia, 1970 (Yvonne Thompson)

The family returned to Australia in 1972 and built a lovely new home, but they were posted back to Butterworth in 1974. They have fond memories of this time:

> [We] drove a lot around – and it was interesting. We'd drive down to Singapore … it was so different. It was spotlessly clean … those years were great years because we would travel across to the east coast and scuba dive off Pulau Pontian … in the South China Sea and … we would hire a little Malay fishing boat and there [were] the Aussies, the Brits, a couple of Chinese and an Australian rubber planter, and we would dive.[16]

Yvonne, Gordon and Scott Thompson outside the home where they lived in Malaysia between 1969 and 1972, taken on their return in 2002 (Yvonne Thompson)

Yvonne and Scott Thompson catching up with old friends in Malaysia, 2002 (Yvonne Thompson)

After Gordon was promoted to warrant officer in 1976, the family returned to Australia. Gordon was discharged from the RAAF in 1979 and the couple remained in the Newcastle area, getting civilian jobs in printing. In 2002, they returned to Malaysia and had the 'loveliest reunion' with the friends they had made during their years living there.[17]

Yvonne has remained active in attending WRAAF reunions in Sydney and Newcastle: 'Whoever is able turns up for lunch … and we just all turn 18 [again]. You press the button back, [and] turn 18 again.'[18]

Yvonne and Gordon Thompson on their way to a Returned and Services League luncheon, 2013 (Yvonne Thompson)

'Who's that WRAAF with the beautiful hair?'

I was on parade one day … in my blue–grey uniform, summer uniform, wearing my little pork pie hat, and the wind just took my hat and blew it away. And I didn't know whether to break ranks or keep on marching. I thought, 'Oh well, the obvious thing is [to] keep on marching.' And when we came off the parade ground, there was the Warrant Officer Disciplinary Norm Gray, with my hat in his hand. And because I was a little ACW [Aircraftwoman; the most junior rank] … I was in trepidation. I thought I was going to be shot at dawn. And I said, 'Well, what did the OC [Officer Commanding] say?' And he said, 'Oh, the OC said, "Who's that WRAAF [Women's Royal Australian Air Force servicewoman] with the beautiful hair?"' And that was it.[19]

Yvonne Tebay (Yvonne Thompson)

THE 1960s

INTRODUCTION

Following the optimistic and prosperous 1950s, the 1960s witnessed many changes to Australia's social and cultural identity.

The 1960s started with a 'credit squeeze' (reducing economic activity by restricting money supply) from Australia's new central bank, but development soon led to the country's biggest resources boom since the 1850s gold rush. During this decade, Japan replaced the United Kingdom (UK) as Australia's biggest export customer, predominantly for wool, iron ore and coal. Australia was connected coast to coast by rail for the first time, and new universities were established, including Flinders, La Trobe and Curtin.[1]

The release of the contraceptive pill in Australia in 1961 prompted a move to equal rights for women, as they appealed for equal pay for equal work, better childcare, and freedom from violence. Also, during this decade, First Nations peoples appealed for greater equality and recognition of their rights. In 1962, the Australian Government granted them the right to vote in national elections and, in the 1967 referendum, the Australian public voted overwhelmingly that First Nations people should be counted in the census. An increase in migration from 'non-white' nations during the 1960s further contributed to Australia's multiculturalism, with potential immigrants no longer being assessed from 1966 according to their race or nationality, but according to their skills and potential ability to contribute meaningfully to Australian society.[2]

Also in 1966, Australia received its first visit from a serving United States (US) president, with crowds gathering to welcome Lyndon B Johnson, and many more viewing his visit on television. This was, indeed, the decade in which TV became mainstream. With family programs often scheduled around dinnertime, families started to eat in front of the TV, which led to increased sales of stain-resistant furnishings and durable crockery – along with TV dinners. Many churches ceased evening services as more and more members of their congregations stayed home to watch TV, while restaurants and entertainment venues offered specials to entice people to go out.[3]

TV brought foreign accents, fashions and ideas into Australian living rooms, with commercial TV stations sourcing most of their programs from the US, and the Australian Broadcasting Corporation sourcing most of its programs from the UK. But locally produced variety and pop programs were also extremely popular during the 1960s and included *Bandstand* (1958–72) and *In Melbourne Tonight* (1957–70), which made host Graham Kennedy a household name. Daytime variety show *It Could Be You* (1961–69), received so much fan mail (18,592 letters in just one day in 1961!) that a new post office was built to process it all. Yet the TV highlight of the decade was unquestionably the televised moon landing in 1969. Retailers experienced a run on TV sales in the lead up to the landing, children were released from school early on the day, and people who did not own TVs of their own squeezed into living rooms of friends or neighbours who did. No one wanted to miss this historic event![4]

During the 1960s, the Royal Australian Air Force Nursing Service (RAAFNS) and the Women's Royal Australian Air Force (WRAAF) continued as the two avenues for women to join and serve in the Air Force.

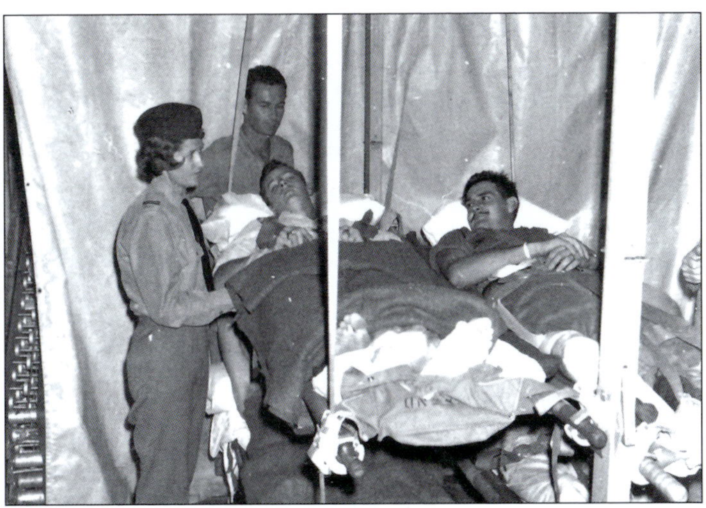

A Royal Australian Air Force Nursing Service nursing sister tends to patients in a medical tent in Vietnam (RAAF Museum)

RAAFNS personnel served overseas during the Vietnam War (1962–75) while WRAAF personnel continued to serve back home in Australia. Between 1965 and 1972, 106 RAAFNS nursing officers deployed to No 4 Hospital at RAAF Base Butterworth in Malaysia. They also cared for sick and wounded Australian military personnel during medical evacuation flights from Vietnam to Australia via Butterworth.[5]

Former Royal Australian Air Force Nursing Service nursing sister Faye Bryce peruses historical photographs of her time in service, 2015 (Department of Defence)

Former Royal Australian Air Force Nursing Service nursing sisters during a 75th anniversary commemorative service at Royal Military College Duntroon, Australian Capital Territory, 28 November 2015 (Department of Defence)

During the 1960s, RAAFNS and WRAAF servicewomen gradually started to benefit from Australia's social move towards equality for women. From 1965, female officers were offered permanent commissions and, from 1969, servicewomen could marry and remain in service. From 1967, WRAAF servicewomen could join their RAAFNS counterparts by serving overseas, with some deploying on Exercise *Southern Cross* to New Zealand.[6]

Women's Royal Australian Air Force (WRAAF) members visiting a Maori meeting house in Rotorua, New Zealand, February 1967. WRAAF personnel served outside of Australia for the first time when 11 members participated in Exercise *Southern Cross* with the Royal New Zealand Air Force (Department of Defence)

Women's Royal Australian Air Force personnel (Department of Defence)

A Women's Royal Australian Air Force equipment assistant (Department of Defence)

Leading Aircraftwoman Lynette Mitchell (née Kyte)

Clerk General

Service number: W112917
Date of birth: 22 June 1946
Place of birth: Brisbane, Queensland
Date of enlistment: June 1965
Date of discharge: 19 February 1967

Lyn Mitchell at RAAF Base East Sale, Victoria, 1965 (Lyn Mitchell)

Lynette ('Lyn') Kyte was born on 22 June 1946 in Brisbane, Queensland. Her father was a taxi driver and her mother sold shoes. During the Second World War, both of Lyn's parents had served as drivers in the Army:

> I blame them for my fast driving – it's genetics! Dad was a 'Barnardos Boy', from a child immigration scheme, and he fought in just about every field of war during WWII, including … New Guinea. He went all over the world except for Italy … So he survived the war, and came home, and he drank. I think he had PTSD [post-traumatic stress disorder] and maybe he drank because he was abandoned as a child, and because of the war. He became a monster at home … my childhood was difficult; the abuse became too much. My mother called him a street angel/house devil. And my brother left to go into the Navy because he couldn't deal with it. He left six months before me … I was 19 [when I joined the WRAAF] because I'd … previously left home … I went to [work as a governess for] probably one of the poorest [families in Charleville in] Western Queensland … it was drought time.[1]

However, the girl Lyn was teaching in Charleville 'was so difficult … [I] had to leave' and she returned home. Lyn then got a job with the Returned and Services League:

> [But] Dad was no better … It was pretty awful … I wanted to go into the service, into the Air Force … and Dad wouldn't sign the papers … My story is not singular. It's not unique. So many young girls were dealing with this type of situation at that time. On this particular night I will never forget … Mum and Dad were in the kitchen, and I was listening at the door, and Mum wanted him to sign [the enlistment papers], and he said, 'No'. He said, 'In six months, she'll be just like you. She'll be a whore', and I could never forget it. It was just horrendous. He wouldn't sign. His disrespect for women [was] so obvious. The next day, Mum signed … [and] leaving home … was self-preservation [for me]. It was freedom.

Lyn had considered joining the Army like her parents, but the 'beautiful planes in the sky', paired with the elegance of the RAAF forage cap, proved far too alluring.[2] She enlisted in the WRAAF in June 1965 and was flown to RAAF Base Edinburgh in South Australia for her 'rookies' with the other new WRAAF recruits. Her adventure began with her first-ever ride in an aircraft since, owing to the distance, Queenslanders were flown south while the women from other states had to be content to travel to Adelaide by train. Hailing from northeast Australia, Lyn found that Edinburgh:

> Was bloody cold. I could not feel my toes. The blocks of ice at the bottom of my legs were my feet, but they did not feel connected to my body at all … [I could only] assume I still had ten toes, heel and arch encased in the shiny – so [shiny] you could see your face – low-heeled, black lace-up shoe.[3]

Lyn was on the first WRAAF course at Edinburgh – No 151. The women were housed in a 'two-storey brick building set apart' from the men's accommodation, with long corridors and bedrooms that housed two.[4] During their rookies course, the WRAAFs were taught to march, 'right turn with precision, and about turn with clear effect'.[5] They also learned to:

> Iron, clean and wash clothes, floors, walls, beds – anything that could be cleaned we did. Drains, ablutions [bathrooms] … and [we would] wax with a sticky yellow paste that shone … those floors to a mirror image with the biggest and wildest machine to ever grace a dormitory.[6]

No 151 Women's Royal Australian Air Force course members arriving at RAAF Base Edinburgh, South Australia, 1965 (Lyn Mitchell)

Monday nights were 'panic nights' when the building had to be made spotless prior to an inspection by the WRAAF officer known as 'Madam'. If it did not pass inspection, the women had to clean it all over again. They otherwise spent their evenings in the recreation room, singing along to tunes played on the piano, chatting and catching up on the news:[7]

> We sewed our skirts to a length that befitted the service rules but did nothing for the fashionable figure of the emerging 60s. We learned about ranks in the service and how to talk to the men on the base, even though we weren't supposed to. We quickly devised ways to pass messages in the Cornflakes at breakfast.[8]

After rookies, Lyn was mustered as a clerk general and posted to RAAF Base East Sale in Victoria, which was 'a lovely place to work':[9]

> East Sale had a magic all of its own, and those who were posted to Sale … [who had initially] felt as though they had been exiled to some gulag, left the place with a sense of having been given a gift … because East Sale was then a truly beautiful base.[10]

Graduation parade for No 151 Women's Royal Australian Air Force course, RAAF Base Edinburgh, South Australia, 1965. Lyn is in the front row on the left (Lyn Mitchell)

There was also a real sense of esprit de corps and friendship among all of the service personnel. One time, the Maintenance Section pulled an April Fool's Day stunt on Lyn, who was stationed in the Orderly Room. A phone call came through to Lyn with the speaker claiming to be a technician from the telephone company:

> 'We're doing job maintenance ... And there's too much cord on this end of the phone. Could you check on how much you've got on your end of the phone?' It was a curly one. And I said, 'But I can't hold it and take a measurement.' 'Oh, well, get the other WRAAF to take the measurement.' So I said, 'Jenny. Hold the phone, will you?' We pulled the phone out, right across the room. We actually measured the cord and then they said they had too much and could we pull some through our end, and we tried. It's the dumbest story in the world ... It was such a dumb moment ... But I've laughed about it all my life.[11]

Lyn had a bad habit of barging into rooms without knocking:

> It must have got to them in the end, because I barged in this [one] day, and just opened the door ... and said, 'Hey, Lorraine' ... and they all looked at me, and they said, 'Down here, we knock before we walk into a place.' So it taught me manners as well.[12]

On 10 September 1965, at a baseball game function, Lyn met the man who would become her husband: Ian 'Mitch' Mitchell, a 'framie' (airframe fitter) in the jet section.[13] As per the policy of the time, Lyn knew she would have to discharge from the WRAAF if she married:

> I wanted to stay in, but I couldn't ... [on] 19 February [1967] I went home to Brisbane and I cried, and my mother said ... 'Well, why are you getting out?', and I said, 'Because I love him.' ... It was a choice ... [And] 56 years later we're still together.[14]

Fancy-dress party at RAAF Base East Sale, Victoria, 1966 (Lyn Mitchell)

Lyn's roommates at RAAF Base East Sale, Victoria, 1966 (Lyn Mitchell)

Lyn and Mitch married and had three daughters. Together, they were an Air Force family who accompanied Mitch on his postings, including one to Papua New Guinea in the early 1980s:[15]

> [W]e used to complain about being posted every two years, because you couldn't put roots down … [they] moved the men around … [and the family] had to go where [the men] went; we were hangers-on – because they had to be ready for war, so it was said, at a moment's notice.[16]

Lyn and Mitch, 2017 (Lyn Mitchell)

Lyn is of the opinion that joining the WRAAF saved her:

> [I have] been grateful ever since [I joined] … I was brought up in a very unhappy household, and I had to escape … I loved growing [in the WRAAF], and I loved the way of life, and the friendships … it made an enormous impact [on me].

Her time in the WRAAF left such an impression on her that, since leaving the service, Lyn has been proactively working to preserve its history. At the time of writing, she is very active in the ex-WRAAF Facebook group, is an author and administrator of several websites which chronicle the history of the WRAAF and has written stories about her time for publication. 'My participation in being an ex-WRAAF is a way of me giving back to the WRAAF.'[17] She has also been active in organising and attending WRAAF reunions since 1980. Her fondest reunion memory is of the one in 2011 which was attended by Dame Quentin Bryce. A thank-you letter on behalf of the WRAAF to Dame Quentin led to the privilege of Lyn being published in the book *Dear Quentin: Letters of a Governor General.*

Lyn describes the WRAAF as being a 'sisterhood' which has stood the test of time. Their close bond has seen the servicewomen gather time and time again for reunions, informal meet ups, and formal branches of Air Force associations:

> We burnt toast over the radiators, we sang together the same tunes sung by our wartime predecessors, we worked side by side, we laughed at jokes, we cried and others comforted, we played tricks, our most famous [being] wrapping our Commanding Officer's car in toilet paper. We were – and are – there for each other.[18]

Lyn considers herself to be 'no different to any other clerk, or any other officer or whoever went into the WRAAF. But I'm proud of what I've given the WRAAF and [in] being a major contributor … [and advocate for] the ex-WRAAF movement.'[19]

Although she had never been issued with the 'romantic and jaunty' forage cap,[20] Lyn's time in the WRAAF equipped her with:

> An inner glow that the world outside could see when I walked down the street, proud with my pill box [hat] and laced up shoes and seamed stockings and skirt 3 inches below the knee, hair an inch above the collar and leather gloves. I found I was Lyn Kyte, a woman of the 60s, a woman who would one day teach her three girls the joy of knowing who you are. I was a WRAAF.[21]

Women's Royal Australian Air Force reunion at RAAF Base East Sale, Victoria, 2007 (Lyn Mitchell)

Leading Aircraftwoman Sandra Perry (née Guy)

Communications

Service number: W113853
Date of birth: 8 October 1947
Place of birth: Brisbane, Queensland
Date of enlistment: 15 June 1966
Date of discharge: 15 July 1968

> I love[d] the marching. I love[d] the parade. I loved all the pomp and the … spit and polish and all that sort of thing. I thought it was great …[1]

Sandra Guy (second from right) being inspected by Air Vice-Marshal Hannah and Group Captain Rose at RAAF Base Richmond, New South Wales, 1967 (Sandra Perry)

Sandra Agnes Guy was born in Brisbane in 1947 and attended the local Catholic school. After finishing school, she got a job working at a supermarket in Fortitude Valley, and later secured a secretarial role with International Harvester. Sandra enlisted in the WRAAF on 15 June 1966, in search of 'adventure, independence [and] freedom':[2]

> I had a very strict … father. I was 18-and-a-half when I joined the Air Force. [I had] probably only been allowed out on one or two outings with young gentlemen … I just decided I wanted to have some freedom. I suppose I picked the Air Force because Dad was [in the] Air Force during World War II, but one of the reasons was I didn't like the Navy's hats. I didn't like the Army's [uniform]: green. So, the Air Force was my first choice … And I loved it … I [would] join again today, if I could.[3]

Her adventure began on her first day! Sandra and her cohort of about 18 WRAAF recruits were sworn in at Brisbane and then found themselves aboard an aircraft. 'None of us [had] ever been on an aircraft before. None of us had ever been away from home before. So, that was a real adventure.' Late that afternoon, the group arrived at RAAF Base Richmond, New South Wales (NSW), where the skies were overcast and rain was falling hard upon the tarmac:

> [I saw] this thing, standing out there. Black raincoat, big hat … a greatcoat over her, and it's standing there in the dark, and this voice says, 'Alright, you girls, off the bus and double it up the path.' … we were all terrified … she turned out [to be a] real old softie … we double[d] up the path and got taken into the common area [and] met the WRAAF officer. [A cup of] tea and bickie, then I think we must've been dispersed to [our] rooms, and we start[ed] off the next day … [by getting our] uniforms and shoes and injections.[4]

Sandra recalled a lot of marching:

> [We] had to march everywhere, whether we were going to the mess, whether we were going to lectures, whatever. We had to go in a flight [group] and we would see the airmen as we [were] approaching the airmen's mess; you would see them … come running from everywhere. And I said to someone, 'Oh, they must be coming to see us?' And they said, 'No, they just want to get in before us' because otherwise they had to stand back and let us go first.[5]

On account of all of the marching, before lunch every day, the girls had their feet inspected:

> You had to go wash your feet … [with] some sort of anaesthetic stuff. Then you had to paddle in it and they had to inspect your feet to make sure you weren't getting ingrown toenails or blisters or anything like that. Then you went and changed your socks and shoes … then you went to lunch.[6]

Sandra was mustered to communications, a restricted mustering which saw her complete an encrypter's course and sign the *Official Secrets Act*:

> I had to … put down details of someone to check me out. And my parents worked for an electrical store, Kennedy's Electrical in Brisbane. My mother was horrified that

> someone … went and interviewed my father's boss to make sure that I was a good upstanding Australian citizen … I [still] don't talk about what happened in the secret room … [we used] more sophisticated equipment and people had to do the special course to be able to do it.[7]

Women's Royal Australian Air Force Teleprinter Course, 1966. Sandra Guy is seated on the left (Sandra Perry)

After completing her training, Sandra remained at Richmond to take up her first posting. She lived in the two-storey 'WRAAFery', which was a short distance from the sergeants mess where they dined. The Communications Section's work routine involved eight-hour shifts. The day shift was from 8am until 3pm, the evening shift from 3pm until 11pm, and the night shift from 11pm until 8am. The shift cycle consisted of working a night shift, then an evening shift, then a day shift, followed by two days off, and then the cycle repeated:

> It could be a bit tricky trying to get to sleep during the day [be]cause you put a sign on your door saying … 'Night Shift – sleeping'. [But] People were coming and going all the time; they didn't always respect that … There was a squad of ADGs [Airfield Defence Guards] … and they used to do their drill … every morning, just outside my window. And I was on night shift quite a bit of the time, and I remember, one morning, I lifted up my window and I went, 'Oi, give me a break', because I knew them all … so they just stomped their feet even harder.[8]

A contingent from the United States was stationed at Richmond:

> They would come to send messages, and everything that they sent out was [marked as] extremely urgent, even though it was just routine, and we would get FLASH

messages that would come in and all the bells and whistles would go off. And you had to call … the duty officer out because it was a FLASH. We called one fellow out at least three or four times on one particular evening, and it turns out … it was routine stuff. But everything with the Americans was super urgent. And he said to us, 'Look, you know, you don't have to call me out for this.' And we said, 'Well, I'm sorry, Sir, but we do, because that's what the protocol is. If a FLASH goes off, we have to call you out.' So, we did.[9]

Sandra also enjoyed a short stint in Darwin for Operation *High Mars* in November 1967, during which time she wore a starched 'drabs' uniform which was very difficult to put on, along with the famed white socks. The Communications Centre was located at the top of a high-set building which was reached via a flight of 20 stairs, and the air-raid shelter was on the ground below, under a large shady tree. They were each issued with a chit (note) and were instructed that it was a 'rifle':

I can remember one morning, the air raid siren went off about three or four times. So, we all had to file down the stairs, get under the tree with our … 'rifle'. Everybody went to the mess after[wards] … regardless of whether you drink or not, because that was one of the few air-conditioned places on the base.[10]

In 1968, Sandra met Tony, a RAAF fireman, at a pay-night dance:

I saw this fellow across the room with nice blue eyes. And then we sort of started going out. And of course, because we were both on the same base and we could coordinate our shifts, we probably went out a lot more in a short amount of time than what you would do if you were in civilian life.[11]

Sandra and Tony got married in 1968, after which Sandra was discharged from the WRAAF. The couple moved into a house in Windsor, NSW, but then Tony was posted to RAAF Base Butterworth in Malaysia at the beginning of 1969:

I knew about his posting before he did because I used to talk to the people in the Comm[unications] Centre on a fairly regular basis … when I rang up one day … they said, 'Oh, you must be very excited about the posting?', 'What posting?' – oops! And then they wouldn't tell me, so they said, 'Oh, oh, well obviously, you know, Tony's been posted' … It finally came out that we'd been posted to Butterworth for two years.[12]

Sandra and Tony enjoyed their time at Butterworth, where they lived in a tropical home with lots of fans and an amah who looked after the house and made them delicious curries:

We used to ride bicycles to the base … And you knew that it was going to rain, so you'll be pedalling along on your pushbike and … have a downpour of rain – by the time we got to the base to go to the movies, or the pool or anything, you were dry again … because it was so hot.[13]

While they were in Malaysia, Sandra and Tony had their first daughter in the British military hospital at Minden Barracks, which had modern facilities. In 1971, Tony was discharged from the RAAF and the family moved back to Australia and settled in Brisbane.

Both Tony and Sandra had fulfilling civilian careers after retiring from service life. They have been active members of the veteran community through the RAAF Association and Returned and Services League, and they enjoy travelling and spending time with their children and grandchildren.

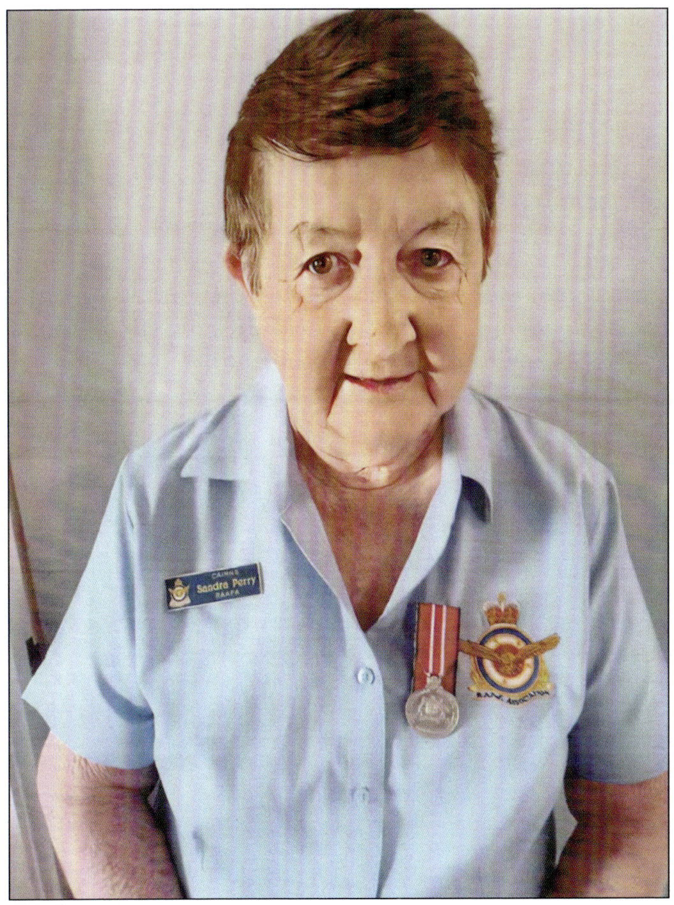

Sandra Perry wearing her RAAF Association uniform (Sandra Perry)

Squadron Leader Patricia Furbank

Nursing Officer

Service number: N225095
Date of birth: 11 March 1942
Place of birth: Lithgow, New South Wales
Date of enlistment: 5 November 1968
Date of discharge: 14 July 1983

> I was always a compassionate person but I think coming out of that experience [Vietnam] I became more compassionate and more understanding of people.[1]

Pat (centre) and colleagues at the Medical Operation Support Unit, RAAF Base Richmond, New South Wales, February 1969 (Australians at War Film Archive)

Patricia ('Pat' or 'Furby') Furbank's sense of adventure was evident from the time she was a child growing up in the coalmining town of Lithgow, west of Sydney in New South Wales (NSW). Her grandfather and father were both coalminers, and she remembered being taken down into the mines by her grandfather:

> I just loved it. You'd go down in a big cage and when you got down to the bottom, it was just pitch black … the miners with their hats and lights on, that's the only light you would have … I used to walk around with my grandfather, and I guess to some people it would be pretty scary, but I must admit I was never frightened …[2]

Pat's recollection of her childhood was a happy and loving one: playing with her sister and four brothers, enjoying school, and playing a range of sports, including swimming and hockey. The idea of training to become a nurse took hold as a career option after she was hospitalised with appendicitis during a hockey tournament at Bathurst, NSW, around the age of 16:

> I came down with appendicitis, very badly, and I was taken off the train and straight to hospital … when I was convalescing, I just fell in love with all the nurses and the sisters. That's when I made my mind up that I would become a nurse and I'm very glad I did.[3]

Before she could start her training, Pat needed to have permission from both of her parents due to her young age:

> My father refused to sign [the permission form]. He had some strange idea that nursing was very hard and a bit tough. Somehow my mother talked him round, which he never regretted after.[4]

Pat started her nursing training at Lithgow Hospital as a cadet, carrying out basic tasks such as cleaning. Her general training started after one year, and after a full year of nursing training, she was 'more or less running wards' and gaining experience that her friends in Sydney hospitals were not given. She lived in the nurses' quarters close to the hospital:

> We had lovely quarters; Brook House, it was called … It was a two-storey building right on the premises of the hospital grounds. The nurses lived upstairs and the sisters lived downstairs … Our bedrooms were very nice and compact. We had a very large common room, where lots of fun was had and, of course, the sisters' area was off limits to us but, naturally, if you have a staircase you're not supposed to go down, you go down it … Underneath the quarters in Brook House was a very large air-raid shelter, [which] they turned … into a drying room because we had central heating … all the big boilers were under there, and it was also a very good canoodling area too, in the winter![5]

Pat recalled that the matron-in-charge, Doris Ashurst, was very strict. Pat came to acknowledge that the matron's approach stood her in good stead as she developed as a nurse:

> In those days our uniforms used to be starched, and I often used to think that [the matron] never sat down because her uniform was just the same when she came on [shift] as when she went off … [she was] very strict, but she taught us a lot [about] respect … she made us a little bit tough, but I realised later that it was good to control our emotions.[6]

It was during her third year of nursing in Lithgow that Pat considered joining one of the arms of the military. The idea of military service had attracted her since she was a child:

> In the old *Women's Weekly* [magazines] – my grandmother used to buy them – they always had a photo of a female in the armed forces. I used to dream and think, 'Oh wow, this would be great.' When I was doing my training, my friend Cathy Prior and I took ourselves off to Sydney … we went down to have an interview and the guy that interviewed us just told us to get back where we came from, and finish our training, and I'm grateful he did that![7]

Once she finished her basic nursing training in 1963, Pat headed off to the 'big smoke' of Sydney to study obstetrics at St Margaret's Hospital in Darlinghurst (obstetrics was deemed an essential skill for nurses due to the high likelihood of them being sent to a country town). Pat had had little experience with babies up until that point, and she found herself having to look after up to 40 in a ward. Despite her hectic schedule, Pat and her friends still squeezed some fun into their busy days:

> One of my big experiences when I was down [in Sydney] was when the Beatles came to Australia. I wasn't particularly interested in them but we did go to see them … One place we did go quite a bit was the Tivoli, where they had different shows.[8]

Once she had finished her midwifery training, Pat spent time back at Lithgow Hospital, before moving to Condobolin, a small country town in the west of NSW, where she was promoted to matron of the hospital in 1967. It was while she was here that she learned about the Vietnam War and could not understand the anti-soldier sentiment she saw on the television or in articles in the newspaper. She decided it was time to apply to enlist as a nurse, to be able to look after the troops who were being injured during the conflict. In 1968, Pat travelled back to Sydney to interview twice for the RAAFNS. She received a telegram offering her a four-year short-service commission, with a 12-month probation period at the rank of section officer. While there was still a view within the community that women should not be on the frontline in Vietnam, nurses were considered in a different light:

> It wasn't on [for women to be involved in war] in those days, but nurses were different, very different … It's just taken for granted that they are … I certainly flew into all sorts of places and the American girls were certainly on the front line, and our Australian Army nurses were too.[9]

On Melbourne Cup Day in 1968, Pat travelled to Melbourne by train and was taken to RAAF Base Laverton. After being measured for her uniform, she received some initial nursing training at No 6 RAAF Hospital, as well as officer training at RAAF Base Point Cook, where she learned to march, salute, and shoot a weapon:

> We learned to shoot but we were always told we were non-combatant and we would never carry arms; however, we had to learn how to use one, and fire drill, and those basic things of being an officer.[10]

In February 1969, Pat was posted to RAAF Base Richmond, west of Sydney, to conduct medical evacuation (medevac) training for six weeks. She had to learn about the different types of aircraft she would operate in, including the C-130 Hercules, and how to treat patients in an aircraft that was losing pressure inside the cabin:

> We'd go into the decompression chambers and we'd have this special equipment on, and they'd slowly bring down the altitude, and you'd do things. You thought you were wonderful. It was in a little way like having a few too many glasses of champagne.[11]

Flight Officer Pat Furbank (right) following a 'wet ditching' exercise, 1969. Royal Australian Air Force Nursing Service nursing sisters trained to survive in water in case their aircraft was forced to land in the ocean (Australian War Memorial, P10261.001)

Treating a patient inflight was completely different to anything Pat had experienced before. It was critical to understand the impact of altitude on certain injuries, with aircraft limitations being another factor to consider when planning missions:

> There were a lot of things that were different to nursing on the ground … with oxygen, you had to know if you were going to take a patient somewhere, [and] how much oxygen they would need. We couldn't load up to 20 oxygen cylinders because we always had to think of weight. 'Will we get from A to B with so much oxygen?' It was a very different type of nursing.[12]

While she was at Richmond, Pat first assisted injured service personnel who were being evacuated from Vietnam. They were evacuated via the 1st Australian Field Hospital in Vũng Tàu in Vietnam, through No 4 RAAF Hospital at RAAF Base Butterworth in Malaysia, and then offloaded at Richmond:

> We had a terrible lot of amputees coming through, [caused by] the boys standing on landmines mainly, terrible … the majority of them were very traumatised. Also, in those days, they didn't get a good reception coming back to Australia, which was very sad, but it was a very big challenge and one I think we met very well.[13]

After four months at Richmond, Pat was sent to Butterworth to operate out of No 4 RAAF Hospital, a 'very large hospital right on the beach.'[14] It was the first time Pat had been out of Australia: 'I found it very strange. I found it very difficult to cope with the smell and odours to start with, and the heat.'[15]

She started with surgical nursing in the hospital; patients included the Gurkha regiment assigned to the security of Butterworth, the Australian personnel serving on the base, and the wounded from Vietnam. Pat recalled the beauty of the base buildings: 'a big open mess [where they ate and socialised] … we had parquetry flooring … we had a cocktail lounge, a bar and a beer garden, and the quarters were attached to this area.'[16]

The flying cap which Pat Furbank wore during her service (Australian War Memorial)

It was not long before Pat commenced missions into Vũng Tàu to escort wounded personnel from Vietnam. She would leave Butterworth at 4am on a Hercules and fly for four hours to Vũng Tàu, having received an estimate of the number and types of wounded who required evacuation. Once at the 1st Field Hospital, the medevac team would meet the Australian Army doctors and nurses to receive a handover of information on the patients:

> We always tried to take nice food up to the Australian girls [the Army nurses] like frozen meat pies because they didn't get many niceties up there. We had a very good liaison with the sisters.[17]

The C-130 could take up to 74 patients on litters set up in vertical rows and, on many occasions, the small medical team had to monitor more than 50 patients on litters and more sitting on 'webbing' seats. Patients would spend one or two days at Butterworth before travelling back to Australia, through the Cocos Islands and Perth in Western Australia (WA) and then on to Richmond. These flights would take 15 hours, with only two nurses to monitor the wounded, checking intravenous drips, dispensing medicine, and allowing those who were able to stretch their legs. Pat recalled not sleeping much on those flights:

> We'd start coming through Derby [in WA] just as the sun was coming up and it was beautiful. The sky was red and it was just wonderful. So we'd tell the boys that we're over Australia and it was amazing to watch the transformation on their faces, and they became quite happy, and I guess they felt safe.[18]

On arrival at Richmond, Pat would spend at least another four hours offloading the patients and handing them over to the resident personnel. Her parents, who had moved to Dapto in Wollongong, NSW, would always travel to Richmond to collect Pat for the night, before she travelled back to Butterworth to repeat the cycle. She rarely spoke of her experiences, not wanting to worry her parents. Her father's reaction when she would come home surprised Pat: '[On my] first trip home to Australia with the wounded, my parents were waiting at Richmond, and my father was very overwhelmed. I'd never seen my Dad like that.'[19]

After four months at Butterworth, Pat was selected to work with the United States' (US) 902nd Aeromedical Evacuation Squadron (902nd AMES), which operated out of Clark Air Base in the Philippines. Only one Australian nurse and one Australian medical orderly worked there at any one time on a base which had a population of more than 30,000. Throughout the war, the 902nd AMES would conduct daily runs into Vietnam to evacuate patients to Clark or to other locations around the world. These secondments gave Australian nursing sisters the opportunity to increase their skills by working on large and complex evacuation tasks.

Pat recalled that the base was 'massive':

> It had about three high schools. It had motels. We lived in what they called the Bachelor Officer's Quarters which was a six stor[e]y building … it had a six stor[e]y hospital.[20]

Pat had been on base for less than a day when she was put on alert to fly her first task into Vietnam, with little instruction from the US medical personnel regarding their procedures or what to expect. She recalled having to learn different names for drugs and medical terms. Even the term 'sister' meant something completely different to the Americans! Pat remembered a time at a social function when the language differences became very entertaining:

> 'Sister' to them was a nun … I'd been on a flight with the Americans, and we were in one of the clubs, and I'd been dancing and jumping around, and [word of] this went back to the table, and one of the guys said, 'Oh my God! I can't believe these nuns from Australia!' He really thought I was a nun![21]

Pat's medevac tasks into Vietnam would consist of a 'milk run': travelling a set route to a number of bases to collect patients. She operated on a number of different aircraft depending on the route and end location, including the DC-6, C-130 Hercules and the C-141 Starlifter, which could hold 103 patients on litters, the scale of which she had not experienced before.[22] Pat would frequently fly with patients and other passengers to Japan, South Korea and the

US during her secondment. She recalled that despite the Starlifter being much larger than a C-130, it was greatly affected by turbulence:

> In a Starlifter, just hitting a little bit of turbulence was pretty rough … on one flight, one of the American girls just went up and cracked her skull on the roof of the aircraft … we used to have seatbelt bruising and bruising from parts of the aircraft, the litters, the stanchions [upright supports] … [but] you soon got over it.[23]

Pat Furbank's flying jacket, with squadron leader rank slides, which she wore during medical evacuation operations (Australian War Memorial)

Pat returned to Butterworth after two months in the Philippines and, after a two-year posting away from Australia, she returned to No 3 RAAF Hospital at Richmond. While the Vietnam War was coming to an end in the mid-1970s, Pat remained in the RAAFNS for several more years, serving firstly at RAAF Base Wagga Wagga in NSW, and then on a second tour to Butterworth from 1974 to 1976. In all, Pat conducted 84 aeromedical trips with the RAAF, most of them during her time in Vietnam.[24] She came back to Australia to work at RAAF Amberley, near Brisbane, and after several more postings throughout Australia, retired from full-time service on 14 July 1983, taking up a position at St Stephen's Hospital in Maryborough, Queensland.

Pat remained connected to the RAAF as a Reserve member for five years after she discharged, ready to be called up in time of need. In 1995, she became the President of the Returned and Services League Sub-Branch in Macksville, NSW. It was not until 1994 that Pat's service during the Vietnam War was recognised by the Australian Government and she was entitled to receive the Vietnam Medal and the Australian Active Service Medal.[25] Pat passed away on 27 January 2006.

The Vietnam War: the silent contributors

During the Vietnam War, 106 nursing officers from the RAAFNS were deployed to No 4 RAAF Hospital at RAAF Base Butterworth in Malaysia. Their role was to care for the military personnel based there, and to assist with evacuations of injured Australians from Vietnam. The hospital was designated as the transit medical facility for Australian battle and non-battle casualties. The nurses would travel on medical evacuation (medevac) flights into Vietnam, tasked with transporting wounded Australian personnel to Butterworth prior to being assessed for movement back to Australia. At the height of the conflict, these frequent evacuations played a critical role in increasing battlefield casualty survival rates.

Royal Australian Air Force Nursing Service nursing sister Squadron Officer Harriet Hardy Fenwick tends to an Australian Army casualty during a medical evacuation flight from Vietnam to Australia, 20 August 1965 (Australian War Memorial, MAL/65/0083/03)

The first medevac flight was conducted on 9 July 1965, with Squadron Officer Harriet Fenwick and Sergeant Don Percy, a medical escort, as the two personnel dedicated to monitoring the patients on board a Douglas C-47 Dakota. Harriet recalled, 'The Vietnam conflict had started much earlier but now *we* were involved.'[1] In the early days, there was no specific timetable for medevacs, and the number initially varied from two to six per month. The number of soldiers able to be evacuated was increased when fortnightly C-130 Hercules runs commenced from Richmond. These medevac flights would depart Butterworth and travel via the Cocos Islands, through RAAF Base Pearce in Western Australia, before arriving in Richmond.

Margaret Sutherland (née Curgenven) recalled the sensory impact of the medevac flights into Vietnam, where the aircraft would leave Butterworth at first light:

> The aircraft would be loaded to the hilt with cargo, spare parts and supplies going into Vietnam. The arrival at Vũng Tàu was memorable – I can still hear the noise of the Hercules landing on the airfield … my bones shaking and the back door opening and the heat rising off the tarmac … We would meet the Army nurses, exchange news from Australia and receive a report on the patients we were to evacuate.[2]

The schedule for medical personnel in Butterworth was anything but routine: they were on call at all times, and it was common straight after a full shift to be directed to head back to the hospital. The requirement for flexibility came in handy when being assigned to urgent medevac tasks, and from 1966 when short-notice secondments to the United States Air Force (USAF) were put in place.

From July 1966 until April 1971, 32 RAAFNS nursing sisters and 14 male medical orderlies were seconded to the USAF 902nd Aeromedical Evacuation Squadron (902nd AMES), based at Clark Air Base in the Philippines. They joined the United States (US) teams of nurses and medics flying into Vietnam to evacuate large numbers of American military casualties. The 60-day assignments gave the nurses invaluable large-scale medevac war experience, flying up and down the length of Vietnam collecting patients with varying injuries, with some missions having to remain overnight in Vietnam if aircraft became unserviceable. The C-118 Liftmasters (the military version of the Douglas DC-6), C-130 Hercules and C-141 Starlifters were used by the USAF for these missions, with regular flights across to Japan, South Korea, Thailand and the US. By the end of the first year of attachments, the nursing sisters had nursed and helped to evacuate more than the equivalent of the entire number of Australians who would be wounded during the Vietnam War.[3] Due to security restrictions, RAAFNS personnel were directed not to disclose information about their operations into and out of Vietnam. Nursing sisters were also directed not to wear their uniforms in public after returning home; anti-war sentiment from many members of the public led to the poor treatment of many who returned from the conflict.

The nurses also did not receive any type of psychological or medical debrief after they returned to Butterworth from their deployments to Clark Air Base, or after they redeployed to Australia. This is in stark contrast to current-day deployments, where Australian Defence

Force personnel conduct medical and psychological screening just prior to returning to Australia, then again several months after their return.

Given the secrecy surrounding their deployment, and with no official record of their service during the Vietnam War, the significant role the members of the RAAFNS played during the conflict was not recognised. It was due only to the continued efforts of a small number of women, in particular Flight Officer Gaynor Tilley, through the submission of diaries, letters and 902nd AMES flight mission records, that all members were recognised for their service. Gaynor recalled in her submission that 'Former RAAFNS sisters remained alienated, their service contribution to the Vietnam War ignored and disbelieved by many, or else completely misunderstood.'[4]

In 1989, their contribution was recognised in part, and they were awarded the Returned from Active Service Badge. It was not until a submission to the Committee of Inquiry into Defence and Defence Related Awards in 1993 that the nurses were awarded the Vietnam Medal and the Australian Active Service Medal.[5] Importantly, this allowed the women to be eligible to apply for appropriate entitlements through the Department of Veterans' Affairs, to ensure their medical needs would be met. Those seconded to the 902nd AMES were also awarded the US Air Medal: Margaret Sutherland was the first recipient in 2021.[6]

Incredibly, not all of the nursing sisters were officially advised of the decision: some heard about it through the grapevine years later. Section Officer Bev Millner recalled the first time she became aware of the decision was when she was invited to the US to attend the opening of the Nurses Memorial at Arlington Cemetery in 1997.[7] She applied for her medals and they eventually arrived in the mail. Despite this disappointing treatment of the RAAFNS 'silent contributors', Bev said deploying in support of the Vietnam War had been the best experience of her life: 'It was challenging, fulfilling, interesting and rewarding and it gave me a maturity I hadn't had prior to going.'[8]

THE 1970s

INTRODUCTION

The 1970s were a volatile period in Australian political history. Mass demonstrations took place to protest the increasingly unpopular Vietnam War, which ended for Australian servicemen and servicewomen by 11 January 1973. In December 1972, the Labor Party, led by Gough Whitlam, came to power after 23 years of Liberal–National coalition government. Australian multiculturalism emerged with the abolition of the White Australia Policy in 1973 and the introduction of the *Racial Discrimination Act* in 1975. Feminist issues, gender equality and First Nations people's activism reached new heights in the ensuing years.

In 1972, the Aboriginal Embassy was established on the lawns opposite Parliament House in Canberra, as a site of protest and advocacy of land rights. It remains as the longest continuing protest in Australia's history.

In June 1978, in Darlinghurst, Sydney, a group formed to protest against the treatment of gay and lesbian community members, calling for an end to discrimination. The group grew to around 2000 protesters, and resulted in police violence and arrests for many. This event is considered the birth of the Sydney Gay and Lesbian Mardi Gras.[1]

The officers mess at RAAF Darwin, Northern Territory, after Cyclone Tracy struck the city on Christmas Day 1974 (Department of Defence)

Women were positioned to benefit greatly from the social and policy changes of the Whitlam government. Whitlam sought to ensure workplace pay and conditions for women were in keeping with the principles of social equality that guided his agenda. The United Nations declared 1975 as International Women's Year, acknowledging the global women's liberation movement. Whitlam responded with significant funding to support women's health and welfare services, and the status of women. This began to be reflected in the opportunities for women in the armed services.[2]

Among this landscape of political and societal upheaval, the whole of Australia, including the Royal Australian Air Force (RAAF), banded together after Cyclone Tracy devastated Darwin on 25 December 1974.[3]

The British royal family visited Australia as part of celebrations for Queen Elizabeth II's Silver Jubilee in 1977, reaffirming Australia's willingness to remain within the Commonwealth.

The RAAF commemorated its 50th year in 1971, with the Queen reflecting how far the Air Force had come and looking forward to what it was going to achieve in the future:

> In this Golden Jubilee Year the Royal Australian Air Force can look back with pride on its achievements over the last half century. The Service has played its part with distinction in times of peace and war, and has won a world-wide reputation … The future will present many challenges, but I am confident that the Royal Australian Air Force, because of the high calibre, professionalism and purpose of its men and women will meet and overcome these challenges and will continue a story of development and success which will be an inspiration to new generations.[4]

Her Majesty Queen Elizabeth II in Canberra, Australian Capital Territory, 1970 (Department of Defence)

Air Vice-Marshal Julie Hammer AM CSC

Engineer

Place of birth: Brisbane, Queensland
Date of enlistment: 21 February 1977

I'm just an ordinary person who works very hard – I wanted them to see that someone who is not extraordinary can actually reach very senior rank and achieve in a male world.[1]

Official portrait of Air Vice-Marshal Julie Hammer on her promotion to two-star officer, 2003 (Department of Defence)

During her school and university years in Brisbane, Julie Hammer always loved science and maths, and she placed eighth in the state in the Senior Public Matriculation Examination in 1971. She went on to complete a Bachelor of Science with post-graduate Honours in Physics at The University of Queensland. Julie reflected that her parents, Colin and Shirley, always encouraged her along the road to success: 'They believed girls should have as much opportunity for education as boys and went without comforts themselves to enable their daughters to pursue university educations.'[2]

While her father had served in the RAAF as a wireless operator/air gunner during the Second World War, his experience was not a significant influence for Julie to join. It was only during her final Honours year in university that she went along to a careers day to discover the only employers of physicists were the Bureau of Meteorology (who were not taking on anyone new that year), the Australian Public Service and the RAAF:

> The RAAF wanted maths and physics graduates as Education Officers. And I thought, 'Oh well, that might be a good option for a year or two until a proper job comes along.' I really thought about it mainly as a short-term opportunity.[3]

Julie joined in 1977 at a time when the RAAF was opening a number of traditionally male employment areas to women. Even though the Women's Royal Australian Air Force (WRAAF) still existed at the time of her commissioning, Julie entered the RAAF as an education officer at the rank of flying officer, the third woman to join the Education Branch:

> While I might have been in a minority group, there were always a number of women in the workplace in a range of roles, and we were all friends. Although perhaps I was a bit of a novelty, I was accepted by the men once they observed that I was willing to work hard and could do the job.[4]

Despite being a RAAF officer, all women were paid in line with the WRAAF pay scale and Julie received approximately three-quarters of the equivalent male wage. In May 1977, the WRAAF was disbanded and all of its members were incorporated into the RAAF. It took another 12 months for all women to start receiving equal pay.[5]

Julie was initially posted to the Engineer Cadet Squadron at RAAF Base Frognall in Melbourne until 1979, then she was posted in as an instructor at the RAAF School of Radio, Laverton. As an instructor, she gave lessons on basic electronics, radar, navigation aids and electronic warfare (EW).

By 1981, the Engineers Branch had been opened to women, and a colleague suggested she consider transferring her specialisation:

> My initial reaction was, 'How can I? I've got a physics degree, not an engineering degree?' He pointed out that a number of cadets who had been unsuccessful as aircrew had gone into the Engineer Branch.[6]

Officer training course graduation, 1977. Julie is third from the right in the front row (Julie Hammer)

Julie reflected on this opportunity as the first major turning point of her career:

> I didn't really see myself staying for a long period of time in the Air Force until I was given the opportunity to transfer to engineering. As an Engineer, I saw that I had a much greater career opportunity than I had as an Education Officer.[7]

Her early engineering postings involved the oversight of aircraft deeper-level maintenance at No 3 Aircraft Depot, RAAF Amberley, Queensland, where she gained experience in 'on the ground' engineering roles with the F-111 aircraft, Iroquois and Chinook helicopters and the Canberra bombers. This was followed by a tour as a sub-section head in the Aircraft Equipment Engineering Division of Headquarters Support Command in Melbourne, where she was responsible for the engineering management of radio and radar equipment in half of the RAAF and Army fleets. After performing this role on higher duties for 18 months, Julie was finally promoted into the role as a squadron leader in June 1985.

In January 1986, Julie was posted to the United Kingdom (UK) to study at RAF Cranwell, where she completed a Master of Science in Aerosystems Engineering. While she found this to be a difficult course, Julie believes it stood her in good stead for her subsequent career:

> It gave me an extraordinarily comprehensive technology update … and gave me a great deal of credibility with my peer group too, who sometimes saw me more as an ex-edo [education officer] than as an engineer.[8]

After returning to Canberra in 1987, Julie was posted as a technical intelligence analyst in the Joint Intelligence Organisation:

> It gave me my first insight into the intelligence community … time after time in my subsequent career, my network in the intelligence community was a godsend … So I was, if you like, a trusted party; not someone on the outside.[9]

Flight Lieutenant Julie Hammer with engineering and maintenance crew in front of a Bell UH-1 Iroquois at RAAF Amberley, Queensland (Julie Hammer)

This became important in her next posting onto the major EW project to fit an electronic-support-measures system to the P-3C Orions: first as project engineer and then, on promotion to wing commander, as project manager. In 1992, Julie was selected as the Commanding Officer (CO) of the Electronic Warfare Squadron in Edinburgh in Adelaide, having gained considerable experience in the EW field in some of her previous postings. She was the first woman to command an operational unit in the RAAF; however, ironically, her specialisation as an engineer was considered to be more of a roadblock to her selection than being a woman:

> It was deemed to be an operational aircrew job in the early days of the squadron. It was actually more controversial that I was an engineer appointed to do an aircrew job than it was that I was a woman being appointed to the first female operational command that the Air Force had had … I visited the posting officer and asked him to broaden the pool of candidates to include Engineers, still using the same selection criteria. Happily, for me, he came to the conclusion that there was logic in doing so, and argued the case to his boss to open the selection up. The rest is history, as they say.[10]

Wing Commander Julie Hammer taking a salute on parade, as the Commanding Officer Electronic Warfare Squadron, at RAAF Base Edinburgh, South Australia, circa 1992 (Julie Hammer)

This was a period when a number of RAAF aircraft were being fitted with EW systems, and the squadron's role was to program the adversary threat libraries (developed to identify an adversary's military capability and develop methods in which to counter threats in combat) and other EW software to support Australian Defence Force (ADF) aircraft in their operational roles in exercises and on peacekeeping operations:

> It was highly technical and highly classified, and very, very deeply involved in the operational world. It gave me a huge amount of knowledge and a great many insights that really stood me in great stead for the rest of my career. I then found myself, later on in my career, moving more into the communications and information technology world, working with computer systems and the big command and control systems that were epitomised in the software hosted on those systems.[11]

Post-command, Julie spent the next phase of her career on major projects. In 1996, she was the first woman to be promoted to the rank of group captain in the RAAF. Her first role was as Project Director responsible for the design, development and introduction into service of the secret command and control network and systems for the entire ADF:

> During my tenure as Project Director, we installed a couple of dozen new nodes on the secret network; effectively that became today's secret network. The DSN [Defence Secret Network] grew from that. Up until that time, any little computing

> networks Defence had were in isolated pockets that were not connected to each other … we absorbed them all, until now what we've got is one homogenous secret network throughout the whole department.[12]

Group Captain Julie Hammer (right) engaging with peers during a work luncheon (Julie Hammer)

In 1999, Julie was posted back to the UK as the sole Australian student at the Royal College of Defence Studies, where she completed a 12-month course in strategic and international studies. On her return to Australia, Julie was promoted to air commodore: the first woman to attain star rank in the ADF. Noting that when she had joined the Air Force, women were excluded from many roles, Julie reflected on how far women had come during her time in service:

> As I progressed in my career and got more senior, it was almost inevitable that it was the first time that a woman had served in that role. Of course these days, happily, it's much more commonplace. So I guess that I was used to being the first [woman] in a role. I recall when I was promoted to one-star that not only did a lot of Air Force women make contact with me and rejoice in my promotion along with me, but interestingly, a lot of Army and Navy women also did. They were so encouraged by the fact that a woman had made it to star rank.[13]

Julie's first one-star posting was as the Director General Information Services, a large organisation with personnel in more than 100 locations:

> I had in that job a staff of 1,500 people delivering the day-to-day running support of Defence's communications and information technology systems, both restricted and secret. I must say it was probably one of the most challenging jobs that I had, but also one of the most rewarding. I thoroughly enjoyed working in the tri-Service

> environment and working with civilians. It was a great joy to me that, at the end of my career, I could count among my friends and colleagues people from right across the Defence Force.[14]

Julie married a fellow RAAF senior officer, David Dunlop, in 2000. They had first met when Julie was CO of the Electronic Warfare Squadron, and she said their meeting was a 'little unusual'.[15] The squadron had developed a threat library for the F-111 that was first used during Exercise *Pitch Black* in 1993, to great success. David was the Officer Commanding (OC) of the wing where the F-111 squadrons were stationed, and was extremely impressed, wanting to learn more:

> The OC of the Wing said to his Wing Commander Ops, who was an experienced EW type and a buddy of mine, 'Well, we'd better go down and check out this EW Squadron and see how they do this stuff and learn a bit more about it … you arrange for us to go and visit him.' My mate said, 'Well, it's not a him, it's a her.' So down they came, and that was the first time we met. So I don't think many people meet their future husbands by programming a radar warning receiver threat library for them![16]

They met again a few years after that sole meeting, and eventually married. They spent the last 15 months of David's career in different states, until David transferred to the Reserves and they moved back to Canberra.

In December 2001, Julie was appointed as the Commandant of the Australian Defence Force Academy (ADFA): the first woman to take command of the organisation responsible for the development of the ADF's cohort of trainee officers across the Royal Australian Navy, Australian Army and RAAF. She recalled she was not appointed to the position by chance:

> I was very privileged to be the first woman to be appointed to that role. I lobbied hard to get it, not only with the posters [Air Force's career management agency] but with many of the senior people in Defence, including the Chief of Defence Force of the day. Hopefully I was given that role because they thought I'd do a good job, not just because I annoyed them to get it! But it really was and is a wonderful institution.[17]

Julie sought the role for a number of reasons. Firstly, she had loved the experience she had gained in a command position at the Electronic Warfare Squadron, in being able to develop her team and grow their capabilities. Commandant of ADFA was another opportunity to help develop young military personnel at the beginning of their career:

> That was its core role. But there was another reason that I wanted to be Commandant of ADFA, and that was because I wanted to be a role model for the young future officers of the ADF. In particular, a role model for the young women, so that they could see that someone who wasn't extraordinary – I'm just an ordinary person who works very hard – can actually reach very senior rank and achieve in a male world. It was important to me to show that senior women are achieving and that they don't have to be untrue to their own personalities to be able to do that. As well as that, I actually wanted to be a role model for the young men. A lot of young women have

> male role models. Why can't young men have female role models? And I wanted them to get used to seeing women in very senior roles so that that was something they considered the norm rather than the exception. I spent as much time in an informal atmosphere with the cadets as I could, where I could just sit and talk to them and where they could get to know me, and see that senior officers are not aloof, they are accessible, and that this is something for them to aspire to.[18]

Julie was promoted to air vice-marshal in 2003, the first woman to attain two-star rank in the ADF. Her role was as the Deputy Chief Information Officer in Defence Headquarters:

> I accepted that it might take a male workforce a little bit longer to get to know me and accept me and make the judgement that I was actually a competent person … I would give people in a new environment a little bit longer to get to know me. Of course, as I progressed through each rank and as I got to much more senior levels, I recognised that I was being watched by men as well as by women. For women, they wanted to see how a woman was being accepted in a senior role and how a woman was performing in a senior role, because this was what they had to look to in the future.[19]

On promotion to senior levels, Julie was tasked with representing a female perspective on a range of issues, providing input to a committee group or contributing to certain papers, which she considered to be a great privilege:

> But I was sensitive to the fact that all these extra opportunities I had could be seen to be positive discriminatory behaviour or positive selection … I was always very, very careful that whatever I did was very well considered. I never did anything rash. You might even consider I was boring.[20]

On 26 January 2004, Julie was appointed a Member of the Order of Australia for exceptional service in the fields of electronics engineering in Defence, and military education as the Commandant of ADFA. She retired in 2005, after a stellar career of 28 years. While she considers herself ordinary, her career achievements certainly demonstrate an extraordinary contribution to the capability of the Air Force.

When asked what she considers to have been the most momentous change to the RAAF during her career, Julie believed it was the opening of aircrew categories to women in 1987:

> This was a truly momentous milestone, and an even bigger milestone was achieved when all RAAF combat roles were opened to women in 1992. It took quite a few years after those policy changes for women to progress into many of those areas, but it is pleasing to see that this is now more the norm than the exception.[21]

Group Captain Jenny Fantini OAM

Engineer

Date of birth: 1960
Place of birth: Sydney, New South Wales
Date of enlistment: 16 January 1978

It is a great lifestyle with almost limitless possibilities, if you are willing to work hard and be part of a team.[1]

Flight Lieutenant Jenny Fantini prepares for a back-seat flight in an F/A-18B Hornet at RAAF Base Williamtown, New South Wales, 1986 (Jenny Fantini)

Jenny Fantini was born in Sydney in 1960 to a father with Italian heritage and a mother with Anglo–Danish heritage. With one younger sister, Jenny was the tomboy of the family:

> I preferred to play with boys' toys. Mum tells the story of me stubbornly refusing to enter my first kindergarten class when I was five, until the teacher offered me cars and trains to play with![2]

Her upbringing was reasonably strict, with her parents focused on earning a living (her father worked in real estate), creating a safe home and educating the children:

> Mum always focused on our education as being vitally important and was always very encouraging. She used to tell me that I could do anything I wanted, if I set my mind to it.[3]

Jenny loved science and maths at school and tried to avoid studying traditional girls' subjects. Her father wanted her to attend a Catholic girls' high school, but these did not guarantee to offer the senior high school subjects Jenny needed to get into engineering at university – she dreamed of becoming an astronaut or space scientist. 'This argument won over my father because education was very important to him too (having had only limited education himself as a boy in Italy).'[4] Jenny went to a large co-educational high school and in Years 11 and 12 enrolled in physics, chemistry, mathematics and engineering science, in which she excelled. When she graduated from high school in 1977, she was in the top five per cent of students in New South Wales (NSW).

Jenny was drawn to joining the Air Force because she liked the idea of working with aircraft and also doing something that most other girls did not do. 'I liked the potential for adventure and travel with the RAAF. I liked being in a male environment – and being unique and a bit different.'[5]

Engineer Cadet Jenny Fantini at RAAF Base Frognall, Victoria, January 1978 (Jenny Fantini)

At the time, the RAAF did not accept women in technical or aircrew roles. However, it was just starting to accept women as engineer cadets: this meant Jenny would be able to study an engineering degree and then graduate as an engineering officer in the RAAF. She signed up immediately after finishing high school in December 1977. 'I had a bit of an issue joining up, perversely due to the length of my feet! Yes, I have women's size-11 feet.'[6] The 'feet size' issue delayed her acceptance letter, but she received it just in time to join the RAAF in January 1978. She lived on base at RAAF Base Frognall in Canterbury (in Melbourne) and commuted each day to the Royal Melbourne Institute of Technology, where she studied communications/electronics engineering.

> There were very few females at Frognall when I arrived. But being [one of] so few among so many boys felt normal to me – I had often been the only girl in my high school physics/chemistry/maths/engineering classes.[7]

Jenny quickly settled into life on base, undertaking military drill in the mornings and playing soccer with the boys, while studying for her degree. But during her first year, cadets were confined to the base on weeknights:

> Occasionally, we would go stir crazy and jump the back fence (there was a guard at the front gate) to escape for a time. I did that once to visit a university friend, whose father (coincidentally a Second World War ex-RAAFie) kindly dropped me back afterwards and gave me a knee-up to get back over the fence. I think he understood what being confined to base did to your head sometimes![8]

No 23 Course Engineer Cadet Squadron (third year) as the Quarter Guard in support of the graduating course at RAAF Base Frognall, Victoria, December 1980. Senior Air Cadet Jenny Fantini is in the front rank wearing a skirt and holding a rifle (Jenny Fantini)

All cadets, male and female, undertook the same training at Frognall, including weapons handling and shooting practice. However, the rules around the carriage of weapons on parade changed around 1981: Jenny suspects this was because she had paraded with a service rifle in 1980 while wearing her uniform skirt (women in the RAAF were not yet permitted to wear trousers). After that, females were not permitted on parade with weapons, meaning she was not allowed to carry a sword for her graduation parade in December 1981. 'This was a major disappointment for me at the time.'[9]

Jenny remembered that uniforms were always problematic for the female cadets, with the mandatory skirts and dresses being impractical in a technical environment around aircraft:

> There were other silly things that were irritating. During our first year, a fellow female cadet and I stood on parade in the pouring rain without raincoats because the supply officer would not issue us with 'male' raincoats. The only difference is that they button up on the opposite side! So we were ordered to wear our civilian raincoats – to much mirth from the other cadets when we reappeared in our yellow raincoats on parade![10]

Otherwise, Jenny believes the female cadets were treated the same as the male cadets:

> My philosophy was to get on with my job and show that I could do it. Whatever physical training or activity we did, I always made sure that I finished, even if I finished last. And, quite often, not all of the boys finished.[11]

Jenny was the first female engineer cadet to graduate from the RAAF's Engineer Cadet Squadron at Frognall. Just two other women (Margaret Maxwell and Julie Hammer) had previously commissioned as engineers via a different pathway. 'I was told that the number of women applying to join the engineering cadets skyrocketed after I graduated in December 1981.'[12]

Jenny's Air Force career has been filled with other 'firsts'. She was the first female engineer posted to RAAF Base Butterworth in Malaysia in support of Operation *Gateway* with the RAAF P-3 Orions in 1982 to 1984; she was the first female engineer posted to an operational fighter (F/A-18 Hornet) squadron in 1986; and she was the first female Base Commander of RAAF Base Wagga Wagga in NSW in 2006. In 2010, she was the first female to be appointed as the senior engineering and logistics director for Air Combat Group at RAAF Base Williamtown in NSW, where she oversaw maintenance and logistics performance and standards for the RAAF's F/A-18 Hornet, F-111, Hawk 127 and PC-9 Forward Air Control squadrons.

> During my career, I learned to ignore anyone who predicted what women could/couldn't/should/shouldn't do. Fortunately for me, Air Force gave me some great opportunities and allowed me to be myself and, over time, Air Force itself adapted to those of us in non-traditional roles.[13]

Her career in the RAAF took Jenny all over Australia, as well as overseas on deployments to Malaysia, the Philippines and New Zealand. She was posted to the United States twice: the first time to be trained on the technical and engineering aspects of the new F/A-18 Hornet (as the only woman in the detachment) and the second time as an exchange officer with the USAF, working on a VIP aircraft acquisition program.

She cited as her most rewarding time her posting to No 3 Squadron (3SQN) at Williamtown from 1986 to 1988, where she served as the inaugural Flight Line and Aircraft Maintenance Officer when they re-equipped the squadron with the F/A-18A Hornet. The introduction of a new aircraft type was a particularly exciting time, both professionally and personally, for Jenny:

> For most of the personnel whom I commanded (around 80, including only two women), I was their first female boss. An interesting coincidence is that during WWII, 3SQN flew over the part of Italy where my father lived as a young teenager. Who would have guessed that on the ground below the aircraft was a young boy who would grow up to emigrate to Australia, and whose daughter would become the squadron's engineering officer 50 years later![14]

Flight Lieutenant Jenny Fantini in front of Hornet A21-012 with her two Warrant Officer Engineers, 1987 (Jenny Fantini)

During her time in the RAAF, Jenny has seen many changes for the better. These include the RAAF eventually recognising that its members are a diverse group. For Jenny personally, this included the RAAF recognising that female engineers can do the job just as well as male engineers, and acknowledging same-sex couples and a more diverse workforce:

> The RAAF has managed to change and, while some will struggle with those changes, I am proud of us in the RAAF for the strides we have taken. Treating others with respect and expecting the same in return are important traits, as is a willingness to muck in and get the job done.[15]

Jenny is proud to wear the RAAF uniform, which she sees as a reminder of the standards and values military personnel need to uphold, as well as being a symbol of belonging. Plus, these days, women are permitted to wear trousers!

> The values taught to me by my parents as a child blend very well with the Defence values of Service, Courage, Respect, Integrity and Excellence, and the application of these within Air Force.[16]

Jenny believes a career in the RAAF can lead to great heights, and considers the greatest honour of her career was being awarded an Order of Australia Medal in the military division of the Queen's Birthday honours in June 2020:

> If someone was to ask me for advice about joining the Air Force, I would tell them that it is a great lifestyle with almost limitless possibilities, if you are willing to work hard and be part of a team. Air Force is a huge interconnected family – one that will change your life. I would also tell them that I envied them their choice, because I would like to do it all again![17]

Group Captain Jenny Fantini with Deputy Chief of Air Force Air Vice-Marshal Gavin 'Leo' Davies, 2014 (Department of Defence)

Society's attitudes and national policies: the impact on women in the Air Force

The professional opportunities presented to women throughout the Australian Defence Force's (ADF) history are largely reflective of societal norms, public attitudes and government policies of the time. It was only at the turn of the 20th century that some Australian states had even recognised women as citizens, thereby allowing them to vote.[1] At the start of the Second World War, a woman's role in Australian society was still considered to be one of wife, mother and homemaker. Employment options for women were limited to what would be considered traditional female occupations, such as clerical workers. A long-term, professional career was rare.

However, the early years of the Second World War highlighted the increasing requirement for Australian women to contribute to the nation's war effort. With a significant number of men being deployed to operational areas in Australia and overseas, the need for personnel to join supporting roles drastically increased. The use of women in these roles was the logical choice; Great Britain paved the way by signing up large numbers of women to its armed forces.

Despite some resistance by members of the War Cabinet, and after considerable lobbying by women who wanted to serve, the WAAAF was formed in March 1941.[2] Previous policy restrictions on women contributing to military service (albeit in an auxiliary capacity) in a range of different roles were temporarily lifted. Towards the end of the war, women were employed in 73 different fields in the WAAAF and did 'everything but fly'.[3] They were also serving as nurses in the RAAFNS.

The employment of women in other Commonwealth departments during the war largely echoed the opportunities which were provided to women in the military, demonstrating the start of a slight shift in attitude towards a female workforce. However, it did not take long for political pressure to mount to reduce the number of women in military roles, even as the war continued. In 1943, Prime Minister John Curtin assured male employees that all women who were employed under wartime conditions would be removed from this employment after the war ended, but he also stated that was what women would want![4]

The WAAAF was disestablished in 1947, in large part so that men returning from conflict had opportunities for continued employment. As a consequence, many women returned to their homemaking roles. Only the RAAFNS remained as an arm of the military in which women could continue to serve. As it turned out, many positions vacated by women were not filled as anticipated (by men), leaving the RAAF short staffed, with some considering that the disbandment of the WAAAF had been too hasty.

In July 1951, one year after the commencement of the Korean War, Cabinet approved the re-establishment of a women's air force, albeit with limited available roles. As was the case in other government departments, the salaries for women were not on par with their male counterparts, and the requirement for women to resign if they decided to marry lasted well into the 1960s. Air Force regulations also capped the percentage of women able to join at no more than 10 per cent of the male established strength.[5] By 1975, nearly 25 years after the establishment of the WRAAF, women made up only five per cent of Air Force numbers.

The issue of marriage and employment

To join the WRAAF, women had to be between 18 and 34 years of age and, if under 21, they required parental consent. They had to be single, widowed or divorced without dependents.[6] It was only in 1966 that a change to national legislation started to open up opportunities for women to remain in employment if they decided to marry. A Parliamentary Bill to remove the ban on married women entering the Commonwealth Public Service was introduced in 1966 and, not long after, the *Public Service Act* was amended to allow for the permanent appointment of women in the Commonwealth Public Service. However, it took a few more years for the Air Force to catch up. In 1967, the Air Board determined that retaining a woman who chose to marry 'should be on a permissive basis to be decided in each case by the respective Service'; the final say was held with the personnel agency. This ruling was altered to an entitlement in 1969. Even though women were now able to remain in service if they chose to marry, they still had to agree to the service requirements of unmarried members, such as postings and short-term duties. They also had to provide an undertaking that they would not fall pregnant! Already-married women were finally able to join the WRAAF under this determination in 1969.[7]

Regardless of these policy changes, some senior members of the ADF did little to argue on behalf of their female counterparts for equal employment opportunities. Indeed, in 1978, the Chief of the Air Staff, Air Marshal Sir James Rowland, said to a joint parliamentary committee (referring to the likelihood of women pilots in the RAAF), 'Do you want me to spend $1 million of your money producing a Mirage pilot who is going to leave in a couple of years?'[8]

Equal pay for equal work

While policies around marriage and employment were improving opportunities for women, the right of equal pay was lagging behind. In a Commonwealth of Australia Finance Circular dated 19 March 1965, the significant disparity in the daily rates of pay was evident when calculating an adjustment of contributions to the Defence Forces Retirement Benefits Fund. To assess the contribution towards the fund, a daily rate was used; on average, women at that time were earning slightly more than half the wage of their male counterparts.[9] Even work tasks allotted to women could be different from men in the same employment field, perhaps reflecting a societal view on what a woman 'should' be carrying out in the workplace.

In 1969, a National Wage Case was developed which established the principle of equal pay for equal work, regardless of gender.[10] With this policy in mind, the issue of Defence pay was re-examined. While rates of pay for airwomen (general enlisted servicewomen) were finally increased to match their male peers in 1972, officers and non-commissioned officers had still not gained wage parity.[11] It took until 1978, after the WRAAF and RAAFNS were integrated into the RAAF, for women of all ranks to receive the same pay and conditions as their male counterparts.[12]

Equal employment opportunities

Pay and conditions of service were changing, yet the opportunity for women to serve alongside their male counterparts in all employment fields was still far from being achieved. Many employment categories, including aircrew and ground-defence roles, remained closed to women throughout the 1970s and 1980s. It took the social agenda of Prime Minister Gough Whitlam (1972–75) to champion the role of women in the workplace and, by extension, in Australian society. His aims were to achieve equality of opportunity between men and women, and to remove discrimination against women.[13] In 1975, Whitlam and Defence Minister Lance Barnard agreed that, as a basic human right, women should be able to 'hold all public office on equal terms with men'.[14] This included the question as to whether women could serve in combat zones or in combat-related activities. Defence was directed to investigate new employment opportunities for women, with recommendations from the working party including female participation on active service at home and overseas, but not in combat roles. Ironically, the RAAFNS had, for several decades, already operated within conflict zones, treating the injured in a combat-related role.

Flight Lieutenant Emily Walker during Operation *Tanager* in Dili, East Timor, April 2001. She was part of a volunteer group helping to rebuild a local children's school and refurbish a memorial pool, which had been built by Australian veterans in the 1960s (Department of Defence)

In 1984, the Hawke government passed the *Sex Discrimination Act* (SDA), thereby prohibiting any form of discrimination on the basis of sex, marital status or pregnancy. While this was a turning point in the employment of women, exemptions included in the SDA provided for the ADF to exclude women from positions 'involving performance of combat or combat-related duties'. Combat duties are defined as duties requiring a person to commit, or to participate directly in, an act of violence against an adversary in time of war. Combat-related duties are defined as duties requiring a person to work in support of, and in close proximity to, a person performing combat duties.

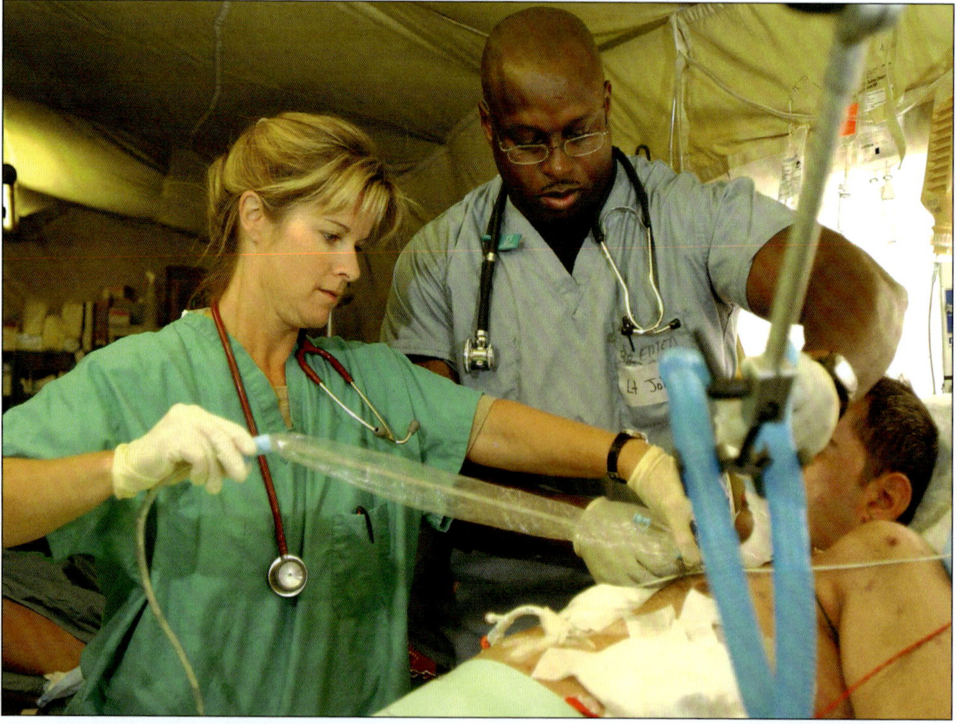

Flight Lieutenant Belinda Ball treats a patient in the medical facility at a coalition air base north of Baghdad, Iraq, during Operation *Catalyst*, 2004 (Department of Defence)

It took until 1987 for women to be eligible to join the RAAF as a pilot or aircrew on 'non-combat' aircraft, and until 1992 for women to be eligible to join as combat-aircraft crew. In September 2011, the Gillard government announced it would remove all gender restrictions from ADF combat employment categories.[15] For the Air Force, this policy change opened the door for women to join as Airfield Defence Guards and Ground Defence Officers. It took several more years for the first females to graduate in these roles.

THE 1980s

INTRODUCTION

The 1980s were marked by defining events that resonated throughout the world. The Soviet Union began to collapse, AIDS emerged as a deadly pandemic, and a little technical system called the Internet was developed.[1] For Australia, it was a decade of contrasts; there were radical economic reforms and spectacular corporate collapses, as well as events that placed the nation on the global map.

The Great Barrier Reef gained United Nations (UN) World Heritage status in 1980. Tim Macartney-Snape and Greg Mortimer were the first Australians to reach the summit of Mount Everest in Nepal in 1984. And the movie *Crocodile Dundee* was an international success in 1986. However, the global economic climate had a significant and negative impact on everyday Australians. The 1987 share market crash, tax evasion by some wealthy businessmen, and soaring inflation rates, led to a recession 'we had to have' (according to the Treasurer of the time, Paul Keating). Unemployment rates soared, the 'big four' banks wiped considerable amounts of debt, and major companies crashed spectacularly.[2]

For Australian women, policy changes regarding their status in the workplace were considered a positive step in increasing their opportunities. In 1983, the Hawke government ratified the UN Convention on the Elimination of All Forms of Discrimination against Women and introduced the *Sex Discrimination Act* a year later.[3] In 1986, Joan Child became the first female Speaker of the House of Representatives.[4]

Royal Australian Air Force recruits graduating from their training course, 1987 (RAAF Museum)

Royal Australian Air Force Officer Cadet Christine Bufalino marching in unison with two Australian Defence Force Academy colleagues, Canberra, Australian Capital Territory, circa 1989 (Department of Defence)

Royal Australian Air Force Officer Cadet Mel Steel in the engineering laboratory at the Australian Defence Force Academy, Canberra, Australian Capital Territory, circa 1988 (Department of Defence)

Representation of women in the Australian Defence Force (ADF) was still comparatively small; however, there was a slow and steady increase in numbers. In 1980, women represented six per cent of the ADF workforce and 7.4 per cent of the Royal Australian Air Force (RAAF). By the end of the decade, the ADF consisted of 10.8 per cent women and the RAAF 13.7 per cent.

In October 1986, the RAAF advertised for suitable female applicants to start pilot training. Flight Lieutenant Robyn Williams and Officer Cadet Deborah Hicks became the first female pilots to graduate from No 2 Flying Training School on 30 June 1988. By the end of the decade, the RAAF increased the number of roles available for women to 87 per cent of all specialisations (the exceptions being combat and combat-related specialisations). These roles included pilots (non-combat aircraft only), loadmasters and navigators.[5] However, this policy change did not see an immediate and significant increase in women's numbers in these occupations for many years.

Officer Cadet Deborah Hicks (middle row, left) and Flight Lieutenant Robyn Williams (middle row, right) with their fellow Royal Australian Air Force pilot graduates, June 1988 (Department of Defence)

Aviation pioneer Nancy Bird Walton (centre) congratulates Flight Lieutenant Robyn Williams (left) and Officer Cadet Deborah Hicks (right) on their graduation from Royal Australian Air Force pilot training, June 1988 (Department of Defence)

Flight Lieutenant Robyn Williams, 30 June 1988 (Department of Defence)

Air Vice-Marshal Tracy Smart AO

Medical Officer

Place of birth: McLaren Vale, South Australia
Date of enlistment: 1 February 1985

It was a very different life from the one that I led in Kangarilla where I picked grapes for 50 cents a bucket, jumped into wool bale boxes to press the wool and helped Dad with our sheep.[1]

Wing Commander Tracy Smart during an exchange posting to the United States, 2001. A self-professed 'space nut', Tracy visited the Kennedy Space Center in Cape Canaveral, Florida (Tracy Smart)

Tracy Smart was born in 1963 and grew up on a farm in Kangarilla, a small rural town in South Australia (SA), which quite suitably in Kaurna language means 'nurturing place'.

However, staying to work on the family farm was never on Tracy's agenda; an initial interest in joining the Royal Australian Navy (RAN) was fostered by a love of the sea, her father's 'nasho' (national service) stories and hearing the legacy of her uncle's service as a pilot and early death during the Second World War.

But when Tracy explored the option of joining the RAN in the late 1970s, she discovered women were not allowed to go to sea. 'Why would you join the Navy and not go to sea? It didn't make sense.'[2] Tracy said that, in retrospect, this recruitment limitation was not surprising; it was still only a few years after a policy change that allowed women to remain in service if they became pregnant. Instead, she decided on medicine as a career, although she joked there was not much thought put into it. Once she was at university, she discovered she could join an undergraduate scheme as a RAAF member, and her career as an Air Force doctor started to take shape.

Tracy joined the RAAF as an undergraduate in 1985 as a fifth-year medical student, having already spent four years at Flinders University in SA. Now in uniform, she finished her degree, completed an internship year at Flinders Medical Centre, then a resident medical officer (MO) year at the Repatriation General Hospital in Adelaide. Her first Air Force posting was in 1989 to RAAF Amberley in Queensland.[3]

Tracy spent her junior postings at various RAAF bases throughout Australia, rapidly taking on senior medical roles in her units. As a self-described 'space nut' (she has several pieces of space-related Lego, a framed montage of the 'Doctors of Star Trek', her original Apollo 11 scrapbook from school, and has even met Neil Armstrong), the idea of aerospace medicine held enormous appeal.[4] In 1992, she was selected for a posting to the United Kingdom (UK), where she completed a diploma in aviation medicine. She remained in the UK as an aviation medicine instructor at RAF North Luffenham, becoming the first female instructor in the UK in that role.[5]

While aerospace medicine was an enduring focus and interest throughout her career, some of Tracy's most challenging experiences came during her operational deployments. In February 1995, she deployed with the second ADF element as part of Australia's contribution to the United Nations Assistance Mission for Rwanda. She deployed as the Officer in Charge of Clinical Services and as the Aeromedical Evacuation Operations Officer, one of 21 RAAF personnel in a task force of around 300. She was working out of the Central Hospital in Kigali when the Rwanda Patriotic Army began killing Hutu minority Rwandans at an Internally Displaced Persons (IDP) camp in Kibeho, located approximately three hours away. Within two days, an estimated 4200 people had been killed:

> I was back at the hospital when the massacre occurred and we received several patients from Kibeho. I actually deployed down to the camp about two weeks after the massacre. There were still a lot of IDPs that weren't leaving, so we went down to provide support. And the good thing was that they actually closed the camp when my group were there, which was quite a positive experience.[6]

Squadron Leader Tracy Smart while deployed with the United Nations Assistance Mission for Rwanda, 1995 (Tracy Smart)

Tracy recalled that a number of ADF members who deployed to Rwanda have had ongoing mental health issues:

> It thrust a lot of people into a very alien world – many had never left Australia before, and they ended up in the middle of Africa, interacting with a culture they couldn't understand and where people were killing each other, so that was very difficult. But I think for others – and I am in this group – we saw it as an opportunity to do really full-on medicine, really make a difference in people's lives and have perhaps a positive impact on the country in a small way as they tried to rebuild after the genocide. I see it as a positive life experience – it changed me, but in a positive way. I think it made me appreciate my strengths and weaknesses – I figured if I could survive that, I can survive anything.[7]

After her Rwanda deployment, Tracy was posted to the RAAF Institute of Aviation Medicine and took on the role of chief instructor, and later as Commanding Officer after her promotion to wing commander in 1997. She was the first woman to take on each of these roles.[8]

Wing Commander Tracy Smart during an exchange posting to the United States, 2000. She completed the 'Top Knife' course, an F-16 course for flight surgeons (Tracy Smart)

In the early 2000s, Tracy embarked on a two-year exchange posting with the United States Air Force at Langley Air Force Base in Virginia as Chief of Flight Medicine Operations in Air Combat Command. This was another memorable posting for Tracy as it included attending courses such as 'Top Knife' (the F-16 course for flight surgeons), where she got to pull 9G (nine times the force of gravity) in a centrifuge, and 'Space Medicine Operations'. She was also involved in developing solutions for inflight bladder relief for female fast-jet pilots, and experienced the dramatic events of 11 September 2001 when the United States was attacked and its military geared up for war.

Not long after returning to Australia, Tracy deployed to East Timor in 2002, as part of Australia's contribution to the United Nations (UN) Transitional Administration in East Timor.[9] She was 'dual hatted' as the UN's Chief Health Officer in the Peacekeeping Force Headquarters (PKF HQ), and the Senior Health Officer for Australian forces.[10] At the time, more than 25 nations were contributing military forces to the UN mission; it made for interesting times as different cultures, languages and work approaches had to be taken into consideration:

> I lived in Crocodile Alley which was a multinational accommodation area. This had its issues from time to time but was also quite amusing at times. There were signs on the walls about how to sit on the toilet and not drop things off to the side and that sort of thing, so there were sometimes cultural issues. And there were also the occasional knock[s] on my door in the middle of the night … for instance, when the Kiwis were teaching the Nepalese to play rugby and they needed some urgent medical advice.[11]

Timor Leste gained its independence in May 2002 and Tracy recalled the health system challenges the nation faced in its initial stages of independence:

> The Ministry of Health was beginning to take back control of their health system and so we were in a transition phase. The non-government organisations were starting to pull back and the Ministry [was] starting to recruit international doctors to work for them in the clinics. In some places like Oecussi, the enclave in West Timor, there was still a real lack of basic public health services, let alone surgical services.[12]

Another recollection from her Timor Leste deployment was when she was coordinating the emergency health preparations for the Independence Day celebrations, which involved the Timor Leste Ministry of Health, the Red Cross, and several military medical capabilities. Dignitaries included Kofi Annan and Bill Clinton:

> The naughty Portuguese Brigadier on the PKF HQ offered me US$100 to offer Clinton a cigar (it was only a few years after the Monica Lewinski revelations) and the Force Commander actually gave me the cigar, but I politely declined as I was in uniform!

The experiences and challenges from Tracy's years of service are impossible to convey in a short story, with her involvement in several operational deployments as well as orchestrating the health response to many incidents. Tracy deployed to the Al Udeid Air Force base in Qatar in 2003–4, where she was the Australian medical evacuation (medevac) coordinating officer embedded in the US system ('Validating Flight Surgeon' per the Americans), as well as the Senior ADF Health Officer in the Middle East:

> I don't know if I learned any medical lessons, but it was certainly interesting to look at the US system; the size of it more than anything. Also it was exciting because occasionally there'd be a major incident and you'd have to be working fairly intensely. It was also interesting to see the injury patterns that were occurring – the high amount of non-battle injuries, like people snapping their pec muscles from lifting too much [weight] … A lot of changes have come out of the Middle East wars … It's not automatic that the injured will go to the nearest facility – they will go to the [facility with the] most appropriate level of care.[13]

Memorable moments of that deployment included having her 'man bag' signed by former US President Bill Clinton, and wearing a Xena Warrior Princess costume to the British bar for a New Orleans Mardi Gras-themed night. She also had the chance to ride in the jump seat on an Australian C-130 medevac mission into Iraq:

> It was a true privilege watching our aircrew work as a team while flying low level into a potentially hostile area – some of the most fun flying I have ever done.[14]

By 2004, Tracy had been promoted to group captain as Officer Commanding (OC) Health Services Wing (HSW), where she was in charge of the RAAF's operational health capability. She was instrumental in the coordination of the RAAF's medical response to the Indian Ocean tsunami in 2004, the second Bali bombings in 2005, and earthquakes in Pakistan and the Solomon Islands. In 2005, Tracy experienced one of the most challenging events of her career after an earthquake struck the Indonesian area of Nias on 2 April 2005. She had sent four of her Air Force team as part of the Australian response to provide humanitarian assistance, and it was the first time she was confronted with the deaths on duty of people under her command. Three of the four were killed when a RAN helicopter crashed on land:

> It was really difficult for me, but it was even harder for their colleagues who had perhaps taken for granted the risks involved in some of the stuff we do as military personnel. But I was able to push through and put my feelings aside … and focus on the team. Helping them process their grief and supporting the families was my priority.

Wing Commander Tracy Smart outside Saddam Hussein's palace in Baghdad, Iraq, 2003. Tracy was on deployment in Al Udeid, Qatar (Tracy Smart)

Tracy revealed that her resilience comes from being tested through these traumatic times:

> I don't think I would have got to the position I did [Surgeon General of the ADF] without having gone through these experiences, as terrible as they were at the time.

Key lessons she has drawn from these traumatic and challenging events include finding a sense of purpose in the work she was doing. In Rwanda:

> I had a mantra that I would say to everybody: 'we're here to help and we're doing a good job.' It changed my narrative of my time there, when I look back at it.

A healthy sense of humour has also been critical. When in Rwanda, she organised t-shirts with the slogan 'Doctors without a clue', noting that medical personnel were seeing many different tropical diseases they had never treated before. 'Having a sense of humour even in the darkest times was helpful.'

Tracy is a firm believer in the power of talking about stressful incidents as a method to make sense of them. In true doctor speak, she refers to this as 'letting the pus out'. In 1999, Tracy was sent to Malaysia as part of a team investigating an F-111 accident in which both crewmembers had been killed:

> I was the MO on that accident investigation. That's probably the hardest time in my career, in terms of having very difficult conditions in the middle of the jungle and having to recover the guys involved. I knew both of them and their wives, so that was probably one of the hardest things I've done, physically and emotionally. When I returned to Australia, I realised I needed some help and I went to see the psychologist on base – I just let the pus out and talked about how I was feeling. I was able to get some techniques and [I] worked on that.

After finishing her time as OC HSW and attending Higher Defence College as a student, Tracy was promoted to air commodore and posted as the Director-General of Air Force Health Services. In subsequent years, she undertook a number of roles in Joint Health Command. In December 2015, Tracy was the third woman to achieve the rank of air vice-marshal, and her final military posting was as the Surgeon General of the ADF and Commander of Joint Health. As Surgeon General, she was the senior doctor in the ADF, and provided strategic advice to Defence and the government.[15]

Tracy Smart on her promotion to air vice-marshal, 2015 (Tracy Smart)

Tracy's experience and lessons on personal and organisational resilience were fundamental to the evolving policy for which she was responsible as the Surgeon General, to ensure ADF personnel were not only 'fit to fight', but also 'fit for life'. Tracy continues to talk to numerous organisations on resilience and leadership, a topic she said holds significant interest.[16]

When reflecting on her more than 35 years in service, Tracy recalled how the ADF has changed in positive ways since she joined. She reflected on how the organisation, while still conservative, is much more inclusive of members from diverse backgrounds and sexuality:

> I know a lot of women have struggles, especially in non-traditional roles. But generally speaking, I've always found it hasn't been an issue for me being a woman. I was in the health world of Defence – it's the most female-dominated part of a male-dominated organisation.[17]

Air Vice-Marshal Tracy Smart with members of the Royal Australian Navy at the Sydney Gay and Lesbian Mardi Gras, New South Wales, 2017 (Tracy Smart)

She said being a gay woman has been even less of an issue. 'I've felt nothing but support. Sometimes over-the-top support,' she laughed. 'I haven't done a lot of activism. I think just being visible and high ranking has had an effect.'[18]

Tracy led the ADF contingent at the Sydney Mardi Gras in 2013, the first time members in uniform were allowed to march. She marched again as an air vice-marshal in 2019. 'And apparently I am still the highest ranked LGBTQ+ member ever – who knew? I have always been myself: being authentic is very important to me.' Through this visibility, Tracy was also able to influence strategic policies relating to diversity, such as allowing people who are HIV positive to deploy on exercises and operations.

Since retiring full-time from the Air Force, Tracy has not put her feet up. At the time of writing, she is Professor of Military and Aerospace Medicine at the Australian National University (ANU), and was the Public Health Lead of the COVID-19 Response Office at the ANU from August 2020 to February 2022. She is also co-chair of the Veterans' Advisory Group for the Australian War Memorial's Gallery Redevelopment. Tracy is still giving back to the ADF as a member of the Defence Honours and Awards Appeal Tribunal and the Australian Institute of Health and Welfare Veterans' Advisory Group. She also assists her partner, Lisa, with her work for the Lifeline Bookfest, a charity that provides support to Australians who are experiencing emotional distress.

Air Vice-Marshal Tracy Smart with national treasure Hugh Jackman AC at an investiture dinner for the Queen's Birthday Honours List, 2019 (Tracy Smart)

Warrant Officer Melinda Skinner CSC (née Banks)

Mover

Place of birth: Sydney, New South Wales
Date of enlistment: 2 November 1987

> I can honestly say that I grew up in the Air Force. I am the epitome of what I would hope [for] if you're going to send your child off to the join the Defence Force – some things are tough, but life is tough – it was definitely a good experience for me.[1]

Sergeant Mel Cotton unloading equipment off a C-130J Hercules during Exercise *Bersama Shield*, RMAF Butterworth, Malaysia, 2007 (Department of Defence)

Melinda ('Mel') Skinner's motivation to leave Western Australia after she finished school was a driving factor in seeking a career in the ADF. Mel grew up in what she called a 'village', considering family friends as having a significant positive influence on her and shaping her lifelong values from an early age. Wanting to 'help people', Mel initially considered a career as a nurse or ambulance operator; however, having to wait to complete Year 12 was not appealing for her. At the end of Year 10, she started exploring military career options, having seen what the son of her mother's partner was achieving in the Royal Australian Navy:

> I think I just woke up one morning and went 'Heck, I'll go to [Defence Force] Recruiting and just see what they've got.' I just didn't see that Army jobs had anything that I could bring … So I applied for Navy and Air Force.[2]

Three weeks after applying, and having just turned 17, Mel received a letter of offer from the Air Force as a supplier, a wide-ranging specialty incorporating warehousing and distribution, explosives management, aircraft refuelling, and the loading and unloading of transport aircraft. After getting a signature from her mother agreeing to the terms of recruitment, Mel was on a bus heading to RAAF Base Pearce, north of Perth, to take a flight to Adelaide for her recruit training:

> I think the defining moment of my career was getting on that [C-130] Herc and flying to [RAAF Base] Edinburgh, and that was the moment I knew that's the stuff I wanted to be involved in [working closely with transport aircraft] … I still remember who the loadmasters were, and they were the ones that I think really encouraged me that movements – what it's called now – was where I wanted to go.[3]

Mel remembered a sense of being overwhelmed when disembarking the aircraft at Edinburgh to start her recruit training:

> Here I am, five foot five, climbing in the back of a Unimog [truck], and being yelled at, 'Get going, get your bags, drag them into your rooms.' It was really, really exciting … I remember they gave us an SLR [self-loading rifle] for the first time. And I was a pretty weedy, tiny little kid back then, and the weapon itself is nearly as tall as me with the bayonet fixed.[4]

Mel recalled those foundational weeks as ones where strong bonds were formed, based on the shared challenges which she and her colleagues faced. After graduating, these friends continued on to RAAF Base Wagga Wagga in New South Wales (NSW) with Mel to start the Supplier Initial Employment Training for 10 weeks:

> There's a few grey moments there that I can't remember very well, but I do know that I did enjoy it. I enjoyed everything; I love a challenge. And I still do, but more so, because I had youth on my side … everything was, 'Wow, this is great. I'll give it a crack.' I was concerned, I think, when it got to the school side of the house … but I did really well. So I was really happy and I was interested.[5]

Aircraftwoman Recruit Mel Banks (bottom row, middle) at No 1 Recruit Training Unit, RAAF Base Edinburgh, South Australia, 1987 (Mel Skinner)

After graduating from the supplier course, Mel was posted back to Edinburgh – the 'real Air Force', as she recalled. She vividly remembered the first conversation she had with her warrant officer, one that was reflective of the way women were viewed in the RAAF at that time:

> His first words to me were, 'Are you here for a career or are you here for a husband?' Now, God forbid we say that these days. But I think it comes down to that was the perception of what was going on in the Air Force at that time. Now, I never took offence to that, because, in time, I've worked out that [the] effort he put into me was probably because of the basis of my answer. So I said, 'I'm here for a career, Sir.'[6]

With the firm direction and guidance of her senior enlisted team, Mel spent her formative years gaining experience and skills in a range of different supplier roles. She met her husband, and by 1991 had given birth to her first daughter, Jessica. She recalled how the policies to support mothers, and also attitudes in the workplace, have changed since she was a new mother in the early 1990s:

> As the manager of young women, I'm like, wow, we've come such a long way, and I'm grateful to see that and those opportunities being afforded, irrespective of being a mum. Because [motherhood] doesn't define you or restrict you; it probably enhances your ability.[7]

Mel's interest in working in the air movements environment had not diminished since her first days of joining, and she was given that opportunity when she was pregnant with her second daughter, Shannon. While on an air movements course at RAAF Base Richmond, NSW, Mel initially chose not to disclose her pregnancy because she did not consider it to be an issue. However, when she did eventually inform her male instructors that she was pregnant, the response was almost comical:

> They sat me down and they were like, 'Are you sure you want to do this?', and I said, 'It's a baby, it's not a brain tumour; I'm quite capable of doing this. There are no issues' … They were not being prejudicial; they were just being concerned … Back then, they wouldn't have understood that this was my choice and this is what I wanted to do. Because they said, 'Did you want to come or did they force you to come?' And I said, 'No, I wanted to do this.'[8]

Once she completed her courses and gave birth to Shannon, Mel commenced at the air movements section at Edinburgh. She recalled it was her Air Force 'village' who helped her manage being a mother of two children, especially since she had separated from her husband not long after Shannon was born:

> All my air movements family, they had something to do with the raising of my children … as a single mum, I was supported … It was always hard, always hard. But that support I had from my choice of friends – and they were Defence people – there are no words for it.[9]

In 1999, after 11 years at Edinburgh and the birth of her third child, Brodie, Mel was seeking a change of scenery. She was posted to RAAF Base Williamtown in Newcastle, NSW, although she spent more than two months working in Darwin at the start of the ADF's deployment to East Timor. This was the start of a period of significant operational deployments for Mel; she was involved in facilitating victims of both Bali bombings back to Australia via Darwin, and later in support of deployed task forces in the Middle East Area of Operations:

> I think the Bali bombing [in 2002] changed everything for the ADF. And especially in our HADR [humanitarian aid and disaster relief] response from the perspective as movers working with the aircrew in a whole different space; working together for that single goal, just knowing that we had to go in and get these people out. To this day … every time the anniversary rolls around, I know that it affects me a lot.[10]

Mel had separated from her second husband not long after arriving at Williamtown, and so it was her Air Force family who again helped to support her with her children while managing a busy job, often with periods of deployment. Her first of five Middle East deployments was in 2003, establishing a military footprint at Al Minhad Air Base in the United Arab Emirates. Mel ended up deploying for five months and 29 days, ensuring cargo and passengers ended up in the right locations throughout the region. She cannot remember having a day off and, despite the fatigue she experienced, she could see the positive effect which her work was having on the mission. The most difficult part of that deployment was the separation from her children, who were too young to understand why 'Mum' was not at home:

> I would write in a diary, they would draw pictures in a diary, and I would post it to them … this went on throughout my whole deployable career … Obviously, mine's a bit sanitised, whereas they'd just tell me what they're doing … to this day, there's a little thing that I do where the kids will tie a little ribbon around my wrist, and I just wear it for the whole deployment, and they get to take it off when I come home.[11]

Warrant Officer Mel Skinner with her 'biggest cheer squad': her children. Left to right: Brodie, Shannon and Jessica (Mel Skinner)

Not long after returning to Australia, Mel deployed in 2004 in support of the Regional Assistance Mission to the Solomon Islands. The focus was different to the Middle East – providing logistics and security support to the Australian Federal Police mission in the country. She recalled how this deployment clarified in her mind the importance of personal and professional conduct when representing the RAAF:

> It gave me that good insight into understanding culture and understanding [that] the uniform that I wear – [it] doesn't matter where I am in the world – has an effect … So the conduct of us is paramount, and I certainly push that to my team here [in Darwin] and anyone that comes through that works for me.[12]

Corporal Mel Skinner with her deployed Commanding Officer, Squadron Leader Kirrily Dearing, in the Solomon Islands during Operation *Anode*, Anzac Day 2004 (Mel Skinner)

Flight Sergeant Mel Skinner and her air movements team in Tarin Kot, Afghanistan, during Operation *Slipper*, 2011 (Mel Skinner)

By the early 2010s, Mel had worked in every Air Force and joint ADF field in the movements specialisation, including a posting to Malaysia, where she met her husband Craig, the deputy principal of an international school in Penang. She made the difficult decision to leave Craig and her children in Penang while she was posted back to Australia, to RAAF Base Tindal in the Northern Territory. In the space of a few years, Mel deployed three more times to the Middle East, the last being her third deployment into Afghanistan:

> There were certain things that happened that changed my view on how I was seeing things, whether that was because I was emotionally tired as well as physically tired, not having my family around, having a bit of a disaster with relationships prior – I wanted to make that work. I was missing my kids; they were getting older. I just really felt that it was time that I needed to step away, before I really hated something that I loved, and I didn't want that bitterness; I just didn't want to do that.[13]

Mel's last working day was 25 April 2014. She travelled back to Malaysia and reunited with her family, then subsequently won the position of head of boarding at the Penang International School and started Reserve work at RMAF (Royal Malaysian Air Force) Butterworth. She discovered that the skills and experience she had gained during 25 years in the Air Force were transferrable to other professions. It was also a period that allowed her to take stock of the cumulative effect of multiple deployments on her resilience and attitude towards her service. A chance meeting with a senior Air Force officer in Butterworth led to Mel considering rejoining the Air Force. Her daughters were back in Australia, and she and Craig made the decision to leave Penang. Twelve months after her emotional decision to resign, Mel was back serving full time, yet again deploying as a senior aviator and developing the leadership skills of her team.

Flight Sergeant Mel Skinner conducting a reading during the dawn service in St Peter's Chapel at RAAF Base Tindal, Northern Territory, Anzac Day 2014 (Department of Defence)

At the time of writing, as a warrant officer, Mel is the senior enlisted aviator at RAAF Base Darwin. She holds a dual position – the warrant officer of the air movements section and the Squadron Warrant Officer for No 13 Squadron, a unit responsible for providing base support to activities on the base as well as supporting units transiting through it. She takes immense pride in her ability to harness the skills of her team to provide the capability outcomes required for the organisation. Passionate about developing junior team members' leadership skills, she focuses on the foundational values of the ADF as a guardrail and allows her team to learn and grow from their failures:

> My job now is to share [my knowledge], mentor and say to them, 'Look, you're not going to get it right [all the time]; you'll get it as close as you can. But if you learn from that and you share your mistakes – [for] people that don't share the mistakes, it's more detrimental. We've got to accept that we do make mistakes, no one's perfect … if you don't accept it, you haven't learned.'[14]

Mel's aim is to ensure the junior aviators she is charged with leading and developing become better versions of herself:

> If we do not encourage our teams and our aviators to think bigger, we're never going to grow … I want these kids to be smarter than me, I want them to outdo me, because that's how it should be … I'd like to think that there's always going to be a replacement for [ourselves].[15]

Warrant Officer Mel Skinner and her air movements team, No 13 Squadron, at RAAF Base Darwin, Northern Territory, Anzac Day 2021 (Department of Defence)

Mel has reflected on the positive changes for women in the RAAF since she joined. This has included legislation ensuring women can serve in all roles, and the policy changes assisting mothers (and, by extension, fathers) to concurrently work and be parents. However, Mel believes there is still work to be done to ensure future generations want to put on the uniform and serve their nation. Her aim is to continue to instil the values on which she has drawn in more than 35 years of service, into future generations:

> I love the uniform that I wear. I am immersed in the people that serve, so I serve my troops, I am here for them, and the day that stops is the day that I need to get out.[16]

Mel was recognised for her leadership in the movements capability in the 2024 Australia Day Honours list, by being awarded a Conspicuous Service Cross. In typical style, her response was a humble one: 'I do everything for my troops, and I want to be that mentor for them. I'm really humbled, honoured, and speechless.'

Warrant Officer Michelle Hardy

Military Working Dog Handler

Place of birth: Port Pirie, South Australia
Date of enlistment: 1 February 1989

When I put the uniform on every day, I remind myself that I will continue to instil the values and ethics that helped me get to where I am today.[1]

Aircraftwoman Michelle Hardy after graduating from No 1 Recruit Training Unit, 1989 (Michelle Hardy)

Half a centimetre was what initially prevented Michelle Hardy from joining the RAAF as a military working dog handler (MWDH). She had to seek a waiver for her height to join her preferred mustering in 1989, as there was a minimum height and weight entry requirement to be met at the time. Jumping that hurdle was only the start of the physical and mental challenges Michelle has met head on in a career spanning more than 30 years.

Michelle was born and raised in Port Pirie, a small lead-smelting town north of Adelaide, where her father worked on the railway line throughout South Australia (SA) and north towards Darwin. His work meant Michelle, her mother and brother would spend months at a time following the railway work, during which time she was home schooled and spent periods in remote SA. Time back in Port Pirie meant catching up with her many aunts, uncles and cousins.

Seven-year-old Michelle in Leigh Creek, South Australia (Michelle Hardy)

Michelle settled into a stable school life only when she reached high school, after her parents had separated. She spent the following years focusing on numerous sports, and enjoying less-gender-stereotypical subjects such as woodwork and metalwork, in which she excelled:

> I was really more of a practical person in that sense … I didn't want to be pigeonholed … I got to about 14, 15, and thought, 'I need to get out of this town. There's nothing here for me.' I used to say to my Mum, 'I'm not going to be a hairdresser or the manager of the fruit and veg section at Coles [supermarket].'[2]

After finishing high school, Michelle initially scoped the police force as a career option; as an animal lover, she wanted to join as a dog handler. To her disappointment, she was told she would have to wait until she was 19 to join, then spend a further two years in general duties before she could apply for the dog squad. So Michelle started working casual jobs with the aim of saving enough money to leave Port Pirie. It was when she was working at a local hotel that she met a Defence Force Recruiting team. Michelle discovered the Air Force had MWDHs, and she set her mind to joining. She travelled to Adelaide with a school friend to attend the recruitment office:

> We got there, and [my friend] walked through the 'Navy door' and I walked through the 'Air Force door'. She was gone before me, because she joined as a technician on the choppers. She was good to go, because she was very tall … I had applied and they said, 'You're half a centimetre too short', because there was a height restriction.

Michelle had to exercise patience and wait several months for a waiver to be granted; she was also under the minimum weight and so spent time working on putting on the additional two kilograms she needed to meet the MWDH minimum standard weight of 70 kilograms. After she was finally accepted, Michelle was sent to the local working dog section at RAAF Base Edinburgh to gain a better understanding of the role:

> I had to spend a day at the dog section with a whole bunch of men … They walked me through the kennels and pushed me right up close to the kennel, the gates where the dogs were frothing at the mouth, barking. They said, 'Are you scared?' I was like, 'Hell, yes.' And they said, 'So that's a good answer, because people that say they aren't, are wrong.'[3]

Michelle was wondering how, at five foot six inches, she was going to handle a dog that weighed more than half her own body weight.

She started her initial Air Force training at No 1 Recruit Training Unit (1RTU) at Edinburgh in early 1989. Aged 19, Michelle was one of the older recruits, with some in her class as young as 16. Michelle found herself taking on a mother role to 'sort them all out'. After graduating with the 'Personal Qualities' award, Michelle spent Christmas at home before her MWDH Initial Employment Training was due to start. Her memory of that time was of feeling very different to her school friends and family, after having experienced the formative weeks of her career.

Michelle was sent to RAAF Amberley, Queensland (Qld), to commence what she thought was going to be her MWDH initial training; yet on arrival, she was met with 'yelling and screaming' airfield defence guards (ADGs). It turned out that her class had to complete a 10-week basic ADG course first. 'I thought, hmm, I don't remember this being in the glossy brochure.'[4]

The course of 30 included both MWDHs and ADGs, and Michelle and a friend from 1RTU, Lynn, were the only women on course at a time when females could not even join as ADGs. Michelle recalled it was clear the instructors struggled with how to integrate them into the course. Even their accommodation proved problematic:

> You went in the shower blocks and there were no walls … [and] no doors. 'How are we going to do this?' So [Lynn] stood guard while I had a shower and vice versa … After a few days, I mentioned it to our corporal and he was horrified.[5]

Field-training policy was different for men and women: a reflection of the time, yet this did not make it any less frustrating for Michelle. Michelle and Lynn were directed to shower every two days, yet the males did not shower at all:

> We'd go out field, and they said we'd be there [for] three days and we were there for a week and they'd turn around and say, 'There's a policy that you have to have a shower every two days as a female.' But you're sitting in a pit with someone who's not going to shower the whole time. So we'd come back smelling like roses and we'd say, 'Phew, you guys stink.'

After passing the physically and mentally demanding ADG course, Michelle finally started her dog handler course at the Security and Fire School (SFS) at Amberley. She was initially teamed with a longhaired German Shepherd called Scotch, who had been given to the school because he was unable to be controlled and, ironically, because he supposedly did not like women! After a few weeks of ensuring they would be a good team, and building trust between woman and dog, Michelle and Scotch began training for all security and response eventualities:

> You had to learn all the animal husbandry; you had to learn all the different types of attack work, and then basics, which is the heeling, learning how to go over all the obstacles. Back in those days, we had fire hoops where the dog used to have to try and jump through the fire hoop.[6]

On graduation, Michelle and Scotch were posted to No 1 Stores Depot in Tottenham in Melbourne. Michelle remembered the reception she received was less than welcoming. It was clear that a woman in the section was neither expected nor wanted and, in effect, she was subjected to exclusionary behaviour:

> I think they all had it in their heads that they didn't really want me there. And I just thought that, once people got to know me, they'd probably change their attitude, and they did.[7]

Michelle said this cycle of having to prove her ability and capacity would repeat itself, to some extent, for each posting.

Michelle had met her husband at recruit training; he graduated as an MWDH after Michelle. Partway through her Melbourne posting, Michelle fell pregnant. Despite there being no policy to guide the decision, Michelle was directed to send Scotch back to SFS to be reteamed, due to the assumption by more senior members that a pregnant woman could not retain a dog. After giving birth to her first son, Joel, Michelle went back to work on posting at Edinburgh. This meant she had to undertake another reteaming trip to Amberley, so her mother came to look after Joel for two weeks. 'That's when I met my police dog, Buddy, who was an amazing dog. We pretty much hit it off straight away; we were great mates.'[8]

Leading Aircraftwoman Michelle Hardy and Buddy at RAAF Amberley, Queensland, 1996 (Michelle Hardy)

Michelle and Buddy spent time on flight line and gate duties, and became involved in display work, attending Adelaide shows and other public events. It was during this posting that Michelle started branching into other roles within the security capability, the first being in counterintelligence work, where she would conduct investigations and surveillance. In the early 1990s, when it was still illegal to be gay in the Australian Defence Force, RAAF police would investigate those suspected of being gay, to potentially discharge them from service.

This was the first of a number of capability restructures Michelle experienced during her career; in this instance, the amalgamation of the RAAF police and MWDH role to Security Police. Her counterintelligence role meant Buddy spent the majority of his time in kennels as a 'pool dog'. Michelle would take him for a run at lunchtimes and sit in the training yard with him while having her lunch. But as Buddy started to get older and developed some health issues, Michelle was advised he would have to be euthanised:

> Back then, you weren't allowed to take your dog home to retire, as they were seen as a threat to the community … Buddy was gentle and kind, a pretty quiet dog who knew when he was working [and] when he was allowed to relax and have play time … Taking Buddy to the vet to be euthanised was one of the hardest things I've had to do in my life. I was taking my mate, my best friend and my protector to be put down – [this was] a decision that I still struggle with today.[9]

Retiring Military Working Dogs now undergo a three-month transition course and an assessment by the Royal Society for the Prevention of Cruelty to Animals. Many are successfully rehomed and live out the rest of their days in a domestic environment, often with their former handlers.

After having to make this heartbreaking decision with Buddy, Michelle continued in the intelligence field, this time at the Electronic Warfare section at the Aircraft Research and Development Unit. When it was discovered she was an MWDH out of her mustering, she was subsequently moved back to her core job, 'kicking and screaming'. During a reteam with yet another dog (coincidentally also called Buddy), Michelle was informed she would be posted to RAAF Base Wagga Wagga, New South Wales – a base that did not even have a Military Working Dog section. By this stage, Michelle was separated and had two young boys, so she decided to move, without a dog, and start up the counterintelligence section at the base. It was here she met her second husband, who ran a family company in the town.

After being given a posting to Darwin, her husband made it clear he did not want to move. Michelle resigned herself to staying in Wagga, remaining in the Reserves and taking on civilian jobs, while also having her third child, a daughter, Bridie. While on maternity leave, Michelle realised her current life was not making her happy. She rang an old boss to ask how she would go about rejoining the RAAF as a permanent member. Before long, she was moving yet again, back to Amberley with her children, taking on an instructor role at SFS. While she was posted there, Michelle was approached about deploying with a largely Army unit to Tarin Kot, Afghanistan. She made the difficult decision to send Bridie to her father in Wagga, while her sons, who were in their late teens, remained in her house in Brisbane. With a three-month pre-deployment period in Darwin, and ultimately an eight-month-and-three-week deployment, Michelle was gone for close to a year. She was unexpectedly promoted to flight sergeant during her pre-deployment training:

> I was thinking, 'What have I got myself into?' They treated me like the token RAAFie, [that] is what they would call me. The token RAAFies just get on these deployments because they have to share as a joint force. They put me in the role of the ops warrant

> officer … I pretty much controlled any type of movements, operations on the ground, if anyone needed anything. I also conducted the force protection in-briefs to Tarin Kot and scheduled the contracted Mi-26 helicopter to resupply the Forward Operating Bases.[10]

Flight Sergeant Michelle Hardy at Tarin Kot, Afghanistan, with the crew of a Russian Mi-26 helicopter contracted for resupply tasks, 2013 (Michelle Hardy)

Michelle came home to find out the grocery money she had been giving to her boys (at that stage aged 18 and 21) had gone towards tattoo 'sleeves'! 'They lived on two-minute noodles.' She concedes that at least it was good artwork.

After five years at Amberley, Michelle was told it was time to move and she accepted a role in Canungra, Qld, at the Defence Intelligence Training Centre with the 'Conduct after Capture' program. This included having to spend five weeks on a resistance to interrogation course, on which she would later be an instructor:

> You go through all the different types of interrogation methods so that you understand what is happening to you if you're going to do that to other people. That was very interesting; I learned a lot about myself.[11]

Michelle's ex-husband relocated from Wagga Wagga to the Gold Coast for business, so she was able to spend more time with Bridie, with her sons remaining out near Amberley.

Her performance and capacity were recognised in 2020 when she was promoted to warrant officer: the pinnacle of the enlisted aviator community. This happened not long after another restructure of the RAAF security capability, and Michelle was posted as the

Squadron Warrant Officer of No 2 Security Forces Squadron: the first woman to achieve such a posting. With yet another review into the capability, Michelle could sense the impact that uncertainty was having on the unit:

> I could see there were a lot of people struggling, and it was because of that constant change, the unknown, and what was coming … I would say to them, 'My door is always open. You can call me, if you need a chat.'[12]

Warrant Officer Michelle Hardy celebrating the Royal Australian Air Force's centenary with No 2 Security Forces Squadron team members, 2021 (Michelle Hardy)

Michelle believes the Air Force can improve how it retains members, by using the option of a transition to a different role to increase their longevity within the organisation:

> There's been so much talk of how do we sustain and maintain [personnel] … you can only go at that level, 100 miles an hour [for so long] … without breaking yourself at some stage. We need to find some sort of rotational role for them because we won't be able to keep them … I've been lucky in my career … if I was continually going to be a dog handler for the whole of my career, I would probably be in a body brace. It's unsustainable.[13]

After a career spanning more than three decades, and with experience in many different facets of the security capability, Michelle's next focus is on transitioning out of full-time service. Having purchased her 'forever home' west of Amberley, she is thinking of completing a celebrant's course and using the property and its gardens for weddings: 'something that's a joyous occasion for somebody'.[14]

Warrant Officers Michelle Hardy (right) and Fee Grasby with a member of the Royal Society for the Prevention of Cruelty to Animals and working dog puppies, RAAF Amberley, Queensland, 2011 (Michelle Hardy)

When asked about what could be done to continue to improve the culture and capacity of the Air Force, Michelle believes it comes down to how people treat each other: developing a culture that recognises an individual's contribution and being open to other options within the service.

> From a female's point of view, in Defence, we need to be kinder to each other as females … If we're ever going to evolve into having females in Defence that are happy in their jobs and don't feel like they always have to prove themselves, I think we need to do that as a united front … I'm all for finding the right person for the job – [but] it might take a few goes until you find it.[15]

THE 1990s

INTRODUCTION

Against the backdrop of global optimism due to the collapse of the Soviet Union in 1991, Australians experienced both hardships and lifestyle improvements during the 1990s.[1]

The early years of the decade were characterised by Australia's 1991 economic recession and high interest rates, but these gave way to increasing prosperity as the decade progressed. Terms such as 'corporate restructure', 'downsizing' and 'globalisation' entered the Australian vernacular, due to the privatisation and outsourcing of government entities and industries including Telstra, Qantas, public transport, and electricity and gas services. Many local manufacturing industries shut down due to overseas competition during the 1990s, but it was not all bad news: new industries and opportunities arose in the tourism, retail, education and health sectors.[2]

Ongoing international trade and immigration contributed to the ongoing multiculturalism of Australian society and efforts were increased to achieve reconciliation with First Nations Australians. Key achievements for the indigenous rights movement during this decade included Eddie Mabo's landmark land-rights case win in 1992, and the Australian Human Rights Commission's acknowledgement in 1997 of the forced removal of indigenous children from their communities during previous decades (the Stolen Generations).[3]

The globalisation of Australian society was further enhanced in the 1990s by new media which allowed 24-hour access to other cultures and societies. These included the dominance of sitcoms – often from the United States, with *Seinfeld* and *Friends* among the most popular – and pay TV airing dozens of channels from around the globe. But the most enduring new technology proved to be the internet, which became increasingly accessible to homes and businesses as the decade progressed.

The Royal Australian Air Force (RAAF) experienced a time of review and cost rationalisation during the 1990s, driven by the 1991 *Force Structure Review* which recommended a significant reduction to the Australian Defence Force (ADF) workforce. Within three years, the numbers of ADF military personnel had been reduced by 15 per cent and Defence public servants by 16 per cent. Yet due to increasing global unrest during this decade, the ADF was kept busy, deploying on many peacekeeping and humanitarian aid and disaster relief missions. RAAF personnel were involved in peacekeeping missions in nations as varied as Bosnia, Cambodia, East Timor (now known as Timor Leste), Rwanda and Somalia, and assisted in the evacuation of United Nations personnel, Australians and foreign nationals from nations experiencing conflict, including Cambodia, Iraq and Timor Leste.[4]

Supply clerk Leading Aircraftwoman Julie Jardine with medical supplies at the Kigali Central Hospital, Rwanda. She was deployed with the Australian Medical Support Force which provided medical care to United Nations troops and Rwandan civilians, early 1990s (RAAF Museum)

Flight Lieutenant Sandy Riley treating East Timorese children at a clinic in Suai, Timor Leste, 1999. Sandy was deployed as the Air Medical Evacuation Coordinator as part of the United Nations International Force East Timor (Department of Defence)

The 1990s represented increasing equality for RAAF servicewomen. Before the end of the decade, in December 1999, Air Commodore Julie Hammer became the ADF's first female one-star officer, while Flight Lieutenant Joanne Mein became the first female pilot to fly in the tactically challenging RAAF Roulettes aerobatic team.[5]

Royal Australian Air Force Officer Cadet Cheryl Perry on parade at the Australian Defence Force Academy, Canberra, Australian Capital Territory, 1990 (Department of Defence)

The graduation of the Royal Australian Air Force's first female Warrant Officer Disciplinary, 1992 (RAAF Museum)

Group Captain Hannah Jude-Smith AM

Intelligence Officer

Place of birth: Canberra, Australian Capital Territory
Date of enlistment: January 1999

The people who have inspired me … are the ones that you've got that human connection with … who show you that you don't actually have to be task focused all the time to be a good leader … people who have shown me you can be a 'normal' human being and still do great things.[1]

Flight Lieutenant Hannah Jude-Smith during her deployment to the Middle East Area of Operations, 2007 (Hannah Jude-Smith)

One could assume Hannah Jude-Smith was predestined to join the ADF. Her grandfathers and her father all served in the Royal Australian Navy (RAN), and her stepfather was a career Army officer. Hannah said 'keeping it all in the family', with her mother marrying a RAN officer, made sense at the time. However, not long after she was born, her parents separated. Hannah spent a significant period of her early years with her mother's parents, while her father continued to serve at sea. Hannah's mother and father each remarried, with her mother marrying a 'young Army chap' called Gerry. Hannah spent the remainder of her school years living with her mother and Gerry, moving regularly due to his postings:

> I was living in an Army officer household, then I would go on weekends and school holidays to a naval officer household, and I had grandparents who were very conscious and aware of the Navy. Gerry's postings drove my upbringing, which led to [us living in] 14 houses in 17 years.[2]

Hannah Jude-Smith and her stepfather, Gerry, while he was posted as an observer to the United Nations Truce Supervision Organisation in Lebanon and Syria (Hannah Jude-Smith)

Hannah attended 10 different schools and spent time overseas. She spent time in Washington, DC, and a year in both Lebanon and Syria, while Gerry was an observer to the United Nations Truce Supervision Organisation:

> Reflecting on that, it was pretty formative because I've always had an interest in the Middle East. It wasn't terribly foreign to me by the time [the ADF] started doing all the deployments there.[3]

Despite the strong Navy and Army influences during her formative years, Hannah's decision to join as a RAAF intelligence officer was in part influenced by a number of books she loved. The first was the children's book *Harriet the Spy*, which she read in Grade 6. The others were all of the James Bond novels, written by Ian Fleming, which she read in Year 9. When she told Gerry she wanted to 'do what James Bond does', he explained that to follow in Bond's footsteps, she would have to serve as a Navy intelligence officer first, then transfer out of uniform to work in an intelligence agency. Given the RAN did not have a professional qualification for intelligence at the time, Hannah had to consider the other ADF services. Gerry gently persuaded her to consider attending the Australian Defence Force Academy (ADFA) and, at the age of 14, Hannah decided to aim for a pathway to intelligence through ADFA.

In 1999, she started her career as an officer cadet, with useful advice from Gerry on what to expect:

> Gerry was obviously hugely influential in my whole life; we used to wash up dishes together, and he used to tell me his RMC [Royal Military College] stories, and he used to tell me what I needed to be aware of … he said, 'I'll give you the worst case. If it's better than this, you'll be fine.' So he would tell me his stories, and he would very much say things like, 'It's all a game, Hannah. You've just got to play the game.' And I'd already had a quite structured life. We lived a structured life, so routine was something that I was very comfortable with.[4]

But Hannah's experiences at ADFA did not reflect her expectations, largely because of significant changes to the ADFA organisation and the method by which trainees were treated. She recalled that while expecting to be 'yelled and screamed at' from day one by senior cadets, the reality was very different. She felt she was not given the opportunity to 'prove myself to the second and third years, because they all thought, and rightly so, compared to their stories, that you had it easy.'[5] Despite the initial letdown, Hannah's experience at ADFA was positive. After spending a fourth year as an Honours student, Hannah graduated and was posted to No 3 Control and Reporting Unit (3CRU) – a surveillance unit responsible for conducting surveillance of airspace and air-battle management for flying squadrons – at RAAF Base Williamtown, near Newcastle, New South Wales.

During her early years as a junior officer, the RAAF intelligence structure was immature, and it was 'just the luck of the draw what unit … and what supervisor you got'.[6] Hannah was lucky enough to finalise her initial intelligence training not long after graduating from

ADFA, and she gained significant exposure to intelligence operations. Hannah also met her husband, Jeremy, while she was at 3CRU:

> I had five reasons not to date him, one of which was the fact that I had a divisional officer in the first year [of ADFA] who was like, 'Don't go out there and date the first people that you meet in the unit.' But I was very hard-nosed. I didn't date [Jeremy] for at least four months … For six months, actually. And he was 19, and I was 22, so he was way too young for me, and that was gusting 20 years ago now.[7]

Officer Cadet Hannah Jude-Smith, graduating with Honours from the Australian Defence Force Academy, Canberra, Australian Capital Territory, 2002 (Hannah Jude-Smith)

In 2004, while at 3CRU, Hannah deployed on the first of her six overseas operational deployments. She deployed to the Combined Air Operations Center (CAOC), a United States (US)-led organisation in Al Udeid in Qatar, where she worked in an Australian cell which provided intelligence products to RAAF aircrews. 'I really wanted to go. I really wanted to do my job for real. I wanted to have an adventure.'[8] Jeremy, whom she was dating at that stage, had deployed to Baghdad in Iraq the month before her, which spurred her on even more.

After her return to Australia, Hannah spent the next few years working in support of the majority of Air Force flying elements, thereby gaining extensive tactical-intelligence experience. This included yet another deployment to the CAOC in 2006, and a deployment to Darwin, looking for fugitives in East Timor. She was 'up for adventure and I was literally away all the time. And I loved it.'[9] But after five years of working in tactical roles, Hannah was looking for a new challenge. She was seriously considering resigning from the RAAF when she was offered a posting to the Australian Signals Directorate (ASD):

> I was just jettisoned straight from very tactical intelligence work right into strategic intelligence. And given my interest from the outset had always been intelligence,

> and I'd sort of forced myself to like planes, this was perfect timing, because it really reinvigorated me. And I had a huge learning curve.[10]

During her time at ASD, Hannah deployed to Afghanistan in support of the Mentoring and Reconstruction Task Force (MRTF) in Uruzgan Province. She had married Jeremy three weeks prior to deploying. Hannah said this deployment rivalled the best experience she had had in the service to date:

> [The MRTF] would make a decision on whether they would do a patrol based on the intelligence you were collating with other agencies who were there. It was the first time I'd been in a job where I felt that my intelligence directly meant something.[11]

Squadron Leader Hannah Jude-Smith on deployment in Uruzgan Province, Afghanistan (Hannah Jude-Smith)

After returning to Australia, Hannah's parents noticed a change in her demeanour:

> They definitely felt that I was tense, and on edge … because of that pressure [of deployment], and that desire not to make a mistake, I came back and my parents commented to me that they felt that I was changed.[12]

On reflection, and after assessing her strengths and weaknesses during a professional development course, Hannah realised the anxiety she was experiencing post-deployment was linked to a fear of failure and a sense of imposter syndrome. She called her mother:

> 'Mum, I've just had this massive epiphany that I'm really anxious about failing', and my Mum goes, 'Oh darling, you've never failed anything in your life. There's no need to worry about that.' I said, 'That's the problem.'[13]

After seeking assurance from her loved ones and friends that it is okay to fail, Hannah used that understanding to focus on how to manage her fear of failure. She recalled that having children was one way of 'curing' her of that anxiety. A few years later, while she was studying on the Australian Command and Staff Course (ACSC), Hannah said she placed zero pressure and expectations on herself, as she had 'taken herself out of the rat race' (her sole focus on her career) to raise her children. She was just happy to 'be here with some grownups, having some grownup conversation, and going to the toilet by myself [unescorted by her young children]'.[14]

Hannah talked about her partnership and strong communication with Jeremy as being critical to her career success. Some of their postings were focused on his career, others on hers – 'yin and yang', as she puts it. Her stipulation when she agreed to marry Jeremy was that they would not spend time posted to different locations, which is a reality faced by many married serving couples. She spent time on leave without pay while he was completing a training course in the US after re-categorising his specialisation from air defence to air combat officer. She took 'whatever job was going' when he was posted to RAAF Amberley near Brisbane. Over the years, they have both made their marriage work by being flexible and open in whichever roles each of them can occupy.

Hannah and Jeremy even deployed at the same time, when their son Sebastian was only 17 months old and Hannah was working three days a week. Jeremy's parents agreed to look after Sebastian for the four months the couple would be away. After less than a week of being told they could be deploying, Hannah left on her sixth Middle East deployment, in support of the 'Defeat Daesh' operation (Operation *Okra*) based out of Al Dhafra Air Base in the United Arab Emirates. It was not an easy decision for either her or Jeremy to make. She recalled being torn between leaving her young son for so long, and doing her job:

> I was very motivated because it was doing my job as a flight commander and taking an intel team over, and every night I would come home and I would put Sebastian to bed and I would sob, and I would say to Jeremy, 'I can't go. I can't go', and he'd go, 'Okay', and I'd get up in the morning resolved to tell them I can't go and then I would be like, 'Well, no, this is my job. I'm going to go', and I did that until I got on the plane. And I got on the plane, and then the decision just happened, but that didn't make it easy.[15]

After having their second child, Annabel, Hannah was posted as a student to ACSC in 2017. Jeremy took on the role of primary caregiver during that year, working part-time:

> A few weeks into that year, he said to me, 'This is really, really hard, and it's not very fun,' and I said, 'You're right. It is really hard, and it isn't really fun, but it's really great that you're doing it.'[16]

She said this shared responsibility and clear communication between the two influenced their leadership: empathising with personnel who have to juggle work, parental and personal responsibilities.

Wing Commander Hannah Jude-Smith and her children on her son Sebastian's first day of school (Hannah Jude-Smith)

Hannah was promoted to wing commander after the course and subsequently posted as Commanding Officer of No 87 Squadron at RAAF Base Edinburgh near Adelaide. Here she was in charge of a number of intelligence flights throughout Australia in support of flying Force Element Groups. She says it was not an automatic decision to say yes to this role, not just because of the weight of responsibility, but also because she had firm ideas of what needed to be changed within the unit. Ultimately, her focus was on her team and how she could support them to carry out their role:

> I had an incredible sense of relief when I finished command, because I was very conscious of the responsibility I held for those people, and that I was responsible for the trajectory of their careers … I felt very obligated to enable them.[17]

In 2021, while serving as the Assistant Air and Space Attaché in the Australian Embassy in Washington, DC, Hannah was promoted to group captain. Jeremy's posting was the first of the two US postings to be locked in, and Hannah commented on the advantage of 'working for one boss' (the RAAF), which also enabled her to be assigned an overseas posting. The couple had to establish themselves during the height of the COVID-19 pandemic, home schooling the children while developing professional and personal relationships virtually.

Hannah also suffered the devastating loss of her cherished mentor and role model, Gerry, to a form of blood cancer, 14 months after his diagnosis. Hannah was about to leave for Australia to assist Gerry and her mother with a treatment program when she was informed he had passed away. After two weeks of quarantine in a Sydney hotel, Hannah was able to help her mother with Gerry's funeral arrangements, and spend time supporting the family. Despite seriously considering cutting her time in the US short, Hannah and Jeremy persevered, and Hannah enjoyed the different challenges of working in an environment where relationship building and 'messaging' government initiatives were critical.

Wing Commander Hannah Jude-Smith with her son Sebastian and daughter Annabel, while Hannah was Commanding Officer No 87 Squadron (Hannah Jude-Smith)

Reflecting on her remarkable career so far, Hannah said that two reasons have contributed to her remaining in the Air Force. The first is her true partnership with Jeremy, in which they continually communicate and 'debrief' on events and challenges they face as a family. The other is the total workforce model they have both been able to use, moving in and out of full-time and part-time service over the years:

> The change to the flexible total workforce model is the reason I'm still in service. The ability for me to go to part-time when I had my children on return from maternity leave, then to go back up to full-time service.[18]

Hannah and Jeremy returned to Australia at the end of 2023 to take on new roles and, true to the deal they had made early in their marriage, they negotiated postings in Canberra to ensure they remain together in one location. Hannah's new challenging opportunity is as the Chief of Staff to the Chief of Defence Force. To her surprise, she was also recognised in the 2024 Australia Day Honours and Awards list, being awarded a Member of the Order of Australia for her significant contribution during her career to date. As always, Hannah considers her recognition as a family one.

Wing Commander Hannah Jude-Smith with her husband, Jeremy, in Washington, DC, United States (Hannah Jude-Smith)

The evolution of women's uniforms

Women's uniforms have evolved significantly during the eight decades in which women have served in the RAAF and its preceding women's services.

The changes have been driven by factors such as cost, fabric availability (consider wartime restrictions), safety, comfort, practicality and even societal expectations: no woman wants to join an organisation with an old-fashioned or 'ugly' uniform.

The following is a brief glimpse into one of the most obvious indicators an Australian woman was serving in the Air Force: the uniform she put on each morning.

Royal Australian Air Force Nursing Service 1940–77

While on duty in RAAF hospitals and medical sections, Royal Australian Air Force Nursing Service (RAAFNS) nursing sisters wore a working dress consisting of a white cotton ward dress and white organdie veil. A short navy-blue cape was worn when they went outside. In 1974, the veil was replaced with a white organdie cap and the cape was replaced with a longer blue-grey cape with a red lining.[1]

The white ward dress made nursing sisters highly visible while on deployment in the South Pacific during the Second World War so, in early 1942, the dresses were dyed with strong tea.[2]

Senior Sister Wheatley caring for an injured civilian, New Guinea, December 1942. She wears a tea-dyed ward dress and veil (Department of Defence)

Due to the prevalence of malaria throughout the South Pacific, tropical working dress was introduced for nursing sisters to wear between sunset and sunrise, and consisted of a long-sleeve khaki shirt, khaki trousers and khaki fur-felt hat.[3]

Royal Australian Air Force Nursing Service nursing sisters wearing tropical working dress, New Guinea, circa 1945 (Department of Defence)

Royal Australian Air Force Nursing Service nursing sisters, wearing tropical working dress, disembarking from a Royal Australian Air Force aircraft (RAAF Museum)

The tropical working dress was adapted for use as medical evacuation dress, with the khaki fur-felt hat replaced with a navy-blue cap, and a blue fur-lined flying jacket added for warmth.[4]

RAAFNS nursing sisters wore a 'walking-out' uniform when they were in public. The winter walking-out uniform consisted of a navy-blue tunic, straight navy-blue skirt, white blouse, black tie and navy-blue felt hat. A woollen navy-blue greatcoat or belted raincoat was worn in wet weather. The summer walking-out uniform was similar in style, with a khaki jacket, khaki skirt and khaki felt fat. A white blouse was later replaced with a khaki blouse.[5]

Royal Australian Air Force Nursing Service nursing sisters, late 1960s, wearing (left to right): ward dress and cape, summer walking-out dress, medical evacuation dress and winter walking-out dress (Department of Defence)

The RAAFNS walking-out uniform later changed to a blue dress with jacket.

Royal Australian Air Force Nursing Service walking-out uniform with 'air-hostess' cap, 1960s (Department of Defence)

Royal Australian Air Force Nursing Service walking-out uniform, 1970s (Department of Defence)

Women's Auxiliary Australian Air Force 1941–47

Women's Auxiliary Australian Air Force (WAAAF) uniforms were professionally tailored and described in recruitment advertisements as 'uniformly smart'. Because clothing and fabric were in short supply during and following the Second World War, many women wore parts of their uniforms while off duty.[6]

WAAAF uniforms were the same colour as the RAAF (men's) uniforms which had been introduced in 1922. The shade of navy-blue had been chosen by the RAAF's senior officer at that time, Wing Commander (later Air Marshal Sir) Richard Williams, while he was visiting the Commonwealth Woollen Mills in Geelong, Victoria. To make navy-blue serge fabric, it was dipped into indigo dye five times. Wing Commander Williams preferred the colour after the serge had been dipped four times, choosing that shade of navy-blue for the RAAF uniform.[7]

Three Women's Auxiliary Australian Air Force members wearing winter service dress (RAAF Museum)

The WAAAF winter service dress uniform consisted of a navy-blue serge tunic, skirt and cap. The tunic had pressed metal buttons depicting an eagle and a crown, and buttoned up in the male style (left over right) to ensure that ribbons – which are worn on the left – would not be obscured. The skirt was a straight style and ended at or just below the knee. Tan gloves were also issued.[8]

Ena Maude Wilson, who served as a motor transport driver, wearing winter service dress, RAAF Base Richmond, New South Wales, 1940s (Department of Defence)

The WAAAF summer service dress uniform consisted of a khaki gabardine tunic with gold buttons, khaki skirt, khaki shirt and black tie.[9]

Squadron Officer Mabel Miller wearing summer service dress (Department of Defence)

Working dress was worn when performing aircraft maintenance and other physical jobs. It consisted of navy-blue overalls, worn over a light blue shirt and black tie.[10]

Left to right: Sergeants Glennie Morton and Hilary Benn wearing working dress while testing a high-speed aircraft camera in the cockpit of an Avro Anson (Australian War Memorial, 139365)

Women's Royal Australian Air Force 1950–77

Uniforms for the newly established Women's Royal Australian Air Force (WRAAF) were designed by the Commonwealth Government Clothing Factory in consultation with Miss Rita Findlay, a director of Georges department store in Melbourne. These uniforms were a significant advance on the wartime WAAAF issue.[11]

The winter service dress uniform consisted of a navy-blue fitted tunic and navy-blue skirt with a box pleat. Buttons were initially black but were changed to gold in 1954. The WRAAF tunic buttoned up in the female style (right over left). Women were also issued with a navy-blue double-breasted gabardine coat, black gloves and a black leather shoulder bag. In 1963, the field service cap was replaced with an 'air-hostess' cap.[12]

Two Women's Royal Australian Air Force servicewomen wearing winter service dress, 1964 (Department of Defence)

The first WRAAF summer service dress uniform consisted of a blue-grey long-sleeve dress with black buttons, and khaki fur-felt hat. The dress was replaced in 1956 with a blue/white short-sleeve dress with black (later gold) buttons. In 1966, summer gloves were introduced.[13]

WRAAF working dress – worn when performing physical tasks – consisted of a button-through khaki dress, khaki fur-felt hat and optional blue cardigan.[14]

A major revision of uniforms in the early 1970s led to the decision to replace the separate winter and summer uniforms with an all-seasons service dress uniform. In 1972, a blue-grey uniform was introduced for both the WRAAF and RAAF. The WRAAF uniform consisted of a blue-grey tunic, blue-grey skirt, light-blue shirt and two-tone blue hat. Unfortunately, the contract with the fabric manufacturer had failed to include a clause stating the fabric was for the exclusive use of the Air Force. As a result, many other government organisations used the same fabric for their uniforms, with Air Force personnel frequently being mistaken for police and railway personnel.[15]

Women's Royal Australian Air Force uniform, 1974 (Department of Defence)

Royal Australian Air Force 1977–present

New-style blue-grey women's uniforms with greater flexibility for personal preferences were introduced in the 1980s.

Royal Australian Air Force uniforms with skirt, trouser and skivvy (rollneck) options, 1980s (Department of Defence)

The two women in the centre of this photo wear Combined Working Dress with shorts, RAAF Base Tindal, Northern Territory, 1990s (Department of Defence)

In 1982, a Combined Working Dress (CWD) uniform was introduced for women and men, consisting of a blue polyester/cotton collared shirt and navy-blue trousers. An optional navy-blue skirt was also introduced, but was later withdrawn due to its impracticality and unpopularity. In 1992, navy-blue shorts were introduced, followed by the first RAAF maternity uniforms in 1993.[16]

Due to the unpopularity of the blue-grey service dress uniform, in 2005, a navy-blue service dress uniform was reintroduced for both women and men. Today's 'Air Force blue' uniform is a return to the colour originally selected by Wing Commander Williams and introduced in 1922.[17]

This photo shows the difference in colour between the blue-grey fabric which was introduced in 1972 (left) and the contemporary navy-blue fabric which was reintroduced in 2005 (right) (Department of Defence)

At the time of writing, service dress uniform for women consists of a long-sleeve light-blue shirt with navy-blue tie and navy-blue skirt/trousers, or a short-sleeve light-blue shirt with navy-blue skirt/trousers. An optional navy-blue cardigan or jumper may be added. In 2019, a navy-blue wool-blend dress was introduced as an alternative to the short-sleeve shirt and skirt/trousers. This dress is generally praised by its wearers as being comfortable and flattering for all body shapes and sizes.

Left to right: Sergeant Katie Mohapp, Corporal Kathryn Whelan and Flight Lieutenant Jessica Greenway wearing the navy-blue service dress, 2019 (Department of Defence)

An increase in combat duties and deployments from the late 1990s saw increasing numbers of RAAF personnel wearing the Disruptive Pattern Camouflage Uniform (DPCU) – a brown/green uniform adapted from the Australian Army. By 2007, the DPCU had replaced the CWD as the working dress for most RAAF personnel. However, despite being modified with RAAF branding and navy-blue baseball caps, this uniform was criticised for failing to adequately distinguish RAAF personnel from Army personnel. In 2014, the DPCU was replaced with a blue General Purpose Uniform (GPU). The GPU is now the standard Air Force working dress.[18]

From centre outwards: General Purpose Uniform, short-sleeve service dress, flight suit (worn by aircrew) and Disruptive Pattern Camouflage Uniform (Department of Defence)

In recent years, further changes and allowances have been made to female RAAF members' uniform and dress, with a focus on comfort, safety and inclusiveness.

Today's maternity uniforms include both service dress and GPU variants. Both fulltime and Reserve servicewomen are entitled to receive up to four upper and four lower garments (with the service dress counting as one of each), to ensure a comfortable fit throughout the duration of their pregnancy.[19]

Women from various religious backgrounds are now often permitted to modify their uniforms in line with the tenets of their faith, such as wearing headscarves and long-sleeve garments for physical training.

When wearing service dress, women can choose from a range of footwear from high-heel shoes, wedges, low-heel shoes, to flat shoes, including ballet flats. They can also choose from a number of different style hats, including the peaked cap which was traditionally worn only by men. Rules around hairstyles, make up and jewellery are also constantly being reviewed and changed in line with personal comfort and social trends.

Aircraftwoman Katarina Forgan wears a maternity General Purpose Uniform while 31 weeks' pregnant, while Corporal Rhiannon Allum looks on with baby daughter Isla (Department of Defence)

THE 2000s

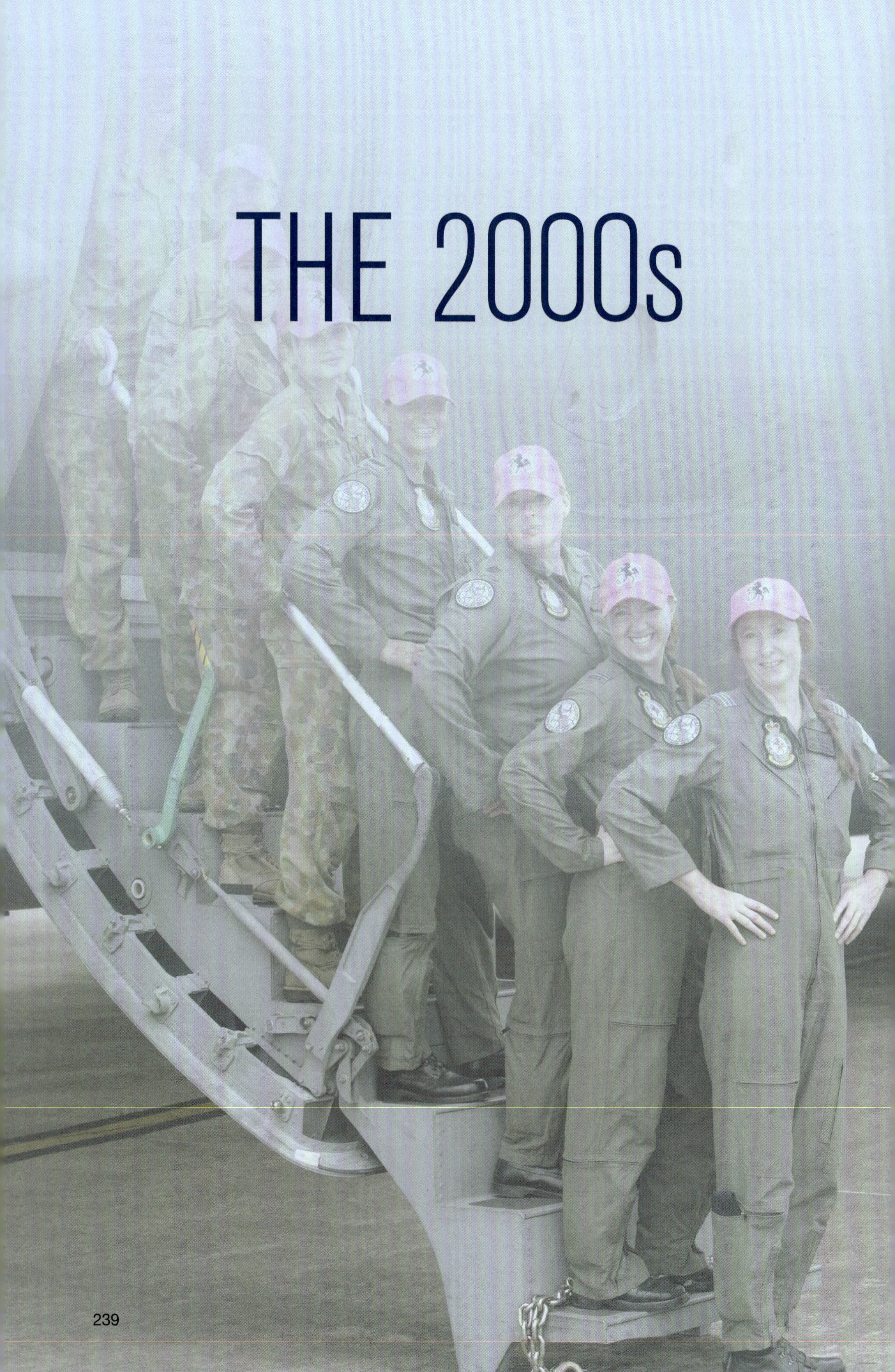

INTRODUCTION

Australia started the new millennium in a spirit of optimism with the Olympic Games in Sydney in 2000, but the 9/11 terrorist attacks in 2001 heralded new security threats, and was the start of a decades-long 'war on terror'. Additional terrorist attacks, including those in Bali in 2002, and Bali, London and Madrid in 2005, changed the security landscape for communities across the globe. Fear of terrorist attacks within Australian territories led to increased security measures – especially at airports – and Australian Defence Force (ADF) personnel were deployed to countries in the Middle East to join the international response to the 9/11 attacks. This global unrest contributed to a reduction in the number of Australians travelling overseas and even gathering in public venues back home, which were assessed as potential terrorist targets. Asylum seekers were detained off Australian shores, and the fear of religious extremism increased, leading to race-related tension and even targeted racial attacks, such as the Cronulla riots in Sydney in 2005. Yet there were moves towards reconciliation with indigenous Australians and, in 2008, Prime Minister Kevin Rudd issued an official Apology to Australia's Indigenous Peoples, particularly the Stolen Generations.[1]

A resources boom fuelled by China contributed to Australia's prosperity in the early years of the decade, with Australian resources companies BHP and Rio Tinto becoming two of the world's largest. While the 2008 Global Financial Crisis triggered the worst worldwide recession since the Great Depression, Australia managed to avoid a recession due to demand from China for our minerals, and prop-up funding from the Australian Government. Nonetheless, many Australians reduced their spending and pursued less-expensive activities, with a focus on family and home life once again gaining prominence within Australian society.[2]

Immediately following the 9/11 terrorist attacks in 2001, the Australian Government committed to what would become its longest war. In 2002, the first Royal Australian Air Force (RAAF) personnel arrived in Kyrgyzstan, where they provided air-to-air refuelling for the more than 350 coalition fighter aircraft striking Afghanistan, the heartland of the Taliban terrorist network. At the same time, the RAAF was operating its F/A-18 Hornets as part of the 'coalition of the willing', aimed at overthrowing Iraqi dictator Saddam Hussein. This was just the beginning of two decades of ADF deployments to combat zones in the Middle East.

While it was engaged in combat operations, the RAAF simultaneously deployed on humanitarian aid and disaster relief (HADR) missions, some of these following terrorist attacks. After the Bali bombings in 2002 killed 202 people (including 88 Australians) and injured 209, specially configured RAAF C-130 Hercules aircraft helped to evacuate the injured. In another key mission, the RAAF deployed to Indonesia only days after the devastating Boxing Day tsunami in South-East Asia in 2004, flying humanitarian relief stores into Bandah Aceh, and supporting the tasks of the Australian Army field hospital and engineering component.[3]

Leading Aircraftwoman Hayley Edwards (front left) and Flying Officer Kim Davey (front right), both of No 6 RAAF Hospital, help carry a Bali bombing victim off a Royal Australian Air Force C-130 Hercules, 2005 (Department of Defence)

Against this often-turbulent backdrop, the 2000s was a decade of ongoing achievements for RAAF servicewomen. In 2003, when Air Commodore Julie Hammer was promoted to air vice-marshal, she became the first woman in the ADF to achieve two-star rank. In 2005, Squadron Leader Ruth Elsley became the first Australian woman to command an overseas contingent (the United Nations mission in Sudan) and, the following year, Wing Commander Linda Corbould was the first woman to command a RAAF flying squadron. In 2008, Wing Commander Corbould also led the first all-female crew of a RAAF C-17A Globemaster III.[4]

Squadron Leader Ruth Elsley prepares to deploy on Operation *Azure* to Sudan as the new Australian Contingent Commander, 2005 (Department of Defence)

Corporal Tricia Reynolds and Duke wait to be hoisted by an Australian Army Black Hawk helicopter in Timor Leste, 2006. The pair were deployed on Operation *Astute*, a mission to help quell unrest and return stability to the region (Department of Defence)

The first all-female crew of a Royal Australian Air Force C-17A Globemaster, 2008. Right to left: Wing Commander Linda Corbould (pilot), Flight Lieutenant Samantha Webster (co-pilot), Warrant Officer Katrina Salvesen, Sergeant Paula Ivanovic, Leading Aircraftwoman Nicole Klein-Essink, Flying Officer Erin Rinaldi, Leading Aircraftwoman A Kay and Corporal E Atkinson (Department of Defence)

Sergeant Jade Evans

Aircraft Technician

Place of birth: Moonee Ponds, Victoria
Date of enlistment: 13 February 2007

My service has made me the person I am today. I am stronger, more resilient, and more people focused than I've ever been.[1]

Leading Aircraftwoman Jade Evans taking a break at Kandahar Airfield during her second deployment to the Middle East Area of Operations (Jade Evans)

By her own admission, Jade Evans's upbringing was not easy. She grew up in a 'tough household' in western Melbourne with her parents and two siblings, Jade being the middle child. She attended strict Catholic schools in primary and high school, where she excelled at a number of sports and academics:

> We weren't privileged or anything like that. Our parents both worked. Our parents focused on making sure that all the kids had an education. As soon as I was old enough, I got a job, because anything we wanted, we had to pay for ourselves.[2]

She started her first job at McDonald's three months before her 15th birthday.[3]

Jade and her sister excelled at pool and ocean swimming, getting up at 4am each morning to train before school, and racing in competitions on the weekends. When that became difficult to juggle with an increasing school load in Year 8, Jade gave up swimming. She was later introduced to lacrosse, and loved its fast pace and team dynamic.

Jade recalled she did not find academics particularly challenging. She hung around with the 'nerds' in her high school, achieving sufficient marks in Year 12 to open up numerous avenues for university courses. Yet while she was accepted into a forensic-science degree, the idea of another six years of study was not appealing, so a gap year to work was an option. However, in Year 12, she listened to a brief by an Air Force Cadets group:

> I'd never even heard of Cadets or anything like that. They advertised that [in the RAAF] you got an education, you could travel, you can get paid doing it, and to me … [I thought] this is it, because I struggled with the idea of having to go back to school for another six years.[4]

Jade started her research, focusing on jobs that had travel opportunities and which sounded 'interesting':

> I wanted to do something physical or active. I knew that I was technically minded so I wanted to do something down that path. I had previously done an introduction placement at Deakin University for mechatronics as part of a program to recruit more females into the technical/engineer workforce. When I saw aircraft technician and avionics technician [listed as career options], I had a look at that.[5]

Jade applied to join the RAAF as an aircraft technician in September of Year 12, and within one month of her initial aptitude assessment, she was contacted by Defence Force Recruiting, who wanted her to start immediately. Wishing to finish her schooling first, Jade came to an agreement to start her recruit training at RAAF Base Edinburgh in Adelaide in February the following year. Jade recalled the excitement of her early days of joining:

> I look back now and it gives me anxiety thinking about that, because it was my first time away from home. But I was super excited. Because at that point in my life, I couldn't wait to get out of the house. I met some people who joined with me and we took the [Defence] oath … It wasn't until we got off the bus at Adelaide [that] it was a bit of a shock … It was like, 'Okay, yes, I'm in the military now.'[6]

Jade said her upbringing and the structure she was used to at home and school helped her to manage the rigours of recruit training, despite being shy and quiet and 'having little to no life [skills] or social skills'.[7] She 'played the game' and loved the physical and sporting elements of the training. After graduating on Anzac Day in 2007, she travelled to RAAF Base Wagga Wagga in New South Wales (NSW) to start her year-long aircraft technician course. Jade does not have the fondest memories of her time there; however, she focused on her units, including mathematics and physics, and enjoyed the hands-on work on aircraft engines:

> My relationship with my family was quite strained and because, at that point, I was still growing and developing … I was very naive, very sheltered and just socially quiet … Just a mixture of things just making for bad interactions, and not really having those barriers up that you would normally have.[8]

On reflection, Jade said those difficult times were 'part of my journey'.[9] On graduation, she opted for a posting at No 37 Squadron (37SQN), home of the C-130J Hercules, which was considered an undesirable posting at the time:

> My approach through my entire career is to be a falling leaf: just go where the wind takes you. I didn't really know much about any of the aircraft, and there was no posting that was ever going to be in Melbourne for me at that time. So I'm like, 'Yes, I'll go to Richmond.'[10]

Aircraftwomen Jessica Johnson and Jade Evans (right) from No 37 Squadron in Sydney, New South Wales, Anzac Day 2009. Between them is Second World War veteran Meg Thomson from the Women's Auxiliary Australian Air Force, holding a photo taken on Anzac Day when she was 20 years old (Department of Defence)

In her second year at 37SQN, Jade deployed on the first of three trips with the C-130 to operations in the Middle East. She turned 21 during that rotation, working on nightshift, changing a part on an engine in a hangar: no fanfare for what is a traditional birthday milestone.

> [I was] changing a PCU [Pitch Control Unit] on one of the engines in the hangar and I went, 'Yay, I'm 21.' [My supervisors and colleagues said] 'Happy birthday; get back to work.'

Jade's travel goals were being ticked in the seven-and-a-half years she was at 37SQN: she travelled throughout Australia and overseas on tasks, including to Hawaii and Guam. During her posting, the C-130H was amalgamated into the squadron, with a training requirement for both aircraft variants. While she was still a leading aircraftwoman, Jade was a specialist at her trade, running shifts designed to be run by more senior technicians:

> You were forced to step up … you'd be running back and forth getting things done because that's what you had to do. The tempo was high but you knew what you were doing.[11]

Leading Aircraftwoman Jade Evans (caught off-guard by the photographer) in a C-130J Hercules, flying into Afghanistan during her second deployment to the Middle East Area of Operations (Jade Evans)

Jade recalled there were few female technicians at the time, and the work culture was not conducive to building a supportive network. In retrospect, she said that having a mentor at the time would have been beneficial and, in the absence of one, she focused on self-protection and getting the job done. Towards the end of her posting, she was promoted to corporal, had developed her skills as a team member and manager, and had settled into a strong friendship group. She was promoted as part of a large group, sensitive to a stigma that females were promoted purely for their gender.

After seven years at Richmond, Jade and her then-partner were posted to RAAF Amberley, Queensland, as he sought a posting to the C-17 Globemaster squadron. Jade again applied her 'falling leaf' approach to life and accepted a position at No 33 Squadron (33SQN) to work on the KC-30A air-to-air refuelling aircraft:

> It was like I had joined a family! The dynamic was completely different to 37SQN and the tempo was less than half. The main difference was the tempo and the technical expertise [that was required] was dramatically lower than 37SQN, and the working environment was much more pleasant. The people were more friendly and accepting and the environment was more harmonious. It was a posting and promotion, so I was seeing a lot of things through a new lens.[12]

While Jade was enjoying a different work dynamic, she was still placing pressure on herself to perform:

> It was a nice change and it made it super easy to thrive and do well. But the kind of person that I am [means that] I want to be good at something immediately, so I was very nervous, because it takes me a little while to become an SME [subject matter expert] on things.[13]

After only a few months at 33SQN, Jade was told she had been placed on a rotation to the Middle East in August 2015; she thought it was a joke because she had not finished her qualification journals on the KC-30A. Despite her expectations of needing to be fully qualified to operate on the aircraft before a deployment, she was placed into a junior position and deployed to Al Dhafra Air Base near Abu Dhabi: her first of two deployments with 33SQN. She spent the next three months with the KC-30A refuelling program in support of the 'Defeat Daesh' operation, honing her technical skills on the aircraft.

Working on a large American-operated base was a different experience from Jade's previous Middle East deployments, and one she admits she preferred. In keeping with the American theme, she travelled numerous times to Hawaii during her time at the squadron, considering it as a second home. She also spent time in Alaska and California while providing support during trials for the KC-30A 'boom': one of the two systems used to refuel other aircraft while airborne. Watching American experts troubleshoot for the trial was 'incredible':

> I thought that [the equipment trials] was more rewarding because you're seeing the full capability of what your aircraft can do, and knowing what contributions we had to other nations as well.[14]

A dust storm descending on the Al Dhafra Air Base, Abu Dhabi, while Jade Evans was deployed with No 33 Squadron (Jade Evans)

Throughout her time at 33SQN, the number of female technicians increased to approximately 25 per cent of the total workforce. As a more experienced corporal, her focus started shifting to a mentoring and leadership role for other women, a role she was initially uncomfortable with due to her own experience of being one of few women on the workshop floor and working largely on her own:

> I realised it's not really about me anymore; it's about growing and developing them … [it's] about 'you're putting pressure on yourself here' … I think the environment is a lot better these days for [women] to be able to be authentic and just be themselves in the workplace, and contribute in their way.[15]

At the end of her seventh year at 33SQN, Jade was promoted to sergeant, despite having no expectations given the competitiveness for promotion in the technician ranks. The year prior, she had applied for a position at the School of Post Graduate Studies (SPS), a unit that delivers professional military education courses to enhance the leadership skills of Air Force personnel. Her reasons for doing so could be considered unique:

> I was terrible at public speaking and I knew that if I was going to get promoted, that's something that I need to start getting comfortable with. What better place to go than SPS to teach you how to do that properly and it's a good environment to learn in.[16]

Jade was successful in winning an SPS posting on her second attempt, joining the unit on her promotion at the beginning of 2023. While still finding her footing in the new role at the time of interview, Jade was struck by the inclusive and supportive workplace. She said they understand the struggles of public speaking, and the challenge of presenting course content in an engaging and imaginative way:

> It's like a resilience growth for myself because I'm very uncomfortable with a lot of things so … if I'm not good at something, I'll go do it so I'm more comfortable with it, and then my stress levels will come down. It's been the same thing throughout my whole career.[17]

Jade's focus in her facilitator role will be on developing aviators' leadership abilities across all work categories. She said young leaders are being taught to understand different types of behaviours and traits, and how to harness those qualities to effect a high-performing team. As a result, Jade has the ability to shape the type of workplace in the Air Force she wants to be a part of:

> I put the uniform on because I want to grow myself. I want to be the best version of myself, and lead, and coach people to do the same.[18]

Flight Lieutenant Ingrid Van der Vlist

Air Mobility Officer

Place of birth: Mildura, Victoria
Date of enlistment: 25 September 2007

I know I can be very driven and focused on a set goal once I have one. I really don't subscribe to the 'such is life' mentality at all or the idea that we should settle for what we've got, even if we're unhappy with it. I'm a huge advocate for change and personal growth, even if it means taking a leap of faith outside your comfort zone. I really do think that an individual can have all the potential in the world, but without a clear sense of direction and some personal grit, potential is just a word.[1]

Flight Lieutenant Ping Van der Vlist standing next to the refuelling boom of a Royal Australian Air Force KC-30A multi-role tanker transport aircraft (Department of Defence)

Ingrid ('Ping') Van der Vlist may have grown up near naval bases, but her career has included time serving in both the RAAF and the Australian Army. Ping spent the majority of her childhood and schooling years in Jervis Bay, a small coastal town south of Sydney and close to two naval bases. Her elder brother's career, firstly in the Royal Australian Navy and then in the RAAF, influenced her while she was in high school to consider a profession in the Air Force:

> By the time I was in Year 10, he'd planted the idea of becoming a RAAF crew attendant [CREWATT] in my head, because he'd worked with so many of them at [No] 33 Squadron on the Boeing 707, and he thought I'd be a good fit for the job. [So] I shaped my Year 11 and 12 electives towards applying once I'd finished my HSC [Higher School Certificate].[2]

Aircraftwoman Recruit Ping Van der Vlist's first official photo while on her recruit course, 2007 (Department of Defence)

During Years 11 and 12, the aviation museum at HMAS Albatross offered engineering aeroskills as an elective, and Ping attended; it was one of the few units at school which she admits she enjoyed. With a CREWATT career as her sole focus, Ping visited RAAF Base Richmond and the Fairbairn establishment in Canberra to familiarise herself with the role and speak to as many CREWATTs as she could, to demonstrate to Defence Force Recruiting her determination to join. Her plan hit a temporary snag when the Boeing 707 was retired and, as a result, few CREWATTs were being recruited:

> I wouldn't say it was great timing for me to want that job specifically. It worked out anyway, in the long run, but there was a solid 18-month gap there [between] finishing my HSC to actually starting recruit training in Edinburgh.[3]

In September 2007, Ping finally started her recruit training at No 1 Recruit Training Unit, the last course to be held at RAAF Base Edinburgh in Adelaide. She recalled 'absolutely loving' the structured environment of the course:

> I had a regimental approach to plenty of other things in my life, so when people were having a difficult time, I found myself confused by it, to be honest. I was like, we're all here together, we can all suck it up. It's not forever. I had, I think, a longer foresight into what a military career could be.[4]

Aircraftwoman Recruit Ping Van der Vlist at No 1 Recruit Training Unit, RAAF Base Edinburgh, South Australia, 2007 (Ping Van der Vlist)

After graduating, Ping started the basic prerequisite courses for all enlisted aircrew at RAAF Base Richmond, with a focus on the skills and qualities required to be an effective member of a crew on board an aircraft:

> Even if you're not the captain or the most senior person [on board], you still need to contribute and value-add, especially in an emergency scenario where you might be the SME [subject matter expert] on a piece of equipment or a situation. So yes, it was a very interesting course.[5]

Ping's CREWATT course was the first to be conducted solely at No 34 Squadron at Fairbairn, Australian Capital Territory, the home of the RAAF VIP (Very Important Person) fleet, after the decommissioning of the Boeing 707. She started serving on the Boeing Business Jet (BBJ), graduating as a 'D-CAT' (the bottom of the skills ladder with 'A-CAT' being a member who has extensive experience and additional skills and responsibilities). Ping's family proudly watched on as she was presented with her first 'brevet' (awarded to aircrew on completion of their qualification course) on graduation, fulfilling a plan that had been hatched as far back as 2004.

Further training on the Challenger 604 aircraft ensured that Ping was trained on both aircraft types, and she spent a total of two-and-a-half years as a part of small crews, flying VIP passengers around the globe and the country. She recalled the posting taught her the importance of flexibility, with regular last-minute changes to tasks and even aircraft types:

> There were many times, especially during an election campaign, where I would be on the BBJ as part of a crew going somewhere, and then the plan change[d] in the background … [and] I would be chucked on the Challenger instead. So I'd literally step off the jet, walk across the tarmac, and jump on a different jet, and go and do something else.[6]

Ping recalled those early years as formative in shaping her future career aspirations, with the next phase serving as a CREWATT on the new air-to-air refuelling capability, the KC-30A. The aircraft itself did not arrive until a year into her posting to No 33 Squadron (33SQN), so she spent time developing operating procedures and the methods in which CREWATTs would operate. She also put that time to good use to start checking off courses and qualifications which she would require to progress in her field. She remembered the first time she walked through the aircraft, she was struck by the sheer size difference to what she had previously worked on, including crew size and the number of passengers on board:

> The jet is just immense. It's a wide-bodied aircraft with these two big, long aisles that just feel like they're going on forever. I wanted to experience the military side of what it was to do the CREWATT job [on the KC-30A]. I wanted to see how different they could be and what a military-focused mindset could be, noting that [No] 33 Squadron's primary role is air-to-air refuelling, but we can also do huge passenger movements and take cargo.[7]

Ping spent five years as a CREWATT on the KC-30A, increasing the level of responsibility she held as a crewmember as the years progressed. A highlight was becoming a cabin manager, thereby holding the responsibility to lead the entire CREWATT team:

> I really enjoyed the moment I got to become a cabin manager … as far as the back end of the jet's concerned, you're running the show. Everyone that is operating with you, is also operating for you, and that was another huge sense of achievement, because I really got to test my leadership skills in that area. There [are] plenty of times where stuff can go very right, or very wrong, and only you, as the cabin manager, can influence which way that goes … That was when I started to get a taste for, 'Oh, maybe piloting

> is where I move professionally in the future', because I started to get a taste for not just the management side of things, but the greater level of responsibility.[8]

Once Ping had achieved a B-CAT CREWATT role, her main focus shifted to checking and assessing other members' levels of competency; the hands-on leadership role she enjoyed as cabin manager was greatly reduced. This was a natural turning point for her to consider what was next in her career. She started exploring options to commission to pilot but did not meet the academic entry requirements for maths and physics to apply. So, her determination to achieve her goal of flying led to Ping taking on intensive courses in aeronautical mathematics and physics, which she funded herself and had to take time off work to complete:

> And I hated every second of it, because I'm not a mathematically inclined person … If something didn't make sense, I had to force myself to understand it in a different way. I saw it as a test: if I can get through this, I should be able to do pilot training … I would say it's another time where that tenacity had to come in, and I had to really grind at getting through those courses.[9]

Ping put everything apart from work and study aside to achieve that goal. She believes that one of her strengths is her ability to accept discomfort as a temporary concept, and this has been a driver throughout her life. 'It's just a drop in the bucket. It sucks, and it's uncomfortable … but that's at least something I'm good at.'[10]

After successfully completing her studies, Ping applied to commission to pilot: not for Air Force, but for Army. She said this was a deliberate decision; she had already decided her end state was to apply as a specialist services officer (SSO) to fly helicopters in the Army. Growing up, she had always had an interest in rotary wing aircraft, believing she had the coordination to fly a helicopter well. The role of a RAAF pilot held less interest for her:

> I could have been one of these people that maybe makes it through all of that basic training, but then spend[s] your time hating your job, or not quite liking the airframe you're posted to; so many things that could influence your mindset moving forwards, and your ability to perform at your best. I was like, maybe that's not it. That's why I was absolutely gunning for SSO [with] Army from day one.[11]

Ping was accepted to commission and spent 10 weeks at the Royal Military College Duntroon in Canberra, completing an abridged version of officer training, before starting Basic Flying Training at Tamworth, NSW. The course focused on the basic principles of flying in fixed-wing aircraft, then additional instrument skills, before Ping travelled to Oakey, Queensland, to commence training in the Kiowa helicopter. Of her experience at Tamworth, Ping reflected:

> It's a very humbling experience, being there. You really do learn a lot about your own strengths and weaknesses. I would say tenacity got me through again, and the ability to study something even if I'm not interested in it, to the required standard to pass a course. And then also I learned – I was already fairly certain of this anyway – [that] my 'hands and feet ability' to fly would far outweigh my academic abilities.[12]

Ping Van der Vlist during her first solo mission as the pilot of a Bell 206 Kiowa aircraft, 2016. She had transferred to the Australian Army in late 2014 (Ping Van der Vlist)

Ping's Kiowa training took up the better part of a year in 2016; when she was completing her second-last flight before graduation, she was involved in a response to a serious motor vehicle accident. It was in the evening, she was wearing night-vision goggles, and so far she'd been meeting the time milestones she needed to pass the navigation element of the task, when she experienced a flash of light. On closer inspection, Ping and her instructor confirmed the source of the light was a fire from a single-vehicle accident. The safest landing zone was quite a distance from the crash site, and Ping had to run up a hill, hurdling several cattle fences, to reach a man who was trapped in the car. After pulling the elderly driver from the car and assessing his condition, she had to race back to her instructor to provide an update, and grabbed some first-aid equipment so she could to tend to the driver. 'I snapped straight back into first-aid mode, and all of that training and drilling as a CREWATT I think is what prepared me best mentally for that.'[13]

Unfortunately, the driver passed away the following day from his extensive injuries, but not before his family had a chance to see him. Ping then had to refocus and repeat her second-to-last check ride, given the accident the night before had prevented her from finishing the task. Yet again, she drew on her determination and ability to compartmentalise, and she passed to go on to her final check ride.

Her family and an unusually large Air Force contingent of friends from 33SQN saw her achieve yet another significant milestone: receiving her second brevet, as an Army pilot. Ping then went on to the regiment which she had initially set out to join and was posted to the 6th Aviation Regiment in Sydney to convert to the Black Hawk helicopter.

However, she faced a significant setback towards the end of her conversion training when she was carrying out underwater escape training. Having caught the boot of her right foot underwater, Ping suffered a significant knee injury to a joint that had already been reconstructed. After another full reconstruction and a significant rehabilitation period, by which time the Black Hawk was being phased out of service, Ping found herself in a position where she had to re-evaluate her career options:

> There was this consideration to maybe pick a career that doesn't involve lower limb coordination and excessive force or pressure needing to be put through either of your feet, especially the right one. So yes, I started to look at other options then. It was very much 'I don't want to relinquish an aviation career if I don't have to', so noting that [an] Army aviation career is quite limited anyway, I'm thinking, 'Hey, if I'm not going to be flying helicopters in the Army, I'd rather be going back to do something aviation-related in the RAAF.' And that's when the AMO [air mobility officer] opportunity popped up.[14]

At the time, the RAAF was developing a new officer aviation specialisation on the KC-30A to manage aircraft refuelling tasking, a role which had initially been carried out by enlisted personnel of various musterings:

> The long-term reason for standing up AMO is leadership potential and the command pathway, and I was like, 'Hey, I'm interested in that. That sounds like a good fit for me.' It's back at a squadron that I love. It's on a jet that I know quite well. I missed the travel, and yes, all of a sudden, this opportunity popped up that I didn't think was going to happen at all.[15]

Fortunately, the RAAF was receptive to Ping transferring service and commencing training as an AMO. By July 2019, she was back in 'blue' to attend a six-month interim posting and, later, the full air refuelling operator conversion course. Within four months of training on a simulator, Ping was back in the KC-30A, refuelling other aircraft in the air, starting with experience on other large aircraft before transitioning to fast-jet refuelling:

> You've got a C-17 [Globemaster] slowly creeping forward, and the sheer inertia of that airframe coming forward … [if] they come too far forward, then you're in a dangerous spot, and [if] they're too far back, you can't reach them at all … it's a very spicy and interesting flying environment to put yourself in.[16]

Ping experienced her third and final brevet ceremony to receive her AMO wings on 15 June 2020, after her completion of the air refuelling operator conversion course. So far, she has enjoyed the new challenge of additional leadership responsibility as an AMO, including being able to positively shape the culture of the specialisation:

> Making the decision to have a commissioned aviator step into the role, I did feel a sense of responsibility, I would say, rather than a sense of obligation, to step us off on the right foot … I did draw on a lot of CREWATT and rotary pilot experience to help make that work.[17]

Flight Lieutenant Ping Van der Vlist at the aircraft-refuelling console of a Royal Australian Air Force KC-30A multi-role tanker transport aircraft during an air-to-air refuelling mission (Ping Van der Vlist)

Ping's next career ambition is to gain experience in a non-aircrew-related role at Headquarters Joint Operations Command, to broaden her perspective within the Department of Defence. As is her approach, Ping believes this will set her up for success in going back to the air mobility environment. She believes the AMO specialisation will provide her with a pathway to achieve her leadership and career aspirations, potentially as the Commanding Officer of a squadron in the future. Ping's intrinsic drivers are evident when she sums up what she wants to achieve:

> I'd say what motivates me is probably just wanting to do the best at what I'm currently doing. It doesn't matter what that is – whether it's a CREWATT, whether it's as a pilot or an AMO, whether it's in my personal life – whatever it is that happens to be the next step … just approaching that as positively as possible with a plan in place. I can't say I've ever gone into something having not thought it through. I'm very much a planner.[18]

Air Force women killed in service

Dozens of Australian Air Force servicewomen have lost their lives in service. These include 57 members of the Women's Auxiliary Australian Air Force (WAAAF) and five members of the Royal Australian Air Force Nursing Service. The majority of these women died in Australia during the Second World War, with their causes of death almost evenly divided between illnesses and accidents (including aircraft crashes).[1]

Sadly, the bodies of two WAAAF servicewomen who lost their lives in Australia have never been found. Corporal Ray Diggles died on 27 February 1942 when Empire Flying Boat A18-12 crashed in Cleveland Bay in Townsville, Queensland, with seven of the 11 personnel on board losing their lives. Aircraftwoman Margaret Carey died on 7 April 1945 when Avro Anson W2244 crashed into the sea between Williamtown and Evans Head in New South Wales, with all five personnel on board losing their lives. Because their bodies were never recovered, Corporal Diggles and Aircraftwoman Carey have never been buried.[2]

A small number of Australian Air Force servicewomen have lost their lives when serving overseas. Sister Marie Craig died on 18 September 1945 in an aircraft accident in Dutch New Guinea in the Netherlands East Indies, and Sister Verdun Sheah died on 15 November 1945 in an unspecified accident in New Guinea. Due to the Australian Government's repatriation policy of the time, these women were buried overseas.[3]

Sister Marie Craig attending to patients in a Royal Australian Air Force Dakota on what would be her second-last flight. The aircraft on which she was travelling disappeared over Dutch New Guinea in November 1945 (Department of Defence)

Until 1966, the policy of the Commonwealth War Graves Commission (CWGC, known as the Imperial War Graves Commission until 1960) for all Australian service personnel who were killed overseas was to bury them where they died. The policy stated, 'deceased Servicemen [and -women] should not be returned to their homeland countries for re-burial but should be buried in the countries in which they died'.[4]

Graves of Australian service personnel at the Commonwealth War Graves Commission cemetery in Singapore, 2017 (Department of Defence)

The reason was to ensure that all who were killed were treated equally. At the time, the Australian Government did not finance the repatriation of bodies to Australia, and it recognised that not all families would be able to afford to bring home their dead. Therefore, it agreed with the CWGC that Australian service personnel killed overseas would be buried overseas in the 'nearest practical CWGC cemetery'. Consequently, Sister Craig is buried in the Port Moresby (Bomana) War Cemetery in Papua New Guinea (PNG) and Sister Sheah is buried in the Bita Paka War Cemetery in East New Britain, PNG.[5]

During the Vietnam War, the Australian public put increased pressure on the Australian Government to repatriate those who were killed in service overseas. In 1966, the government changed its policy to repatriate the bodies of service personnel who were killed overseas during operations and exercises, for burial in Australia. Consequently, RAAF personnel killed while serving overseas are now repatriated to Australia as an acknowledgement of their sacrifice.[6]

Three RAAF health professionals were among nine ADF personnel tragically killed when a Royal Australian Navy Sea King helicopter crashed on the Indonesian island of Nias on 2 April

2005. Two of the three RAAF personnel were women; Flight Lieutenant Lyn Rowbottom and Sergeant Wendy Jones were part of a task force that was providing humanitarian assistance to the local population following devastating earthquakes in the region.

It is a reality that the women who serve in the RAAF today – just like the women who served in Australia's historical Air Force services – sign up knowing that, someday, they may not return home.

Aircraftwoman Breeanna Williams of Australia's Federation Guard during the memorial service for the 70th anniversary of the Battle of El Alamein, held at the Commonwealth War Graves Commission cemetery in El Alamein, Egypt, 2012 (Department of Defence)

THE 2010s AND 2020s

INTRODUCTION

The 2010s and early 2020s have been characterised by both hope and hardship for Australians. While the early years of the 2010s were characterised by poor economic growth and rising debt as a carry-over from the Global Financial Crisis of 2008, by the end of the decade, Australia's economy had grown by 10 per cent. In 2010, Julia Gillard became Australia's first female prime minister, but the rest of the decade saw a rapid succession of five Australian prime ministers within 10 years. There were steps towards greater inclusivity, with legislation for same-sex marriage passing parliament in 2017, and First Nations peoples increasingly receiving recognition of their land rights and sovereignty.[1]

Leading Aircraftwoman Robyn Lamont prepares to load a pallet of bottled water onto a Royal Australian Air Force C-17 Globemaster destined for Japan during Operation *Pacific Assist*, 2011 (Department of Defence)

Australia's economy has long relied on its export of coal, gas and other natural resources, but after years of drought, unprecedented hot temperatures led to massive, deadly bushfires throughout the country in the summer of 2019–20. Australia increasingly acknowledged the need to transition away from fossil fuels and to make efforts to combat climate change. Technological advances in lifestyle, health, media and entertainment continued to transform the Australian way of life in the 2010s and 2020s. New information and sharing technologies led to the rise of platforms such as Uber and Netflix, while routine and manual tasks became increasingly automated or digitised. By the early 2020s, there seemed to be an 'app' (application) for virtually everything.[2]

During these decades, the Royal Australian Air Force (RAAF) continued to deploy personnel in support of active service operations overseas, and humanitarian aid and disaster relief (HADR) missions. In 2010, the RAAF started to take delivery of its first new combat aircraft in 25 years: the F/A-18F Super Hornet, which it deployed to the Middle East on Operation *Okra* in 2014. Two of the RAAF's first female fast-jet pilots graduated from No 2 Operational Conversion Unit in 2017 and, the following year, the RAAF started to receive its fleet of F-35A Lightning II aircraft, a highly advanced 'fifth-generation' stealth fighter.

Many HADR missions were carried out throughout the globe, including Operation *Pacific Assist* in 2011 following an earthquake, tsunami and meltdown of a nuclear power plant in Japan, and to Fiji in 2016 after Cyclone Winston left a path of destruction. When the turn of the decade brought devastating bushfires and the deadly COVID-19 pandemic within our borders, the Australian Defence Force (ADF) was heavily relied upon to provide assistance to the civil community, and members of all services deployed on Operation *Bushfire Assist* from late 2019 and Operation *COVID-19 Assist* from early 2020.[3]

Leading Aircraftwoman Lauren Marshall and Jeep guard a Royal Australian Air Force Wedgetail aircraft at RAAF Base Learmonth, Western Australia, 2014. The pair were deployed on Operation *Southern Indian Ocean* following the disappearance of Malaysia Airlines Flight 370 (Department of Defence)

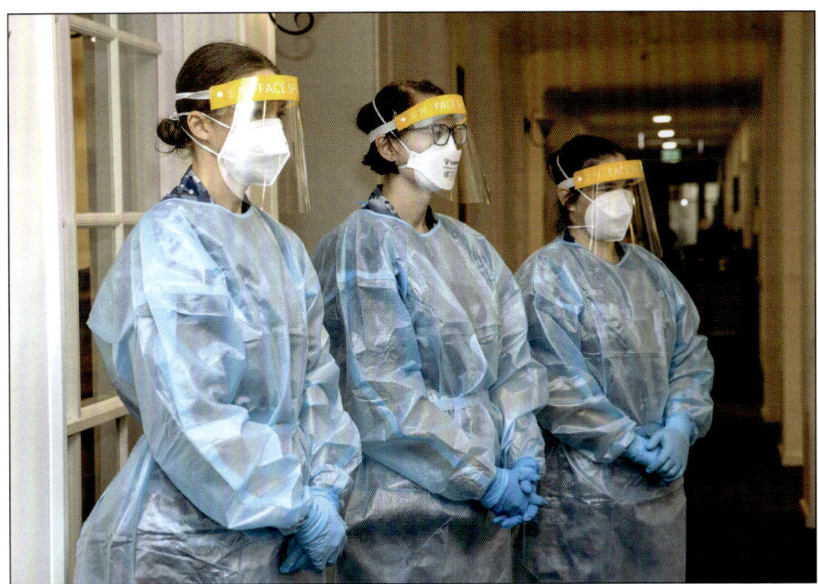

Medical technicians (left to right) Aircraftwoman Kate Ogilvie, Leading Aircraftwoman Laura Devine and Aircraftwoman Taryn Worby from No 1 Expeditionary Health Squadron provide medical support at an aged-care facility during Operation *COVID-19 Assist* (Department of Defence)

With COVID-19 easing throughout Australia in 2021, the RAAF was able to proceed with commemorations for the centenary of its formation on 31 March 1921. The RAAF held events around the country to honour 100 years of the sacrifices and service of Australians – including many thousands of women – and to acknowledge today's highly capable, resilient and resourceful force.[4]

Royal Australian Air Force Indigenous Liaison Officer Flight Lieutenant Patricia Thompson packing donations for Exercise *Christmas Hop* at RAAF Base Townsville, Queensland, 2020 (Department of Defence)

Former Warrant Officer of the Air Force Fiona Grasby (centre) and Leading Aircraftwoman Charlie-Elle McCarthy (right) lay a wreath during the dedication ceremony for the Air Force Centenary Memorial at RAAF Base Point Cook, Victoria, 2022. The ceremony had been postponed due to COVID-19 restrictions, taking place a year after the Royal Australian Air Force's centenary in 2021 (Department of Defence)

Australian female fast-jet pilots

Flight Lieutenant Connie Dixon
Flight Lieutenant Jess Stone

Flight Lieutenants Connie Dixon and Jess Stone, both born in 1993, are two RAAF fast-jet pilots. Both Connie and Jess agree that focusing on their studies was one of the foundations of their success – or, as they both put it, they were self-described nerds!

'I was definitely a nerd so I enjoyed the academic side of schooling,' said Connie.

> Maths, science and tech drawing were my strong subjects. My dad was an aircraft technician on Classic Hornets (F/A-18s) in the late 1980s and early 1990s and, in my early teen years, I became fascinated by my dad's Air Force career. I remember watching the documentary *Speed & Angels*, which is about the last F-14 Tomcat conversion in the United States, and thinking, 'I'm going to be a fast-jet pilot!' I was resolute in that ambition for the remainder of my high school years.[5]

'I enjoyed school and did a lot of mathematics and science,' said Jess.

> I did quite well in most subjects (I'm a bit of a nerd) and had a really good group of friends throughout. I decided I wanted to join the RAAF in Year 12. My first thought was just joining the Australian Defence Force in general, to look at exciting career options. Once I started my research, it became clear that fast-jet pilot was what I viewed as most fitting that category.[6]

Connie and Jess both learned a lot about themselves and their capabilities during their initial training and many courses.

'I joined Air Force via direct entry following the completion of my engineering degree at the University of Newcastle,' said Connie.

> I attended Officer Training School (OTS) in 2016. The course was not difficult, but it was challenging in terms of not knowing my schedule in the early weeks, the sleep deprivation, and the weather out in the field (winter in Sale in Victoria is not fun!). During the course, I learned a lot about patience. The 'hurry up and wait' mantra was a very real training tool during OTS. I remember my mum thinking that I changed a fair bit during those months: I'd always been independent but I became more resilient and willing to roll with the punches.[7]

'I later found pilot's course to be an extremely rewarding experience,' continued Connie.

> It was a challenging and long road to become qualified on an operational aircraft, but I wouldn't have had it any other way. It would be remiss of me not to mention the many times I cried, out of stress or self-doubt after a poor performance. Pilot's course isn't just about building the tangible skills of being a pilot; it's also about moulding the mindset, which is required of military aviators to do their job in the most trying of circumstances. The resilience, humility and mental fortitude I learned on pilot's course was arguably a bigger challenge than the flying itself.[8]

Officer Cadet Connie Dixon helps herself to a hot breakfast at Basic Flying Training School, 2017 (Department of Defence)

'I went through the Australian Defence Force Academy [ADFA] straight out of school at 17,' said Jess.

> There I studied a Bachelor of Technology (Aviation) degree for three years. The structured lifestyle suited my personality, and moving to ADFA that young was probably the best place for me, as I was well looked after. I enjoyed the travel and sport opportunities at ADFA a lot and made a lot of good friends.[9]

'I had an absolutely awesome pilot's course with others who are all still my best friends today,' continued Jess.

> I found the course challenging (as anyone does), with its ups and downs, but it was a great time. [After much training] moving into a single-seat platform (the F/A-18A Hornet) and not having an instructor in the aircraft with me helped me to improve immensely as a pilot and captain. Pilot's course and other training courses take determination and the ability to handle criticism well. Particularly, not taking criticism personally, and having the ability to look at it as an opportunity to improve. Often at fighter squadrons, they run off the adage that to fit in, you need to meet two out of three criteria of: be a good 'bloke', be a hard worker, be a superstar pilot. I definitely tend to fall into the first two before the third and, in my opinion, those are more important – the rest just falls into place.[10]

Connie and Jess describe their typical working day.

'Every day is so different,' said Connie.

> If it's a flying day, there'll be a couple of hours of pre-flight prep (including preparing a mission brief as the flight lead and ensuring products are ready). This is followed by a mission brief two hours before the take-off time. Our walk flow [planning for and executing a flying mission, including checking the aircraft is prepared and ready] to the jet commences an hour before our take-off time and then the mission will vary in length but is on average two to three hours, depending on the mission set we are practising. After landing, our walk flow and debrief will take another two-plus hours. We very quickly run out of work hours to do our other jobs on flying days!

'My secondary role is as an aviation safety officer,' Connie continued.

> This includes investigating aviation safety events, preparing and delivering whole-of-squadron aviation safety training packages, and developing risk-management plans for the many exercises my squadron participates in throughout the year. During an exercise, we'll be on a plan/fly cycle (plan one day; fly the next) and these days will be 12 hours in length. Outside of

> flying and secondary duties, there is always self-managed study required to stay on top of current tactics and emerging systems.[11]

'Currently, my day [as an instructor] will tend to consist of an instructional flight or simulation, teaching the students who are currently on operational conversion [OPCON],' said Jess.

> I may also get to do a staff training mission as well. Typically, flying will take up at least half a day or more, with a brief and debrief. Outside of that, we have secondary duties to perform; for my part, I am the phase commander for part of the OPCON so I work on syllabus updates, mass briefs and standardisation.[12]

Flying Officer Jess Stone in an F/A-18A Hornet during Exercise *High Sierra* at RAAF Base Townsville, Queensland, 2017 (Department of Defence)

Connie and Jess have the following advice for those considering a career in the Air Force.

'Get comfortable with being uncomfortable – it's a challenging job that will frequently put you outside your comfort zone,' said Connie.

> Do everything you can to prepare yourself for that. If you want it badly enough, don't let the system tell you 'no'. Grind every day and never give up. And be humble – I've had days where I've felt invincible and I've had days where I've wondered if I should have [pilot's] wings at all. The important thing is to be able to take on board the feedback which your instructors, supervisors and peers give you. Swallow your pride and learn from your mistakes.[13]

'Putting on the Air Force uniform means having been selected to do a job that requires dedication, commitment and sacrifice in one's personal life,' continued Connie.

> There's an immense pride in wearing a uniform which not everyone has the opportunity to wear and contributing to something greater than myself and greater than a bottom line. It also means being a part of a wider community that's spanned generations and contributed to creating the life we are accustomed to here in Australia.[14]

'I get quite a few emails and phone calls from people who know someone who wants to sign up as a pilot,' said Jess.

> Typically they tend to be young ladies who reach out. My advice is to be receptive to criticism, and understand how you learn best. Getting a strong group of friends early on in training is also a big help. As for joining the Air Force or any service in general, my advice would be to appreciate the benefits we get, especially the opportunities to travel and live in places where you wouldn't normally get the chance.[15]

Flying Officer Jess Stone with Make-A-Wish Foundation recipient Jason, looking over a Hawk 127 lead-in fighter jet at RAAF Base Williamtown, New South Wales, 2016 (Department of Defence)

Flight Lieutenant Olivia Little (née Salvatore)

Electronic Warfare Officer

Date of enlistment: 29 July 2011

I just want to fly jets … I'm not settling for anything else.[1]

Olivia Little's cockpit selfie (Olivia Little)

Olivia ('Liv') Little was born in Carlton, Victoria, and grew up on an 80-acre chicken farm in the small country town of Wallan, surrounded by a quarter of a million chickens:

> It was a very simple, hard-working kind of life. My dad worked 14-hour days on the farm … We didn't really go away very often until Dad started selling off the farm, when I was about 15 or 16.

While trips were few and far between during her childhood, Liv's first exposure to the RAAF was at the age of 10, when her father took her to the Australian International Airshow at Avalon, Victoria. It was there that she first experienced the thrill of a fast jet. While watching the F-111s, Liv thought, 'It would be cool to fly that fast.' From that day on, her focus was set on achieving her wings in the Air Force.

> I just wanted to fly as fast as possible, to challenge myself, and to push myself. That was the goal. Every subject I picked thereafter was focused towards that.[2]

At the age of 16, while still in Year 10, Liv sat the aptitude tests for aircrew, with the intention of entering the Air Force through the Australian Defence Force Academy (ADFA). Unfortunately, she was unsuccessful, and was advised to reattempt the ADFA entry process in 12 months' time. Instead, Liv allowed herself a little more time and completed Year 12, then applied to Swinburne University to undertake a four-year Bachelor of Aviation degree. Although Liv's final results were 'one or two points off' what she needed to be accepted into the course, she sat an interview with the university board and was accepted.[3]

Liv excelled at her degree. As part of her studies, she obtained her private pilot's licence and completed the theoretical and practical components to such a high standard that she could have taken the commercial pilot's test. Although Liv's plan was to 'finish my degree, and then seamlessly transition into Defence after that', the recruitment process took much less time than she had anticipated. Expecting the recruitment process to take up to 18 months, Liv applied for the Air Force in the third year of her four-year degree. Instead, she received and accepted an offer to join as a pilot only six months after applying. While she was studying the final year of her Bachelor of Aviation, Liv also completed an abridged version of Officer Training School (OTS) at RAAF Base East Sale, Victoria, then began her pilot training at No 1 Basic Flying Training School in Tamworth, NSW. To describe the workload as heavy would be an understatement. 'Looking back at it now, I would never do that [again]. I would've solely focused on pilot's course.'[4]

Due to a policy at the time that sought to accelerate aircrew through the training process, Liv undertook an officer training course of six weeks, instead of the usual 16 weeks. Unfortunately for Liv and her fellow trainees, this policy was changed partway through their Basic Flying Training (BFT), and Liv was required to go back to OTS to carry out the full 16-week course from the beginning. Demonstrating her resilient approach to setbacks, Liv considered this as:

> A blessing, because it gave me some time to go back, re-gauge … [and learn] how the Air Force actually worked … I didn't really have a full appreciation of the chain of command … and expectations [of the Air Force] was the biggest thing. Then I got to

> BFTS [Basic Flying Training School], and that kind of slapped me in the face a little bit … I'm Italian, so I'm a little fiery by nature, so being told what to do … was quite challenging for me.[5]

Liv did not return to OTS immediately, however; approximately nine months passed. During this interval, she was posted to RAAF Base Williams at Laverton, Victoria, to work in Education Services. While she was frustrated by this at the time, Liv considered it as an opportunity to finish her degree and gain some valued experience in a unit.

After eventually completing both OTS and BFT, Liv was posted to No 2 Flying Training School at RAAF Base Pearce, Western Australia, for a 12-month course of advanced flying techniques. Reflecting on this aspect of her training, she acknowledges that while it was enjoyable, it was also very stressful, and she thinks she may have managed the stress better if she had joined the RAAF when she was a little older. While Liv was supported by her instructors, who were able to guide her through the challenges of the course, she failed at the last hurdle: the final instrument-handling test. She describes her second attempt as 'savage': 'I still remember walking out of that debrief in tears, and that was it.'[6]

Liv's next three months were spent at Pearce before being posted to RAAF Base East Sale, during which time she started the application process for the Australian Army as a helicopter pilot. At East Sale, she worked in an operations role at the Base Command Post. Her time at East Sale:

> Was wonderful because it was exactly what I needed at the time. I needed motivation to stay in the Air Force, because all I cared about at the time was pilot's course. So, it was awesome to see the other side of the Air Force that I hadn't seen.

Twelve months after failing pilot's course, Liv attended an Army board interview in Canberra, and she admits it did not go well. 'I'm not going to lie. I walked out of that interview in tears, again. They shredded me apart.' The Army board advised her she lacked the required leadership skills to be a helicopter pilot.[7]

By this time, Liv had been in the Air Force for around five years and, deflated, she returned to East Sale where she was informed she had to select an alternative career path, or have her appointment terminated. Reluctantly, she commenced the air combat officer (ACO) course, 'just to keep flying'. Liv's experience on the course was not a positive one. 'I hated it … I was expecting it to be somewhat easy, with my pilot's course experience … but I think I took that for granted.' In spite of this, she was determined to pass: '[I knew] I just want to fly [fast] jets … I'm not settling for anything else. So I pushed for that, and I worked hard enough to get a shot.'[8]

On graduation from ACO course, and seven years after joining the RAAF, Liv was promoted to pilot officer. She was posted to No 76 Squadron (76SQN), whose role is to train the RAAF's fighter aircrew on the Hawk 127 'lead-in fighter' aircraft:

> I got extremely sick on the Hawk. I flew twice a day. [I] threw up twice a day … There was a point where I was going to pull the pin on fast jets in general … that's how bad it was.

However, believing in her potential, Liv's flight commander arranged a flight for her in an F/A-18 Hornet, in which she did not experience any nausea. Liv's persistence yet again paid off and, after nearly 12 months at 76SQN, she completed her conversion on the Hawk and was successful in gaining a role on the EA-18G Growler aircraft.[9]

Olivia Salvatore and her instructor 'Cougar' at Naval Air Station Whidbey Island, Washington State, United States. This was Olivia's first flight in an EA-18G Growler aircraft, at the start of her aircraft conversion course (Olivia Little)

Olivia Salvatore and course mate Flight Lieutenant Dan Storey at Naval Air Station Whidbey Island, Washington State, United States. This was Olivia's first crewed Australian flight in an EA-18G Growler aircraft during her aircraft conversion course (Olivia Little)

Liv was posted to No 6 Squadron at RAAF Amberley, Queensland, to prepare for a 16-month conversion course with the United States (US) Navy. The course took her to 'Whidbey Island [in Washington State] for 16 months … [a] beautiful place … the flying was unbelievable'. The only downside was that 'my partner [Kory] wasn't there; he was doing [conversion training on the F/A-18F] on the other side of America.' The pair had met while on ACO course. At the completion of their courses in the US, they returned to Australia to get married and settle into operational life at RAAF Amberley.[10]

Liv was posted to No 6 Squadron (6SQN), which she described as 'awesome'. The unit simply did not stop: 'Everyone wanted a piece of the Growler because it was such a new capability.' Kory was posted to the equally fast-tempo No 1 Squadron, so the pair had very little time to spend together:

> [We spent only] six months [together] out of the 12 in 2019. We just tag-teamed the whole time. He went away. He'd come back. I'd go away. And we could do that; we didn't have kids at the time. It was hard work. Very rewarding. I loved going away, and I love[d] the squadron, and [I] loved the people. It was fantastic.[11]

Nos 6, 33 and 77 Squadrons flying over a Royal Australian Navy convoy during the Regional Presence Deployment, 2020. Flight Lieutenant Olivia Little is in the EA-18G Growler closest to the camera. She considers this deployment one of the highlights of her posting to No 6 Squadron (Department of Defence)

A standout moment for Liv while at 6SQN was returning to where her dream had begun: the airshow at Avalon. 'Standing in front of a Growler was awesome, given that that's what I [had] always wanted to do – go to Avalon – [and] stand in front of my own jet.' It was also a highlight to have '[my] family come up, and see me in uniform … in front of the jet'. Another career highlight was when Liv was awarded a Chief of Air Force Bronze Commendation in 2020.[12]

In 2021, Liv took six months of maternity leave to welcome her daughter Sophia into her and Kory's lives. The pair decided that Kory would continue flying while Liv would move to a ground posting, so she returned to work after maternity leave to No 82 Wing. This provided Liv with a flexible work routine, so she could pick up Sophia from day care and be there for the childhood milestones which she might otherwise have missed if she was away flying. Liv does admit there is quite a balancing act, but her biggest motivator is clear: to be the best person and mother she can be for Sophia. 'I'm a Mum … Mum comes first now.'[13]

Olivia Little with her daughter Sophia, Anzac Day 2023 (Olivia Little)

Sergeant Brodie Stewart

Loadmaster

Place of birth: Rockhampton, Queensland
Date of enlistment: 2 October 2012

My service life has developed me in ways I couldn't even imagine. If you would've asked me 10 years ago, do I think I would be a Sergeant Loadmaster who has deployed four times and done humanitarian and disaster relief [missions] all over the world, I would have laughed. My personal growth over the last 10 years has been incredible. I have always had a [strong] work ethic and a desire to be the best. My ability to take feedback and adapt is a strength. I think resilience is the key trait that has assisted me in my career.[1]

Sergeant Brodie Stewart during her loadmaster conversion course (Brodie Stewart)

When she was growing up in Rockhampton, Queensland (Qld), the idea of joining the Air Force was not even a remote consideration for Brodie Stewart. Her mother Katheryn was a single parent who worked hard to provide for Brodie and her two sisters, while studying at the same time. Brodie recalls it was her mother who demonstrated that hard work and the courage to try something new would be the key to achieving her goals:

> My Mum has three degrees now – journalism, criminology and law – and then she went into the Police Force. She said to me, 'I can't look back on life and think I did a job I hated for years: I kept challenging myself and opening new doors. That's what life's about.' So my Mum set a good example from childhood.[2]

Brodie's main focus from the age of eight was cycling. She first fell in love with the sport while watching a race at the Rockhampton velodrome:

> 'Rocky' actually produces some of the best cyclists ever – Anna Meares is from Rockhampton. My sister was actually dating a junior world champion from the track and we went to watch him on the velodrome one day and I was like, 'I want to do that.'[3]

With that, she got on a bike in board shorts and started pedalling. She moved with her mother, stepfather and sisters to Brisbane at age nine, where she raced on the velodrome and in road events. Schoolwork and up to 600 kilometres a week of cycling proved challenging. To fit in her riding, she would train from 4 o'clock in the morning on her own:

> Mum was petrified I'd get hit by a car so [she] and my stepdad would drive their car or ride a scooter behind me for two-and-a-half hours. And on a Saturday, I'd do an eight-hour ride up through the mountains. They'd give up their Saturdays to drive behind me. So that was the kind of support that I got.[4]

By the time Brodie was 16, she had represented both her state and Australia in velodrome and time-trial racing. Her accolades included 100 state junior titles and 20 national titles, and she was identified as being on the pathway to represent Australia at the London Olympic Games. However, the sudden death of one of her sisters, a subsequent departure to the United States (US) to race, then a move to Perth in Western Australia to continue with her cycling, was too much for Brodie. At the age of 17, she was away from family support, training for long hours, and trying to complete her Year 12 schooling:

> I was burnt out, and it was a shock [to others] when I pulled the pin [on cycling]. That was a challenging time for me, transitioning out of high school and sport life, because I was a little bit lost, which most people are at that age.[5]

Brodie moved back to Brisbane after finishing Year 12 and for two years she worked odd jobs to pay the bills. It was her mother who suggested she consider joining the military. Brodie began to research options. '[I thought] I'd give it a crack. I thought if the military is not for me, at least I can get a trade.'[6] She initially applied as a diesel mechanic in the Army:

> I had zero idea about cars, but I always wanted to challenge gender norms and decided I could do it, despite having no experience apart from working on my bicycle.[7]

However, Brodie was knocked back by the Army because she has tattoos on her hands. Instead, the Air Force offered her a position as a ground support equipment fitter and, within a few months, she was on her way to No 1 Recruit Training Unit (1RTU) at RAAF Base Wagga Wagga, New South Wales:

> Someone was looking out for me that day, because [the RAAF] was definitely the Service for me. When I joined, I was wearing Doc Martins [boots], I had a lip piercing and did not fit the mould whatsoever. I say now when I'm in my job [with Defence Force Recruiting (DFR)], that there is not a mould for what Defence looks for. You just have to have a bit of drive and self-belief.[8]

Brodie laughs as she recalls her time at 1RTU:

> I had no idea. It was actually a bit of a shock to me – I couldn't understand why [the instructors] were yelling at me. I was told that they had 'Googled' me, and knew what I was capable of. And then I just started to go above and beyond and actually put a lot of effort in.[9]

After graduating, Brodie was posted to her Initial Employment Training (IET) at Latchford Barracks in Bandiana, Victoria, an Army training organisation:

> My naivety is I didn't realise I was going there. When I was at recruits, we were looking at a map of all the Air Force bases. I put my hand up and I said, 'Oh, excuse me, Corporal, there's no Latchford Barracks on here – that's where I'm doing my IET.' He said, 'That's an Army base, good luck with that.'[10]

Brodie was one of approximately 300 trainees at Latchford Barracks, who were all working at different phases in workshops to complete their trade. She was one of the few females in that group, although she recalled her ability to communicate and make friends easily helped her feel like she 'fitted in'. However, not all of her experiences with her fellow trainees or instructors were positive. She was subjected to discrimination due to being gay and said there was still a view that women were not capable of carrying out so-called traditional male job roles. Brodie's view is that her negative experiences 'carried me a long way in my career for resilience and a [strong] work ethic as well'.[11]

After receiving her trade qualification three months ahead of the 18-month schedule, Brodie was posted to RAAF Amberley, Qld. She was disappointed to find her role was not focused on working on vehicles, but on changing filters, and defuelling and refuelling aircraft tankers. When she saw the types of aircraft on the flight line (runway), including the C-17 Globemaster, she thought:

> How do I get on that aircraft? I didn't even know what jobs the RAAF had apart from mine. I was told that there were people on the C-17 aircraft called 'Loadmasters' and I started to do my research … I had a book – it covered all the aircraft specifics – *Women, Peace, and Security*, anything and everything that I thought they could throw at me, it was in there.

Despite resistance from her immediate chain of command due to her junior rank and lack of experience, Brodie started researching the option of transferring to the loadmaster specialisation. It was just the challenge she was after. Integral to a transport aircraft, a loadmaster's main responsibilities include: coordinating the loading and airborne monitoring of cargo loads, ensuring they are configured for safe weight distribution; managing and facilitating airdrops; managing passengers; and liaising with the teams who provide cargo and loads.

Leading Aircraftwoman Brodie Stewart representing the Australian Defence Force in rugby union (Brodie Stewart)

Before sitting her loadmaster interview board, Brodie prepared by sitting a mock board which was run by loadmasters and logistics officers she had met at Amberley. She was successful on her first attempt and was informed of the decision while she was playing rugby for the ADF in the US. On her return to Australia, she packed up her belongings and headed for RAAF Base Richmond, west of Sydney, to start her initial qualification and the prerequisite courses needed for her new role. These courses included a combat-survival course in Townsville, where students were put through a series of challenges to test their ability to survive in any circumstance. Although a self-professed 'glamping gal', Brodie enjoyed the challenge, although she drew the line at catching and eating toads:

> [The instructors had] a little toad on a leash. [They] just jammed a knife in its back and all the poisons started coming out, 'And then you can eat the legs.' And in my head I was like, 'I can go without food. I'm not going to be that desperate. I'm not going to be that hungry.'[12]

After completing all of her prerequisite courses, Brodie commenced her loadmaster conversion course. Having spent her initial mechanic training in a male-dominated environment, Brodie found herself on a loadmaster course of three, all of whom were women. She was the only so-called 'retread' (an existing Air Force member who is remustering to a new specialisation). She recalled how she faced a significant challenge in going straight into an informal leadership role as a newly promoted sergeant, with course mates who had no previous experience in the Air Force:

> It was very challenging, yet rewarding. I loved every moment of it. At times, I couldn't believe that this was going to be my job. I have a framed photo that was taken on my first flight during training; it was over the water with the ramp open. I still think back to that moment. I hadn't studied much since school, so the theory components really required dedication, which I loved. It sparked my desire to study.[13]

Brodie remembers receiving her loadmaster aircrew brevet as one of the highlights of her career:

> It was something I worked really hard for, and I was sacrificing a fair bit. To have my Mum and my stepdad there to share it with them; it was a super proud moment.[14]

Sergeant Brodie Stewart receiving the Dux of the loadmaster conversion course, with her mother Katheryn and stepfather Jim (Brodie Stewart)

On posting to the C-130J Hercules at No 37 Squadron, Brodie hardly had a chance to settle in before she was sent to the Middle East for an aircraft swap, quickly followed by a humanitarian response to a disaster in Papua New Guinea:

> We'd be delivering water or rice, but they didn't have forklifts, so we would be hand offloading 30,000 pounds of cargo and you'd just be in a pool of sweat. But you'd look at the locals, and give the kids Life Savers [sweets], and see how excited they were … the one thing I've found as being aircrew is you have to be adaptable. You can't have in your head, 'this is the way it's going to go', because nine times out of ten, it's a completely different plan.[15]

Brodie spent the majority of the next few years on back-to-back deployments, including several to Al Minhad Air Base (AMAB) near Dubai, in the United Arab Emirates, in support of operations throughout the Middle East. She recalls her first four-month deployment in 2017, during which she was away for Christmas. She flew throughout Afghanistan and Iraq, delivering different loads and having to improvise if equipment was not built correctly. 'I was just like a little kid at Christmas there. I was so excited.'[16]

Sergeant Brodie Stewart (centre) at Al Minhad Air Base, United Arab Emirates (Brodie Stewart)

Her second deployment to AMAB in 2020 rammed home the very real dangers faced by serving members overseas. Brodie's friend Sarah, a medic in the Army, was deployed to Taji in Iraq when the area was targeted by 26 rockets. While all Australians were safe, a number of allied serving men and women were killed. Brodie's crew flew over to evacuate some ADF personnel, before eventually redeploying the entirety of the ADF element from the area:

> This deployment was a turning point for me ... it opened my eyes a lot ... and changed a few ways I looked at things. Speaking to Sarah when she got back and hearing her story ... seeing how much it affected my friend.[17]

Towards the end of her Middle East deployment in early 2020, the COVID-19 pandemic shut down the globe. However, the RAAF's Air Mobility Group and C-130 tasking continued. Brodie and her crewmembers found themselves in some form of quarantine before or after each task for the next 18 months, as Defence missions increased in support of local communities, while still maintaining operational deployment tasks overseas. In August 2021, not long after returning from yet another Middle East deployment, Brodie was asked to turn around again to support the evacuation of Australians, Afghans and other affected people from Kabul after the Taliban organisation regained power in Afghanistan:

> The moment I landed [in the Middle East], everything was just like this [well-] oiled machine. Every cog was turning and it was working together so well ... [But] When I flew in [to Hamid Karzai Airport in Kabul] it was completely different. I still remember seeing the Taliban up on the towers around the flight line. And I was thinking, 'This is not the same airfield.'[18]

Brodie recalled the sheer volume of aircraft at the airport, all being loaded with evacuating passengers. Up to 200 people were being led onto her C-130, all 'combat loaded' (when people sit directly on the floor of the aircraft to increase the number of passengers the aircraft can carry):

> The aircraft was that packed that I had an old guy – I was sitting in the para[troop] door – and he was just cuddled up around my legs; he had his arms around my legs and was sleeping. Mothers had babies and they were passing the babies to be held because they didn't have the room on the ground.[19]

The memory of being a part of a unified effort and seeing the operation come together under very dangerous circumstances will stay with Brodie for a very long time. After that operation, for the first time in five years in her role, she felt fatigued. Her job shifted towards an instructor role, where she could spend time at home. Never one to slow down, Brodie started a degree in psychology, and decided a break away from a flying squadron was in order. She was posted to DFR in Melbourne to be closer to her fiancée Bek, while considering whether to return to flying. While she admitted to enjoying a break from flying, she misses being a part of a crew on missions:

> I miss being a part of something that is meaningful [flying operations] ... what I experience, and being a part of, it really gives you a sense of accomplishment and achievement and community with like-minded people. And I genuinely miss it.[20]

When asked to reflect on the major changes she has witnessed during her 10 years in the Air Force, Brodie believed the changes in how the LGBTQ+ community has been treated has been significant:

> I identify as a lesbian, and I had a hard time early on in my career, being discriminated against for my sexuality, [which is] something that has shaped me today to stand up and be a voice for people who aren't as comfortable [with standing up]. I also had negative comments about being given handouts for being a female. [But] I believe the culture has come a long way since I enlisted. The zero tolerance of unacceptable behaviour and the training and education has been key. I love the initiatives offered for women. I am a big advocate for women in Defence, which is my passion at Defence Force Recruiting. I always ask myself, 'Would I want my daughter or partner to join the military? If no, why?' For me, I would; I feel as an organisation we have come a long way.[21]

Sergeant Brodie Stewart (second from left) with former Minister for Foreign Affairs, Julie Bishop, and Royal Australian Air Force colleagues (Brodie Stewart)

At the time of writing, Brodie planned to finalise her psychology degree while spending time with Bek. In the future, she sees her psychology degree as being useful to understanding people and enhancing her ability to manage and lead in the future. Brodie's contribution to our current-day Air Force remains reflective of her resilience, talent and a willingness to give anything a go – just like her mother demonstrated.

Flight Lieutenant Dani Cornish (née Jorgensen)

Logistics Officer

Place of birth: Numurkah, Victoria
Date of enlistment: 20 January 2013

> It is one of those career paths where you can never truly predict what can happen and what is within the art of the possible.[1]

Officer Cadet Dani Jorgensen receiving the Chief of Air Force Prize from Air Marshal Gavin 'Leo' Davies during her graduation from the Australian Defence Force Academy, Canberra, Australian Capital Territory, 2015 (John Carroll)

Dani Cornish feels she is a 'bit boring' as she recounts her childhood and the 11 years she has served so far in the RAAF. However, her experience of spending five years on a remote Air Force base in Western Australia (WA) is anything but average.

Dani spent the first four years of her life in Waaia, a tiny town of approximately 400 people, surrounded by dairy farms. She moved to Shepparton, Victoria, with her parents and younger sister at age four, when her father started up a marine business. From the age of 13, Dani grew up on acreage, learning to ride and developing a love for horses:

> We were a relatively busy family – if the weekend wasn't filled with a horse event, it would be spent out on the boat fishing, or exploring at our little holiday cabin near Eildon [in the Alpine region of Victoria]. [In] later years, summers were spent water skiing – the perk of owning a boat business![2]

During high school, Dani had not gravitated towards any specific career path. Her friends all had firm ideas of what they wanted to study at university but, for Dani, it was not as clear. It was her mother who suggested she consider the Air Force, despite knowing little, if anything, about the ADF. Dani was initially drawn to 'the idea of the RAAF' for opportunities in humanitarian aid and disaster relief, as well as job variety and travel:

> I quite literally rocked up to the 'You' Session [held by Defence Force Recruiting] with little clue of what [I wanted to do], just that I wanted to join. I recall this so vividly as it was definitely one of those 'sliding door' moments. Once I completed the aptitude test, they asked if I wanted to do the other test for 'ADFA [Australian Defence Force Academy] entry'. Again, I had absolutely no idea what ADFA was! I said 'yes' anyway, and did the test.[3]

After she received her aptitude-test results, she was given a handful of brochures on ADFA and went home to speak to her parents about her options. Much to her mother's delight, Dani discovered that joining through ADFA meant being paid a salary while she completed her degree in Canberra, with no Higher Education Contribution Scheme fees (the deferred payment scheme for university education). She chose to apply for logistics officer, purely with the intention of 'getting my foot in the door', liking the variety of jobs she could complete as a 'Loggy'.[4]

Dani laughed when recounting her Officer Selection Board experience, during which she interviewed for both logistics officer and intelligence officer. She believed she had failed miserably at her logistics entry, and made the decision not to sit for her intelligence officer entry:

> I had so little clue of military terminology that I recall … being asked if I cared what colour I wore, and I answered with, 'no, not at all' – thinking it was an odd question to be asked about clothing. It did not register that I was being asked about what Service [I wanted] to join … I was adamant that I only wanted to join the RAAF and had no interest in the other Services. Only years after, did I twig on to what this question meant![5]

Not long after completing her Year 12 studies, Dani boarded a bus to Canberra to start her Air Force training and her university degree at ADFA. Her first impression was not a positive one:

> I transitioned terribly. I remember it was the first night, I called Mum and said, 'Mum, I want to come home, there's nobody like me here.' I felt very much like I was somewhere where they spoke a foreign language and I didn't fit in. The majority of those in my Division [of 42 single rooms] or Class [one of three years] had some sort of military influence, either coming from a family where parents or siblings [had] served, or they had gone to Air Force Cadets [during high school].[6]

Dani recalled she was the only one from her graduating school year to have joined the military, and she had no immediate family members who were serving, to share their experiences. It took her a long time to understand the environment, such as the rank structure, how to address personnel, and how to focus on her development as a future leader of the RAAF:

> I often felt like people judged me and thought I was dumb so, naturally, I started to feel that I was. I think it was because I was slower to transition from civilian life and mould into an officer that I wasn't taken seriously. I gave myself a little reality check and, instead of having the judgement read true, I chose to prove them wrong and be the best I could be – this feeling of having to prove myself has stayed with me throughout my career and has been a major source of my inner-motivation in every role I've undertaken.

Despite her hesitant start, Dani's determination and capacity to excel meant she completed her three-year Bachelor of Business degree with high marks. She was also awarded the coveted Chief of Air Force Prize at her graduation parade; this is awarded to the trainee officer who demonstrates the most outstanding performance in academic and military achievement, leadership, personal example and service ethos during their time at ADFA.

After graduating, Dani was posted to RAAF Base Townsville, Queensland, to No 383 Contingency Response Squadron (383CRS), a unit whose sole focus is to provide support to military elements in deployed locations. She said the opportunities she was presented with during that posting were 'pretty astounding, in hindsight'.[7] Her roles included travelling to RAAF Base Curtin in WA to prepare the base for its first major exercise after it had long been used as an immigration detention centre. She also deployed to Papua New Guinea (PNG) under Operation *Hannah*, the ADF's contribution to Australia's support to the PNG national elections in 2017. She was part of a task force that assisted the PNG Government to distribute voting material and supplies to remote areas of the country. Her final deployment with the squadron was as part of Operation *Accordion* to a base in the United Arab Emirates (UAE), in support of Australia's deployed forces throughout the Middle East. She was in charge of the Logistics Support Flight, providing logistical support to all RAAF air- and ground-based elements.

Flying Officer Dani Jorgensen meeting local villagers while she was deployed to Papua New Guinea in support of Operation *Hannah*, 2017 (Dani Cornish)

During her posting to 383CRS, Dani met her husband Adam, a fellow RAAFie. She recalled that, at the time, it was seen as rather scandalous, with her a first-year flying officer and Adam a sergeant, both working in the same small unit.

Flying Officer Dani Jorgensen and Sergeant Adam Cornish in Townsville, Queensland, Anzac Day 2018 (Dani Cornish)

> We maintained a very professional relationship, I was 'Ma'am' at work, which didn't hinder us being on exercises together, performing our individual roles to contribute to the unit. I don't know whether many back then would have envisaged that we would last – [that we would] end up married, [go] down the IVF route and have a baby together.

Dani and Adam ended up deploying to the Middle East at the same time, although they were in separate locations within the UAE.

Flight Lieutenant Dani Jorgensen at the Sheik Zayed Grand Mosque while deployed to the Middle East Area of Operations, 2018 (Dani Cornish)

On her return from deployment, Dani was posted to a unit that resided at RAAF Base Richmond in New South Wales. However, Adam was earmarked for the base site-manager position at RAAF Base Curtin, a designated 'bare base', located approximately 170 kilometres southeast of Broome in Western Australia, and only activated during major exercises and other activities. Rather than living and working on opposite sides of the country, Dani was approved to work remotely from Curtin, an option that would not have been available as recently as 20 years ago. She said her circumstances were mutually beneficial to her and Adam, and to the organisation, with the site-manager position being difficult to fill due to the required skill set, and a small pool from which to draw. Likewise, the Air Force is unable to currently fill all required positions for junior logistics officers. Dani's memories of Curtin were typical of the Australian outback landscape: dry and hot, with red dirt. She found herself going from an environment on deployment where everyone was 'in each other's pockets, to a bare base [with a] total [of] four people, with one of those being my husband – it did take some adjustment.'[8] RAAF Base Curtin is one of just three bare bases in Australia.

Flight Lieutenant Dani Cornish (left) in the back of a United States Marine Corps Osprey tiltrotor aircraft over Derby, Western Australia (Dani Cornish)

Flight Lieutenant Dani Cornish and other Royal Australian Air Force members with children from the Western Australia Police Youth Program, Derby, 2019 (Dani Cornish)

Dani spent four years working in the C-27J Spartan asset-management unit, focusing on the 'through life support' contract to ensure the small airlift transport aircraft had the items and systems it needed to keep flying. She said she is extremely proud of her contribution to the capability, and confesses to being 'overly protective' of the aircraft's image, noting it has been criticised as having limited utility in the RAAF:

> I am hugely proud of my contributions [to the] C-27J and what we were able to achieve: turning the Spartan from [a] 'lemon' to a key contributing platform in bushfire and flood efforts. It was hard for me to let go, come [my new] posting.[9]

Dani believed being posted to a bare base made her one of the luckiest RAAF members in the organisation, and she takes great pride in representing the Air Force within the local Kimberley community:

> We have been able to shift the attitude of the Air Force from … being the white elephant, when RAAF Base Curtin operated as the Immigration Centre, to role models [which] Kimberley youth seek out. By getting involved in local community events and taking school groups on Defence excursions, the Air Force is now seen as an enabler and almost like an outlet for a better life, if pursued. A lot of the youth don't know what to do career-wise, and we are showing them there's opportunity beyond Derby.[10]

Flight Lieutenant Dani Cornish (front row, second from right), her husband Adam (back row, second from right) and other Australian Defence Force members, with Years 10–12 students from Derby District High School, aboard HMAS *Anzac*. The group were on a week-long Defence tour in Perth, Western Australia (Dani Cornish)

In early 2023, Dani started in a new remote posting in support of the Defence logistics enterprise, while waiting to commence maternity leave. Their son, Cooper, was born on 2 March 2023, after a lengthy period in a local Broome hospital due to complications she experienced while pregnant. Dani wanted to acknowledge the support she and Adam received from the ADF health organisation during their efforts to have a child through its IVF program:

> Our IVF was covered completely: the jabs, sperm retrieval, egg collection and embryo transfer. I cannot actually explain in words the gratitude I feel for this as, unlike many others, we didn't have the financial burden to deal with on top of the IVF stress.[11]

Flight Lieutenant Dani Cornish with her husband Flight Sergeant Adam Cornish and son Cooper, Anzac Day 2023 (Dani Cornish)

The couple now face the challenge of how to manage their careers in the Air Force as parents of a young child, in a remote location which has limited posting opportunities. Dani recently decided to forego a promotion, as it would have meant having to move interstate with Cooper and leaving Adam at Curtin to manage their newly purchased property and look after their pets (including a needy dog called Bear, an adopted butcher bird called Butch, two horses, and Keith the bullock, who walked across the apparently impassable cattlegrid at the front gate at Curtin and has remained ever since). While she aims to remain full-time in the Air Force and work in a remote role for as long as she can, Dani conceded that, at some point, she may have to transfer from full-time service to a part-time Reserve role. Given their love for the local community, with Adam wanting to serve with the local government in future, a move interstate to further their Air Force career aspirations is not currently on the cards:

> I think my dedication for the RAAF may be questioned because of our situation; however, I would argue it's the opposite. We are so invested in RAAF Base Curtin and what it has to offer. Because we have been here coming up to five years, we have become the face of RAAF Base Curtin like it is our own 'train set' that we advocate for on behalf of Air Force. We are genuinely interested in the development of the Kimberley region, specifically Derby – Minister for Defence visits, the outcomes of the Defence Strategic Review, potential dry-dock facilities, tidal power initiatives – all [are] unique opportunities to be part of, [which] the standard Defence member[s] posted to other bases aren't privy to.[12]

In the meantime, Dani will focus on returning to remote work, looking after her young family, and representing the RAAF in a community in which she has put down strong roots. She believes service in the Air Force is about contributing to a 'greater purpose', and she continues to advocate for the Air Force as a meaningful profession. Her advice to those considering joining is to just give it a go:

> If you don't try it, you will never know what could have been. Just because you [may] feel like you don't fit in, aren't like the others, [or] aren't as well versed in military jargon, that is perfectly okay, and you don't actually need to be.[13]

Leading Aircraftwoman Kate Clarkson (née Lutkins)

Personnel Capability Specialist

Place of birth: Brisbane, Queensland
Date of enlistment: 2 September 2014

The harder you work, the more you're going to achieve, especially within a team.[1]

Kate Clarkson after the Australian Football League Women's grand final, 2021. Kate won a premiership medal for the Brisbane Lions' win and received the 'Best on Ground' award (Kate Clarkson)

Kate Clarkson spent her childhood years on a small hobby farm at Rosewood, west of Ipswich in Queensland, creating games with her younger brother Michael and spending as much time as possible 'running amok' outdoors:

> We'd ride our bikes around the telegraph pole in the middle of the front yard for hours on end while being chased by the goat we'd fondly named 'Butthead', because that's what she liked to do with us.[2]

Kate and her brother Michael on a hay bale (Kate Clarkson)

After 10 years on the farm, Kate moved with her mother, a veterinarian, and brother to the suburb of Karalee, next to Ipswich itself – a stone's throw from where she is currently posted at RAAF Amberley. Throughout her school years, Kate competed in as many athletics, cross-country and swimming events as she could, and was involved in numerous team sports, including touch football, soccer, hockey, cricket, tennis and futsal. Her athleticism and skill on the sporting field was recognised early, and she represented Australia while still in her teens for futsal, competing overseas in two international competitions after she finished school. She loved the speed and high intensity of futsal, and the fact it is a small-team sport.

While Kate excelled at sport throughout her teenage years, her school experience was not as positive. She experienced depression and anxiety, and changed schools a number of times:

> During my adolescence, I dealt with things in a not-so-healthy way. I was diagnosed with depression and anxiety, and partook in self-harm. Due to this part of my past,

> I put a career with the ADF in the back of my mind and didn't pursue it until many years after I finished school. I had gone out and essentially lived my life in every [positive] way I could ... to ensure that when they said 'no' due to those reasons, I had an argument [that I could be of value to the ADF]. I went out, played a lot of sport, held down two jobs for decent periods of time, and was a good employee.[3]

Kate Clarkson (left) representing Australia in the Futsal World Cup in Colombia, 2013 (Kate Clarkson)

After working part-time at Woolworths (supermarket) during her later school years, her brother suggested she interview for a position as an animal technician at The University of Queensland, which would involve looking after animals as part of research projects. A self-described animal lover, Kate enjoyed looking after the animals' welfare and being involved in as many aspects of the research facility as she could:

> Woolworths and that job both enabled me to play as much sport as I wanted. They were great jobs that I thoroughly enjoyed, and allowed me the flexibility for sport at night and on weekends. Some weekends I was playing three games of sport – AFL [Australian Football League], soccer, and Gaelic.[4]

Kate's exposure to AFL during her school years consisted of playing only one game. It was later on, when she was working, that her contacts from futsal and soccer asked her to come and train at a local club in Brisbane. She was immediately impressed with the camaraderie and team atmosphere:

> [I] felt welcomed, even though no one knew who I was – I felt a part of the team already ... there's so much involved with the game and it was so easy to fall in love with [it] ... I kept going back, and the rest is history.[5]

After several years of working her two jobs and playing numerous team sports at amateur level, in 2013, Kate decided to seriously consider joining the ADF. While she had discovered her grandfather had served in the Royal Air Force (RAF) as a pilot during the Second World War, Kate was only focused on joining the Army. She recalled a memory of watching Army trucks travelling on the highway between Brisbane and the Sunshine Coast when she was a child:

> On reflection, it was really interesting, because I knew my grandad [had been] in the RAF, but I didn't know much about the Air Force beyond that. I didn't really know much about the Navy but, for me, it was an interest in the Army as that's what I'd been exposed to growing up. I guess I was inspired by what I could see, and that was Army trucks driving up and down the highway, so that led me to join the Army. As a civilian, I didn't know how many jobs and opportunities were out there.[6]

It was important to Kate to be transparent in her application to join, accepting that her history of mental-health struggles could affect her chances. After an initial knockback and working through the appeals process, Kate was finally accepted into the Army after 15 months. She ended up being accepted into the Transport Corps, and travelled to Kapooka, near Wagga Wagga in New South Wales, to commence her recruit training in September 2014. She recalled she 'quite enjoyed' the experience by the end:

> I thought it was going to be a lot worse. I just thought it would be stricter and tougher … being 26, I just wanted to get in, do the right thing, listen, learn and pass assessments, really.[7]

Kate's aim was to 'remain grey' (blending in with the crowd) while at Kapooka and at her Initial Employment Training (IET) at Puckapunyal in Victoria. She used her team skills to help others, in an attempt to keep the attention off herself, admitting she does not enjoy being the centre of attention:

> I think I enjoy team sport so much because it is about being the best as a group and everyone working together, to enable each other to achieve a common goal.[8]

However, Kate's drive to do her best, and the enjoyment of pushing herself out of her comfort zone, especially physically, meant she stood out. She received the Physical Training award at recruit training and Soldier of Merit during her transport training:

> I did go in and try and remain grey … but this did not work out! I aimed for 'head down, bum up', to work hard both individually and help others where I could.[9]

By the time Kate had applied to join the Army in 2013, she had been playing club AFL in Brisbane for a number of years, with the Australian Football League Women's (AFLW) still a number of years from formation. In that year, Kate was selected to play for the Western Bulldogs, and played the first exhibition match between the Bulldogs and the Demons in Melbourne, but was delisted: 'Dropped on my bum, given a few tips to get better and I worked on doing that.'[10]

On graduation from Puckapunyal in 2015, Kate was originally posted to Townsville in north Queensland, however was able to swap to a role at 2/14 Light Horse Regiment at Enoggera in Brisbane. She believed if this posting change had not occurred, she would not have had the AFL career she has had. She was drafted to the Brisbane Lions in 2016 and played in the first AFLW official season in 2017. Kate recalled that, in the early years, the sport was considered part-time. While a significant impost on her time, Kate managed to balance work (including significant periods away on exercise) with training and playing AFLW and competing in a season that went for a relatively short eight weeks.

Kate Clarkson (right) with good friend and rival Heather Anderson and Forces Commander Major General Fergus McLachlan, 2017. Kate was representing the Brisbane Lions and Heather was representing the Adelaide Crows in the Australian Football League Women's inaugural season (Kate Clarkson)

While the league continued to rapidly professionalise, with longer seasons and a stronger focus on training and conditioning, Kate was posted to another unit at Enoggera. Despite still successfully fulfilling her job role, deploying in support of the government's response to the COVID-19 pandemic, and being promoted to lance corporal, there was some tension between her and her chain of command, with a misapprehended view that her sporting career would somehow interfere with her service:

> I don't at all take anything for granted, or think I have a right to play AFL instead of [doing] my duty for Defence … I'm a Defence member and I serve my country.[11]

With a deteriorating professional relationship at work, Kate applied for a secondment to Defence Force Recruiting and, while there, she applied for a service transfer to the RAAF. After some toing and froing, and a requirement to resubmit her transfer paperwork, Kate was successful, coming across to the Air Force as a personnel capability specialist (PCS). She credits the support of a number of serving women, including the ADF AFLW coach, in helping her to navigate the process. 'I knew that eventually I would most likely have to choose between the ADF and AFL. Thank goodness it wasn't quite time yet.'[12] It would have been a hard decision to make as Kate was excelling on the field as her Air Force career developed. She was awarded the Brisbane Lions' 'Most Courageous Award' in 2017, won 'Best and Fairest' at the club in 2018 and, by 2021, had been selected three times in the All Australian Football League Women's team.

Kate was interested in a number of Air Force roles but chose PCS because she 'quite enjoys paperwork – I know that sounds weird!'[13] She was also seeking a more flexible role, with her wife's Army career likely to require them to move them interstate, and a job that was not as physically demanding on her body. (Kate has suffered a number of injuries during her playing career, including an anterior cruciate ligament tear during the first round of the 2022 AFLW season, just prior to starting her first posting in the RAAF.)

While a relative newcomer to the Air Force, Kate noted a number of differences, both culturally and organisationally, between the RAAF and Army:

> The size of a team can influence the culture that is generated. In Army, I was part of bigger teams, or teams within teams, and this often led to a culture shaped by multiple personalities. When I transferred to the RAAF, I found myself part of a much smaller team. I was immediately welcomed into this team and judged for my ability to do my job and communicate as a 'human'. By being part of such a small team, you are forced almost to respect each other, as you know you have to work together; otherwise the task will be too insurmountable.[14]

She also noticed the difference in the adherence to a hierarchical structure:

> In the Army, your maturity is judged by the rank you wear … In the Air Force, I have found I've been respected for my age and experience, and trusted to make an educated opinion or action.[15]

She sees a number of parallels between serving in the ADF and playing elite team sport. Both require mutual trust, respect and teamwork to properly function:

> As a team, you rely on each other; there's a common goal and you're all striving towards that common goal and common objective. If you're not on the same page, or not going in the same direction, you're not going to get there as a team, and it's going to fall apart.[16]

Kate Clarkson and her wife, Kate, with the Australian Football League Women's premiership cup, 2021 (Kate Clarkson)

Kate Clarkson and her wife prior to marching in Brisbane, Queensland, Anzac Day 2023 (Kate Clarkson)

In early 2023, Kate completed her IET for PCS, and has recently been focusing on a new role with her wife: that of mother. They are now the proud parents of a little girl, born in October 2023. In the lead up to the birth, and during her time on maternity leave, Kate was planning to be involved with the Brisbane Lions as much as possible. She also plans to assist the head coach with the ADF women's team, wanting to pass on her knowledge and experience to help develop the standard and skills of the team. If her body allows, she wants to come back to AFLW to give one more season of AFLW a 'red hot crack':

> My goal is to play again, however, I know that may not happen. Either way, I have had the incredible opportunity of playing and being involved in the AFLW for almost a decade, and I'm very grateful for this.[17]

Leading Aircraftwoman Emma Gall

Explosive Detection Dog Handler

Place of birth: Gosford, New South Wales
Date of enlistment: 30 January 2018

Dogs are such an incredible capability, and I don't think people realise how much work goes into it.[1]

Leading Aircraftwoman Emma Gall with her Explosive Detection Dog, Ash, Anzac Day 2023 (Emma Gall)

Her upbringing near Gosford on the Central Coast of New South Wales (NSW) was anything but conventional for Emma Gall. Her parents separated when she was very young and, along with her older sister, Emma alternated staying with each parent throughout her childhood and school years. Her mother focused on animal rescue and rehabilitation during

Emma's childhood and, at one stage, assisted in running a brumby (wild horse) conservation program. Her father was a caretaker of a theme park and remained behind as the manager of the property after it closed. Time with her father meant living in a shed which had been converted into a home, where she helped out with ground maintenance, riding dirt bikes and exploring the old theme park grounds.

Emma recalled always having rescue cats and dogs at home, which her mother would foster, then rehome. She believes that much of her natural affinity with animals, particularly with dogs, comes from always being surrounded by animals when she was growing up. While Emma and her sister frequently moved between their parents' places, her grandmother was the constant in her early life:

> When my parents wouldn't attend an event because they thought the other was going, my nanna always stepped up to the plate. She is an extremely kind and generous woman, and one of my biggest role models.[2]

Emma had a challenging school period; while academically gifted, in her primary school years she felt 'a bit odd and out of place'.[3] In high school, she focused less on her academic work, but found herself surrounded by supportive friends during some challenging personal times. At the end of high school, Emma recalled she was overwhelmed by the number of options for careers, but knew she wanted to focus on work that would give her travel opportunities:

> I remember I was sitting in my room one day, fretting about it. And my sister's friend came over. She said, 'I'm doing the Navy Gap Year, and it's so good.' I thought, 'I don't want to be at home anymore; I really want to travel, but the money I have isn't going to work.' So I was just like, 'Okay, I guess I'll try for Defence.'[4]

Emma went on the Defence Force Recruiting website that night and applied to undertake an aptitude session. 'I looked at all the jobs and I thought, there's so many, these all look amazing, I didn't know this was a thing.'[5] Within a few months, Emma sat a range of aptitude and other tests, and her results opened up a number of different options for her to select from. She picked the RAAF Airbase Protection gap year and, not long after completing Year 12, she travelled to Wagga Wagga, NSW, to undertake recruit training. Emma recalled that while her upbringing had been unconventional, many of her father's habits, in particular, set her up for success while she was undergoing initial training:

> My Dad would say that, 'You've got to work for it; it doesn't just happen. You've got to have that self-discipline.' My spontaneity comes from my Mum, but the discipline, the hard work, comes from my Dad.[6]

She admitted, however, that her perfectionist nature added to her anxiety while she was on course. On graduation from recruit training, Emma was posted to RAAF Amberley, west of Brisbane, where she commenced her Airbase Protection Initial Employment Training. The course lasted 10 weeks and Emma recalled it was very physically demanding. But despite being exhausted, she continually thought of the positives – one being meals! 'I thought,

"I'm getting a consistent pay cheque, I'm getting free food and getting taught cool things." I loved it.'[7]

Given that one of her aims was to travel, Emma nominated to go to RAAF Base Pearce, just north of Perth, for the remainder of her gap year. However, on arrival, she was placed on shift, patrolling and carrying out basic security tasks. She recalled struggling with the transition, noting that up until that time she had been physically and mentally challenged while training. Despite being disappointed about what she considered to be more mundane jobs, she decided to sign on for further service after her gap year, and was posted to RAAF Base Richmond, on the outskirts of Sydney. Her intent was to look for alternative employment, while being only an hour away from home. One of her sergeants at the security section, Sergeant Hiagi 'Pete' Mario, took her under his wing and introduced her to the military working dog (MWD) capability and the training it entailed. She was teamed with a training dog called Mason, and admitted she 'fell in love' and started to help with his training:

> I immediately became enamoured by it. I was involved in dog work on shift with my colleagues and would walk one of the training dogs every day with my sergeant (even on days off) ... I was constantly pestering them, asking them questions [and I knew], 'Yes, I've finally found what I want to do.'[8]

She resolved to apply as a military working dog handler (MWDH) with the idea of being able to continue her training with Mason. However, after she returned from a language course, Emma was devastated to find Mason had been sent to another RAAF base. She was, in her own words, 'crushed'. While wondering what she should do next, Emma opened an email seeking expressions of interest in training to be an explosive detection dog handler (EDDH). She was intrigued by the different training aspects of the EDDH specialisation, as she had not been previously exposed to it. It meant completing a nine-month course at an Army barracks in south Sydney, as the capability was initially an Army one, and she would be expected to spend three to four years in the role as a fully qualified EDDH. She applied and spent one month at Holsworthy Barracks in Sydney being assessed with a dog prior to being accepted to start the course. Emma was paired with a dog called Ash. She was recommended for the course, and was due to start in May 2020, but COVID-19 put a halt to these plans, with the course cancelled. To her dismay, Emma was informed she would have to reapply the following year. Given the effort she had already put into her physical fitness and preparation for the course, she was determined to win her spot, which she did. She started the course in 2021, alongside a mixture of Army and RAAF students. Emma was one of two women and was one of the youngest on the course and, by her own admission, she found it difficult to be accepted by the group:

> I had a very different mindset. I was more about the dogs; I was there for the dogs, whereas I think a lot of people were there for the capability – and the dog is the tool for that capability.[9]

Emma recalled there was a significant focus on 'soldiering': the course was physically demanding, and an emphasis was placed on basic soldiering tactics and skills, many of which were foreign to her:

> I had no idea what I was in for when I signed up for the course. It was extremely demanding, as most of the skills I acquired from the course I had never even heard of. We were taught Army first aid ... Combat first aid ... Tactical Canine Casualty Care ... basics of search, basics of explosive components, devices and composition, basic dog psychology, how to conduct continuation training with a dog, how to read canines and move them around an area ... The workload was enormous as I didn't even know what an IED [improvised explosive device] was, before applying for the course. The only thing I had going for me at the start of [the] course was my natural affinity with dogs, due to my upbringing.[10]

Students were teamed with a variety of different dogs to learn all the required skills, focusing on not only their own skills but how to read a dog's behaviour. At that stage, Ash, with whom she had been teamed previously during her first assessment, was still at the school, and Emma immediately put her down as her first preference to be teamed with. In a stroke of fate, while having to handle many different dogs in the school's pool, she was successfully teamed with Ash for the majority of the course.

Emma placed an enormous amount of pressure on herself to perform well and sees that time as the most challenging in her life, both physically and mentally. However, she said it helped her to mature and develop into the person she is today. Emma recalled her final challenge and assessment period, which was carried out over a 10-day period. She pushed through her exhaustion and remembered her pride in passing:

> I felt so accomplished, and wow, I've done myself proud. I'm going into a capability that can be taken seriously. I get paid to work with dogs and they're your best mate. I felt so good about that.[11]

The extremely close bond between Emma and Ash is obvious when seeing them together. Emma exudes enthusiasm whenever she refers to Ash (whose full name is Huntogun Black Ash):

> She is an almost-six-year-old black Labrador Retriever. She came from Huntogun in Tasmania. She is extremely bonded with me, and very clingy. She is also the most energetic dog I've ever met. Sometimes, when I turn around to shut a door, I can feel or hear her breath on the back of my neck, because she's just jumping and telling me she's ready to go and work. She is my best friend and if I'm ever having an 'off' day, she is the first to make me smile. She is very funny and quirky when getting pats. She only loves them from me, and ignores everyone else when I'm around. She is the best friend I could ask for, and I count my blessings every day [that I get] to work with such an amazing dog.[12]

Leading Aircraftwoman Emma Gall and Ash receiving a search brief during Exercise *Arras Sprint*, 2022 (Emma Gall)

Emma and Ash were posted to RAAF Amberley to No 2 Security Forces Squadron at the beginning of 2022. She joined the EDDH section with three of the four other RAAF members from her course. She credits Sergeant Marc Douglas (affectionately referred to as 'dog sergeant') as another mentor who contributed significantly to her professional development. She recalled the section was under-resourced, but she was excited to start the next phase of her career, so she was caught off guard when she was informed about a review into whether the RAAF was going to retain the EDDH capability. 'It was absolutely crushing. I took it very personally – I've just put all these years of my young adult life into this job and career.'[13] Emma has continued to learn, develop professionally and provide this unique capability, however still faces the realisation the role of EDDH might be cut from the Air Force, or merged into a different MWD specialisation. She says it is hard to put the uncertainty aside:

> It's hard to compartmentalise, but [I]'ve clearly been able to do that to a certain extent and focus on the job at hand. My way of dealing with that at the time, was like, we still had 18 dogs in the kennel bank. They are high-drive dogs, and they don't know what's going on. They still have a job and a purpose at the moment, so let's just push through … you make it about the dog.[14]

Leading Aircraftwoman Emma Gall and Ash conducting a stadium search during Exercise *Arras Sprint*, 2022 (Emma Gall)

And that is exactly what Emma has focused on. She has continued to hone her and Ash's skills, and has deployed on security exercises in other states, with both Air Force and Army units. She explains the explosive detection capability is unique, and that it is slow and methodical in nature: not necessarily the same as other security elements of the Air Force, which are more fast paced and reactive. She said it would be difficult to integrate both these capabilities into one. However, working with Reserve Army engineers was 'phenomenal. The regiment [in Adelaide] loved us, as they didn't usually get the chance to work with dogs. We got to do searches at different stadiums and locations.'[15]

Leading Aircraftwoman Emma Gall and Ash during Exercise *Arras Sprint*, 2022 (Emma Gall)

Emma was surprised to win her squadron's Dog Handler of the Year award in 2022. 'I was completely gobsmacked. You do get recognised for the hard work that you put in day in, day out.'[16]

Emma continues to focus on her daily routine, starting at 6:30 in the morning. Her training continues with Ash and the other dogs in the section:

> All dogs are unique. Every dog requires specialised care and training, when required to perform a specific role in Defence. They are the equivalent of athletes and have the ability to do a wide variety of tasks. Our dogs are selected for their drive, as they will be required to conduct long searches, constantly using their olfactory system and sniffing for target odours. This is used to prevent the risk of an explosive being detonated near the rest of the team. It takes a lot of time and effort to train a dog from basics such as how to sit, to becoming a specialised, elite canine capable of protecting a Defence asset. It is a lengthy but rewarding process.[17]

Postscript

Since the time of Emma's interview for this book, a decision has been made to disestablish the EDDH mustering in the RAAF and incorporate some of the role into a new capability. As a result, Emma has decided to discharge from the Air Force and take some time to choose a different career path. Ash will be retired as an explosive detection dog and will go home to live with Emma. Emma remains passionate about increasing her skills in working with dogs. This includes the neuroscience behind their behaviour and training, and working on the best ways to communicate with the animal. Looking back at the five years of her Air Force career, she said she achieved so much in that short timeframe:

> Although there have been times where I have been pushed to my limits and felt like I could not have gone on, I've still always been able to dig deep and continue, with help from my support networks through difficult times. I felt I've lived so much life and grown more than I could have imagined when I'd first joined as a young 18-year-old girl.[18]

Leading Aircraftwoman Paige Boyd (née Stockdale)

Aircraft Technician

Place of birth: Traralgon, Victoria
Date of enlistment: 27 February 2018

On Anzac Day in 2017, there was a woman with young children serving – I thought, 'What? You can have a family and work in Defence?' Maybe I should look into this.[1]

Leading Aircraftwoman Paige Boyd standing on the flight line (runway) next to a Royal Australian Air Force C-27J Spartan (Paige Boyd)

Paige Boyd grew up in Traralgon, Victoria, with her parents and three siblings. She calls her upbringing 'traditional', with her father working as an arborist for the local sawmill and her mother staying at home, raising the children. When her parents divorced, her mother had to find work, starting in a retail role:

> It was very different to how it is today, where both parents work. I think that definitely impacted my life because, growing up, I never had that drive that I was going to go to university and do all these great things. I always just thought I was going to get married and have children, as archaic as that sounds today.[2]

Paige recalled she did not apply herself to her schoolwork, and 'went off the rails' a little when she was around 15. She ended up leaving home around the age of 16, moving into her own place with assistance from the government, while continuing with her schooling. She passed Year 12 and found employment in Traralgon in a small discount shop, and then at the retail store Target until she was 21. After three years of living on her own, she moved back in with her mother, who had remarried.

Her mother and stepfather both encouraged her to leave Traralgon, knowing there would be many more opportunities for Paige outside of the small country town. At this time, she was given the opportunity to rent her stepbrother's property west of Brisbane at a cheap price:

> My Mum's always believed I could have done more … I packed up my car and just drove up to Queensland on my own – [at age] 21. It was the best thing I ever did because I'm extremely shy and introverted, and that got me out of my shell quite a bit.[3]

Paige quickly found work in an administration role at a furniture store, using her retail customer-service experience to win the job. From there, she was promoted to the head office and worked in the buyer's office for a number of years, saving her money with the aim of travelling to England on a working holiday. She had also married, admitting it was an 'on again, off again' relationship. In the end, she left for England, but was home within three months, eventually moving back to Traralgon on her own. After buying her own property, working for a financial institution and then at a Monash University campus for a number of years, she met her second husband, Steve, through an online-dating website. After having two children, juggling work and experiencing 'mother's guilt', Paige decided to take her children out of childcare and started working nights at the local Woolworths supermarket. 'I absolutely hated it … I had [my children] during the day, then I'd go off to work of a night when Steve got home.'[4]

After persevering for a year with night work, the family moved to Queensland. While watching an Anzac Day broadcast on TV in 2017, Paige saw an Air Force woman being interviewed:

> There were all of these ADF personnel telling their stories of being in the Defence Force. This lady came on and she had two little children, and I saw her and her story and I thought, 'She's got a family and she's in the Defence Force. I just never would have thought that's something that you could do. Maybe I should look into this.'[5]

Paige reflected that an Air Force career was something she had briefly explored when she was in her late teens. Her grandfather, a cousin and her stepbrother had all served and, around the age of 20, she had caught the train to Melbourne to attend a Defence jobs information day. But she had believed, at that time, that a life in the Air Force was not for her:

> I was just so intimidated by the whole thing. I was like, 'this is not for me'. I can't recall exactly what I thought at the time, but I think I was frightened ... On reflection, it was probably not the best time for me to join ... I really don't think I would have lasted five seconds.[6]

After watching that Anzac Day interview, at age 37, with two decades of adult life and work experience behind her, Paige thought the time was right to reconsider a career in the Air Force. She looked at job options on the Defence Force Recruiting (DFR) website before attending an information session in Brisbane. Having no desire to work behind a desk or in an administrative role, she was drawn to the concept of working on aircraft. She even joined a gym to ensure she could pass her entry fitness test:

> Steve was really supportive; I think because he didn't think I'd actually go ahead with it! Then he was like, 'Oh my God, she got a physical trainer. This is real.' Now he just likes to brag.[7]

With avionics and aircraft technician musterings in mind, Paige completed her aptitude testing, which she 'aced'. She received a score which allowed her the job of her choice, and her first preference was avionics technician. However, the only job available at that time was aircraft technician, so she accepted the offer, and her new career was set in motion.

Her two children were aged five and two at the time she travelled to RAAF Base Wagga Wagga in New South Wales for initial recruit training. She left them with Steve in Brisbane while she started on her new career path. Once she had arrived, her initial thought was that it was a 'little bit more laid back' than what she was expecting. It was only on the second day that she was woken at 5am by instructors yelling at the recruits to get out of bed:

> I just remember standing in that hallway while they're going up and down – I can't even remember what they were yelling. I was too shell shocked. I was standing there thinking, 'What am I doing here? This is real.'[8]

As a self-confessed 'people pleaser', Paige did everything she was instructed to do during her course, learning how to march and how to fire and handle a weapon and going on field-training exercises. She considers her field time as simultaneously one of the 'best and worst experiences' of her career, as she overcame her nerves, and the realisation of what she was accomplishing started to set in. While initially so busy she did not have time to focus on how much she was missing her family, it was when she started having weekends free that she missed her children terribly. Facing an additional year in Wagga alone while on her technician course, she convinced Steve to move down, despite his initial hesitation. After her five-year-old daughter announced she wanted to go and live with 'Mum', Steve relocated ('he would do anything for his kids') and was a stay-at-home dad for the year.

Aircraftwoman Paige Boyd at her No 1 Recruit Training Unit graduation with her husband Steve, children and parents, RAAF Base Wagga Wagga, New South Wales, 2018 (Paige Boyd)

Paige started her course with a group of 20 others: half Air Force, half Army. Ironically, for a so-called non-traditional role for women, only two people on the course were men. As one of the older students, Paige found the retention of information difficult and had to study hard. Despite the challenges and her sense of 'imposter syndrome', she graduated from the course and was posted to No 35 Squadron, the C-27J Spartan squadron at RAAF Amberley in Queensland.

> It was an excellent aircraft to go [to] as a fitter … you've got plenty of opportunities for troubleshooting and ticking things off in your journal [an aircraft-specific series of competencies].[9]

Paige completed her journal in 12 months: half the time allocated to the task. She was working on aircraft, 'swinging spanners', when the COVID-19 pandemic arrived, which reduced her capacity for travelling on tasks. Around that time, Steve and Paige decided to have another child, and their daughter Frankie was born on 9 June 2021.

While having a very positive experience throughout her pregnancy, her workplace was unsure how to best employ her during that period, given she could not be exposed to fuel or other chemicals. She ended up moving into an administrative role, assisting with safety audits, working on the unit website, and learning other aspects of the organisation. She spent six months on maternity leave after Frankie was born, before returning to the workshop floor three days per week on a shift cycle, an experience she admitted was not enjoyable. She was spending time away from work, because Frankie was sick, and feeling a level of guilt for missing work. When the opportunity came up to manage tools for the squadron in a dayshift role, Paige jumped at the chance. She believes a long-term career as a technician is not in her future and is considering alternative roles within the Air Force.

Aircraftwoman Paige Boyd at her Royal Australian Air Force School of Technical Training graduation with husband Steve and children, RAAF Base Wagga Wagga, New South Wales, 2019 (Paige Boyd)

One option is representing the Air Force at DFR. She wants to be an example of what is possible in the service, regardless of background, experience or family responsibilities. 'I think women like to hear other women's stories.'[10]

Paige reflects on her service and comments that women are now more visible. While observing some people in the Air Force still have an old-fashioned view of women and their abilities, a shift is occurring in the mindset of the organisation:

> There's definitely been a shift since I started. When I came to the unit, I was the fourth female 'techo'. Now there [are] at least a dozen, so visually, we're more in your face. I definitely don't hear the comments I used to. I couldn't tell you the amount of times I heard, when I first started, 'You'll get promoted before me because you're a woman.'[11]

Paige wanted to reiterate that her RAAF career so far has been 'fantastic'. Steve continues to be a proud and supportive husband who brags to anyone willing to listen that his wife is in the Air Force. Her friends and family are also incredibly proud of what she has accomplished:

> I see it as a privilege to serve my country, and I feel very fortunate to be given the opportunity to do what I do. I think I joined at the right time; the perfect time for me.[12]

Leading Aircraftwoman Paige Boyd on the flight line (runway) at RAAF Amberley, Queensland (Paige Boyd)

Leading Aircraftwoman Kobey Misios

Firefighter

Place of birth: Sunshine Coast, Queensland
Date of enlistment: 16 March 2021

As much as I'm not in a flying position now, I still feel right at home [in] that I'm right on the airfield and can look out the window and see the aircraft flying.[1]

Aircraftwoman Kobey Misios during her graduation from No 1 Recruit Training Unit, 2021 (Kobey Misios)

For her entire adult life, Kobey Misios has worked in professions that focus on service to people and communities. From registered nurse, to flight attendant in Australia and overseas, and now as a RAAF firefighter, Kobey has sought opportunities to give back to her community.

Kobey grew up on a large property on the Sunshine Coast, Queensland, and was on the move from a very early age. She spent time on her parents' property, riding horses and feeding the chickens, and competed in numerous sports, including surf lifesaving, cross-country running and athletics. She represented Australia in a one-mile track-and-field event in the United States at the age of 16. Kobey knew from her early school years that she wanted to study to be a nurse, and she also had aspirations to travel and become an international flight attendant, due to her interest in flying. 'I was lucky enough to travel internationally for sport and with family, and I always dreamt of travelling the world and hiking major mountains.'[2]

Both of her grandfathers had served during the Second World War; one in the Army and one in the Royal Australian Navy. Kobey had considered a military career around the time she finished school, but decided she was not quite ready:

> I wanted to study first and then I wanted to go and experience and explore freely. I think I always knew that there were these opportunities in the Air Force … I knew that I would potentially have the opportunity to come back and reapply with [life] experience.[3]

So instead of applying for the military, she started studying as a nurse straight after school and, after graduating, worked at Noosa Hospital in Queensland on the surgical, palliative, and medical wards. After two years as a nurse, she became a flight attendant for Qantas, flying to all states and territories with the airline. She recalled flying into the joint military–civilian airport at Newcastle in New South Wales (NSW) and looking across the runway to RAAF Base Williamtown. 'If I saw any of the "firies" [firefighters] attending [medical incidents], I was always inspired by that and wanted to know more.'[4]

After just over four years of flying with Qantas – during which time she attended to Sir David Attenborough on a trip to Bundaberg – Kobey applied for an international flight-attendant position at Emirates, to pursue her passion for overseas travel:

> It was an amazing career, because I wanted to tick off some major bucket [list items] for myself … I'm a marathon runner and a hiker, so I was able to tick off the three major hikes I wanted to complete, and three international marathons.[5]

She spent the next seven years travelling extensively around the world, spending an average of only eight days per month at her base in Dubai in the United Arab Emirates. One trip could be a 16-hour flight to Australia, and the next could be an equally long flight to South America. But in the few days she spent in Dubai, Kobey did not let opportunities pass her by; during one of her short breaks, she flew to India to visit the Taj Mahal and to Egypt to visit the pyramids. Her third hiking goal was climbing to Base Camp at the foot of Mount Everest in Nepal, which she achieved between flying trips:

I was just ecstatic when I made that final hike up to the summit [at Base Camp]. I think that was really inspiring, speaking to the locals. I went around and just shook the hand of those sherpas that are camped up there in the cold extremes … It was great to also immerse in the culture of the Nepalese who are really doing the hard yards and helping us to accomplish our goals.[6]

Kobey Misios working as a first-class flight attendant with Emirates (Kobey Misios)

Kobey Misios at Base Camp at Mount Everest, Nepal (Kobey Misios)

After her busy career at Emirates, Kobey's focus shifted to a new challenge: joining the RAAF and being closer to her family. Noting that serving in the military was always a goal of hers, she 'decided I would finally complete this goal at [age] 38'.[7] Kobey applied as a firefighter, which was her first preference, but she also considered crew attendant, given her passion for aviation:

> I had my mind set on joining as a Firefighter, for the challenge. I have always worked shift work and enjoyed the lifestyle. Being a Firefighter is a physical profession, with each day being different. I've always worked [in] professions serving the community, and looked forward to representing my new Air Force community.[8]

Kobey's recruiting experience was rapid and positive; after being recruited through Maroochydore near her family home in Queensland, she was accepted within months of applying, at the height of the COVID-19 pandemic. Kobey travelled to RAAF Base Wagga Wagga, NSW, in March 2021, to complete her initial Air Force recruit training at No 1 Recruit Training Unit. Pandemic restrictions meant she spent her first two weeks in a form of quarantine:

> We were confined to our accommodation blocks, as there was a full lockdown. We had meals delivered to us. We were marched over to the training headquarters the following morning, woken at 5am by instructors yelling at us to get out of bed, having to make a bed in a military style and be ready for parade within a certain timeframe. It was a bit of a wake-up [call], to be honest.[9]

She recalled her life and work experience helped her while she was there, with the long days as a flight attendant with little or no rest preparing her for the challenges she faced. However, she did find a few training activities challenging. One was weapons handling: having to carry and maintain a rifle for two months while on the course. She also found the marching component tricky, admitting she has 'two left feet'.[10] Always looking for the positives in her circumstances, Kobey recalled enjoying her field phases:

> Finally firing and shooting a weapon … and being up at all hours out [in the] field. It was a really cool experience. Going on ration packs of cold meat, yes, it was a great experience. I loved the physical side of the training, crawling in the mud and in the dirt and completing the obstacle courses. I think I got a lot out of that experience.[11]

She graduated as the 'most improved' on her course, which she recalled was a shock and one of the highlights of her career so far. Her next challenge was at RAAF Amberley where she started her Firefighter Initial Employment Training, a long and gruelling 20-week course along with 19 other students. She had to become proficient in every aspect of the firefighting capability, including emergency first aid, and chemical, biological, radiological and nuclear response training. One of her highlights was exercising on the commercial airfield at Coolangatta Airport and having the opportunity to hone her skills with Air Services Aviation Rescue Firefighter crews. After graduating from her course in late 2021, Kobey was posted to RAAF Base Richmond, west of Sydney. She spent her first Christmas on shift, sharing a barbecue lunch with members of the local Rural Fire Service. Posted in at a relatively quiet time allowed Kobey to spend time learning the processes of the fire section on her first posting:

> [The] quickest way to learn is through on-the-job training. So I feel grateful for the patience of my colleagues when we would train in the watch room, and they would write out notes for airfield radio calls, because we need to follow procedure when we're on the runway, operating on the airfield.[12]

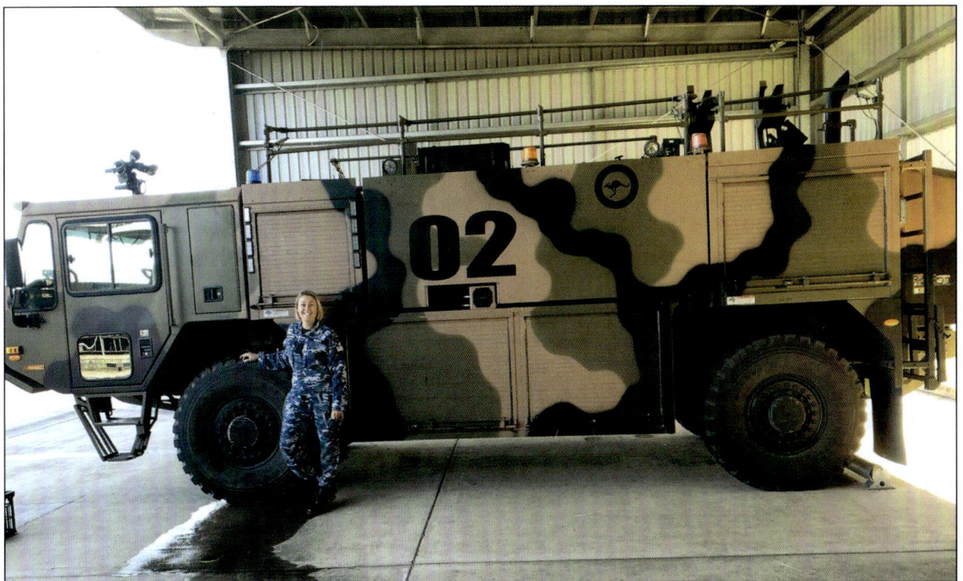

Leading Aircraftwoman Kobey Misios next to an Oshkosh Striker air transportable fire truck, which she crews. These vehicles weigh up to 19 tonnes (Kobey Misios)

She has enjoyed slotting back into a shift system, a lifestyle with which she is comfortable and familiar, given her years as a nurse and flight attendant. Kobey's passion for aviation is apparent, and it drives her motivation for developing her professional capabilities:

> I still get goosebumps when a Globemaster [C-17 air mobility aircraft] lands. I come out of the fire station and just look at it in awe, because I just think, 'Wow, what a machine' … to think that our Panther fire truck that holds 7,500 litres of water can go into a Globemaster – I was just mind blown.[13]

Highlights of her short RAAF career have been varied. Kobey assisted the local Hawkesbury community during a major flood event in 2022, by helping families clear out their waterlogged possessions from homes ruined by the floodwater. She has also jumped at the chance to represent her squadron in the Sydney marches on Anzac Day:

> Knowing that my grandfathers had both served in the Navy and the Army, and then to represent my family and squadron by marching; to be in full uniform [with] members of the public clapping. It was just that feeling of fulfilment … I was very emotional to think I'm walking for my grandfathers.[14]

Leading Aircraftwoman Kobey Misios (left) representing No 22 Squadron in Sydney, New South Wales, Anzac Day 2022 (Kobey Misios)

In 2022, she was selected to deploy to RAAF Base Curtin, a bare base in Western Australia, to carry out firefighting duties as part of Exercise *Pitch Black*, the largest Air Force multinational exercise in the country. While preparing for the exercise in Darwin, Kobey and her team witnessed a car accident outside an Army barracks. Her training in road-crash rescue kicked in and she used her skills to provide first-responder assistance, earning herself and her colleagues a Commander's Commendation in recognition of their rapid response:

> We had completed road-crash rescue and medical training, and with my nursing career prior to joining the RAAF, I had the confidence to respond. I'm passionate about assisting [the] community, so I really got to use all my skills and training in an emergency.[15]

Kobey's recollection of Exercise *Pitch Black* was one of skills consolidation and the privilege of working alongside other nations while using her training, of meeting United States marines and exercising airfield response techniques.

Kobey wants to showcase the Air Force in a recruiting and representational role in the next few years. As a woman who joined in her late 30s, she wants to inspire others and highlight the many opportunities in the RAAF which are available to people from all walks of life. When representing her fire section at the local Hawkesbury agricultural show, Kobey recalled meeting a woman and showing her through the section's fire truck:

> She was around my age and she said to me, 'Oh, you can still join [at our age]?' I think just speaking to her, and seeing how excited she got by looking through the fire truck, I look[ed] back and [thought], 'Wow, that was me' … perhaps I've inspired her to join at an older age, and [demonstrated] that women in their 40s are able to join and pursue whatever mustering or career they want within the Air Force.[16]

Leading Aircraftwoman Kobey Misios with her Commander Combat Support Group Commendation, following her response to a civilian motor vehicle accident in Darwin, Northern Territory, 2022 (Kobey Misios)

As if her role as a firefighter is not enough to keep her busy, Kobey is also volunteering her spare time towards community-based assistance for families who require help with their home tasks. Ironically, she has been paired with an Air Force family on base, assisting them with cooking and other duties. When asked about her future goals, Kobey disclosed she is putting a process in place to ensure she can have a family in future, if that is what she decides:

> I haven't met a partner as of yet. I've had quite a busy career living abroad, but it's still something that I've always thought about. I was lucky enough through the Air Force to receive a padre [chaplain] loan which I then used to freeze my eggs … I went through the procedure … with a very successful outcome, but also with some great support from our medical doctors here helping me.[17]

Regardless of which path Kobey decides to take next, she will no doubt continue her passion of contributing to her community, challenging herself in her work role, and taking advantage of every opportunity in the Air Force that comes her way.

Sport and service

While it may be hard to neatly define Australia's identity, the role of sport and the impact of war on its development can be considered fundamental factors. Qualities associated with both – including courage, teamwork, discipline, mateship and loyalty – have helped to shape Australia's sense of nationhood. By extension, the role of sport in the Air Force has been foundational to its character and history.

Servicewomen's participation in sport has been a regular feature throughout Air Force history. Records show athletics carnivals being held as early as 1942, the year after the formation of the Women's Auxiliary Australian Air Force (WAAAF). However, the types of sport were very much reflective of the time. As an example, a WAAAF sports carnival held at the Wagga Wagga Cricket Ground in New South Wales on 28 August 1944 included wheelbarrow and sack races![1]

Members of the Women's Auxiliary Australian Air Force enjoy a game of leap frog at RAAF Base Wagga Wagga, New South Wales, 11 December 1942 (Australian War Memorial)

During the war years in the 1940s, sports carnivals were usually held in concert with parades and anniversary celebrations, in front of appreciative local crowds.[2] Sporting carnivals provided another opportunity to demonstrate the capability that women were bringing to the war effort. Inter-service competitions were held for cricket, swimming, badminton and tennis, against teams from the Women's Royal Australian Navy and the Australian Army Women's Association.

A Women's Auxiliary Australian Air Force inter-unit sports relay race at Olympic Park, New South Wales, 20 February 1943 (RAAF Museum)

Aircraftwoman Grace MacPherson competes in the cycle leg of an Australian Defence Force triathlon, 2011 (Department of Defence)

The opportunity to participate in sport was considered a positive recruitment tool; many women seeking to join the WAAAF in the early years of the Second World War came from accomplished sporting backgrounds. Sporting capabilities of potential recruits were highlighted in news articles of the time: 'Sporting prowess, however, did not diminish the femininity of these girls volunteering for the W.A.A.A.F.'[3]

During recent decades, women have represented the RAAF in many different sporting endeavours, including rugby league, Australian Rules football, body building, athletics and softball. Inter-service sporting competitions and the opportunity to represent the Australian Defence Force and, in some cases, Australia, in elite sporting teams, now form part of the fabric of the Air Force. Sport embodies teamwork, strength, skill and passion – it also reflects the depth of talent the Air Force has in its ranks.

The women's Australian Rugby Union nationals, held at Lane Cove, New South Wales, 2016 (Department of Defence)

Wing Officer Doris Carter OBE

Director of the Women's Royal Australian Air Force

While several Olympians have served in the Air Force, Doris Carter's story is an especially inspirational one. At the 1936 Berlin Olympic Games, Doris – a high jumper – became the first Australian female track-and-field athlete to reach an Olympic final; she went on to complete more firsts for Air Force.[4]

Wing Officer Doris Carter OBE, the first Director of the Women's Royal Australian Air Force, had represented Australia in the high jump at the 1936 Berlin Olympic Games (Australian War Memorial)

From an early age, Doris played a number of sports before specialising in high jump. While she carried an injury into the final at the 1936 Olympic Games, she pushed on and finished just outside the medal placings. The onset of the Second World War curtailed any further Olympic dreams she may have held, and so her achievements at Berlin were the pinnacle of her athletic endeavours. In 1942, at the height of the war, Doris set aside her athletics career and joined the Women's Auxiliary Australian Air Force (WAAAF).

Her war service finished with her being chosen to lead the WAAAF contingent in the Victory March in London. While the WAAAF was disbanded after the end of the war, Doris was called up to be the first Director of the newly established Women's Royal Australian Air Force (WRAAF) in 1951, with the rank of wing officer.[5] Her outstanding leadership helped shape the WRAAF and this was recognised when she was awarded an Order of the British Empire.

CONCLUSION

Bringing this small selection of stories of Australian Air Force women to the printed (and digital!) page has been a privilege for the women in the small research and writing team. Having reached the end of this journey into the ninth decade, we hope you have come away with a greater understanding and appreciation of the service and sacrifice of the thousands of women who have helped to establish, transform and sustain today's Air Force and strengthen its capability.

The women who enter and serve in the Royal Australian Air Force in the years to come will continue to form part of that exceptional legacy.

ACKNOWLEDGEMENTS

A number of individuals and organisations have played a significant role in bringing *Changing Altitudes: Stories of Australian Air Force Women* to life. The most obvious, and most important, are the women who feature in this book – without them, we would not have been able to create the diverse and rich reflection of women's experiences in all branches of the Australian Air Force since the 1940s. They have generously shared their time, memories and photos.

Dame Quentin Bryce, thank you for graciously agreeing to act as this book's champion and for opening with the Foreword. The interest you have taken in Australian air force women over the decades is significant and appreciated.

We are grateful for the support and guidance of many team members within History and Heritage – Air Force, and across the broader Royal Australian Air Force, who have provided their time and expertise to our team. Among other tasks, their assistance in sourcing images, artefacts and documents is greatly valued.

To those who assisted in the editing and publishing processes: thank you.

Many relatives and friends of the women featured in this book provided their stories, photographs, artwork and artefacts to ensure the memories of their loved ones can be brought to life; we thank them for their generous contributions.

BIBLIOGRAPHY

Published records

'A tribute to the W.A.A.A.F.', *Department of Defence*, 1943.

'Airwoman we thank you', *Department of Defence*, 1943.

Finance Circular No. 1965/10, 19 March 1965, Commonwealth of Australia, Canberra.

Reghenzani, Christine, 'Women in the ADF: six decades of policy change (1950 to 2011)', Department of Parliamentary Services, Parliament of Australia, November 2015.

Report of the Committee of Inquiry into Defence Awards, 1993, Department of Defence, Canberra.

'My Story!', *Radschool Association Magazine* (February 2012).

'Royal Australian Air Force', *Australian Air War Effort*, 10th Ed, 31 Aug 1945.

Tilley, Gaynor, submission to Royal Australian Air Force historical records, Department of Defence, 19 July 1994.

Wilson, Roland (Ed.), 'Commonwealth Bureau of Census and Statistics. Official Year Book of the Commonwealth of Australia. No. 36: 1944 and 1945', Canberra (1947).

'Wyaralong Dam – Environmental Impact Statement.' Queensland Water Infrastructure Pty Ltd (2007).

Archival sources

'Air Board Agenda 2878 (RAAF) - Establishment of a Royal Australian Air Force Nursing Service', n.d. A14487, National Archives of Australia.

'Air Board Agenda 2953 (RAAF) - Royal Australian Air Force Nursing Service', n.d. A14487, National Archives of Australia.

'Air Board Agenda 3341 (RAAF) - Proposed Expansion of Women's Auxiliary Australian Air Force', n.d. A14487, National Archives of Australia.

'Bell Mary Teston Luis : Service Number - 350307 : Date of Birth - 03 Dec 1903 : Place of Birth - Unknown : Place of Enlistment - Unknown : Next of Kin - Bell J', n.d. A9300, National Archives of Australia.

'Benn Hilary Josephine : Service Number - 90664 : Date of Birth - 22 May 1923 : Place of Birth - Carlton VIC : Place of Enlistment - Melbourne : Next of Kin - Turner A', n.d. A9301, National Archives of Australia.

'Brettle Shirley Joan : Service Number - 98395 : Date of Birth - 03 Jun 1921 : Place of Birth - Randwick NSW : Place of Enlistment - Sydney : Next of Kin - Brettle Horace', n.d. A9301, National Archives of Australia.

'Bury Grace Elizabeth : Service Number - N35304 : Date of Birth - 21/03/1929 : Place of Birth - Bairnsdale, VIC : Conflict – Korea', n.d. A12372, National Archives of Australia.

'Clarke Margaret McIntosh : Service Number - 105705 : Date of Birth - 19 May 1924 : Place of Birth - Rockdale NSW : Place of Enlistment - Sydney : Next of Kin – Clarke Leo', n.d. A9301, National Archives of Australia.

'Connelly Dermott Anthony : Service Number - 45 : Date of Birth - 02 Apr 1903 : Place of Birth - Melbourne VIC : Place of Enlistment – Point Cook : Next of Kin - Connelly B', n.d., National Archives of Australia.

'Connelly Dermott Anthony (Wing Commander) : Service Number - 45 : Unit - Royal Australian Air Force Station Sandgate, Royal Australian Air Force : Date of Court Martial - 22 September 1944', n.d., National Archives of Australia.

'Cooke Gordon Oliver : Service Number - 28709 : Date of Birth - 06 Jan 1922 : Place of Birth – Rose Park SA : Place of Enlistment - Adelaide : Next of Kin – Cooke Joyce', n.d. A9301, National Archives of Australia.

'Cooke Norah Pamela : Service Number - 91544 : Date of Birth - 22 Jul 1920 : Place of Birth - Prospect SA : Place of Enlistment - Adelaide SA : Next of Kin - Cooke Percival', n.d. A9300., National Archives of Australia.

'Cooke Percy Bennett : Service Number - S42881 : Date of Birth - 26 Oct 1885 : Place of Birth - Hampshire England : Place of Enlistment - Unley SA : Next of Kin - Cooke Freda', n.d. B884, National Archives of Australia.

'Curnow Thomas Charles: Service Number - 59: Date of Birth - 07 Aug 1911: Place of Birth - Ballarat VIC: Place of Enlistment – Point Cook: Next of Kin - Curnow Claire', n.d., National Archives of Australia.

'Dalzell George : Sern 4763 : Pob Newcastle Nsw : Poe Warwick Farm Nsw : Nok F Dalzell Thomas', n.d., National Archives of Australia.

'Ferguson Eric Robert : Sern 5079 : Pob Repton Nsw : Poe Holsworthy Nsw : Nok F Ferguson George Ross', n.d., National Archives of Australia.

'Ferguson, Joan [Australian Women's Land Army Medical and Hospital Card]', n.d., National Archives of Australia.

'Ferguson, Joan Mary [Australian Women's Land Army History Card]', n.d., National Archives of Australia.

'Ferguson, Sheila [Australian Women's Land Army Medical and Hospital Card]', n.d., National Archives of Australia.

'Ferguson, Sheila Catherine [Australian Women's Land Army History Card]', n.d., National Archives of Australia.

'Ferguson Sheila Catherine: Service Number - 177348: Date of Birth - 07 May 1926: Place of Birth - Paddington Nsw: Place of Enlistment - Sydney: Next of Kin - Ferguson William', n.d., National Archives of Australia.

'Ferguson William Henry : Service Number - N102710 : Date of Birth - 05 Nov 1894 : Place of Birth - Nth Botany Nsw : Place of Enlistment - Marrickville Nsw : Next of Kin - Ferguson Olivia', n.d., National Archives of Australia.

'Gorey Leila Isabelle : Service Number - 93581 : Date of Birth - 29 Jan 1921 : Place of Birth - Leeton NSW : Place of Enlistment - Sydney : Next of Kin - Gorey Herbert', n.d. A9301, National Archives of Australia.

'Haughton-James Audrey Jean Campbell : Service Number - 94177 : Date of Birth - 20 Jan 1916 : Place of Birth - Beaudesert QLD : Place of Enlistment - Brisbane : Next of Kin – Haughton-James Douglas', n.d., National Archives of Australia.

'Jackson Leslie Douglas : Service Number - 270520 : Date of Birth - 24 Feb 1917 : Place of Birth - Brisbane QLD : Place of Enlistment – Point Cook VIC : Next of Kin - Jackson William', n.d. A9300, National Archives of Australia.

'Lang Margaret Irene : Service Number - 500001 : Date of Birth - 23 May 1893 : Place of Birth - Unknown : Place of Enlistment - Unknown : Next of Kin - Kearney J', n.d. A9300, National Archives of Australia.

'Lang Margaret Irene : Service Number - Sister : Place of Birth - Oxley VIC : Place of Enlistment - 3MD [Third Military District] : Next of Kin - (Mother) Lang A', n.d. B2455, National Archives of Australia.

'Mackenzie Lucy Georgia : Service Number - 500358 : Date of Birth - 11 Oct 1918 : Place of Birth - Unknown : Place of Enlistment - Unknown : Next of Kin - Mackenzie James', n.d. A9300, National Archives of Australia.

'McNeil Olive Winifred : Service Number - 93766 : Date of Birth - 23 Jan 1921 : Place of Birth - Gladesville NSW : Place of Enlistment - Sydney : Next of Kin – McNeil Hector', n.d. A9301, National Archives of Australia.

'Organisation & Administration WAAAF', n.d. A705, National Archives of Australia.

'Pearse Alma Sarah Jane : Service Number - 501101 : Date of Birth - 08 Jan 1911 : Place of Birth - Unknown : Place of Enlistment - Unknown : Next of Kin - Pearse G Copies', n.d. A9300, National Archives of Australia.

'Porter Rena June : Service Number - 91859 : Date of Birth - 12 May 1921 : Place of Birth – Yorketown SA : Place of Enlistment - Adelaide : Next of Kin – Unknown', n.d. A9301, National Archives of Australia.

'Stevenson Clare Grant : Service Number - 351001 : Date of Birth - 18 Jul 1903 : Place of Birth - Unknown : Place of Enlistment - Unknown : Next of Kin - Stevenson A', n.d. A9300, National Archives of Australia.

'Volume 1 - RAAF Station, Parafield, South Australia - Personnel Occurrence Reports - 1/1945 - 25/1945, 1/1946 - 6/1946', n.d. A10605, National Archives of Australia.

Books

Brady, Tony, *The Empire Has An Answer: The Empire Air Training Scheme As Reported in the Australian Press 1939–1945*, Big Sky Publishing, Newport, 2019.

Brayley, Annabelle, *Our Vietnam Nurses*, Penguin Random House Australia, Southbank, 2016.

Bryce, Quentin, *Dear Quentin: Letters of a Governor General*, Melbourne University Press, Melbourne, 2017.

Fenton, Morrie, *The History and Stories of 131 Radar Ash Island 1942–46*, Fenton, Lockleys, 1995.

Gillison, Douglas, *Royal Australian Air Force, 1939–1942*, Australian War Memorial, Canberra, 1962.

Halstead, Gay, *Story of the RAAF Nursing Service 1940–1990*, Nungurner Press, Metung, 1994.

Haughton-James, Jean, and Sheila Manley, *"As We Knew It" Transport Section R.A.A.F. Base Evans Head, N.S.W. 1942–43*, Wren Print, Brisbane, 1993.

Haughton-James, Jean, and Sheila Manley, *Wings at War: RAAF at Evans Head, 1939-1945*, self-published, St Lucia, 1995.

Ilbery, Peter, *Empire Airmen Strike Back: The Empire Air Training Scheme and 5 SFTS, Uranquinty*, Banner Books, Maryborough, 1999.

Mexted, Kathy, *Australian Women Pilots: Amazing True Stories of Women in the Air*, New South Publishing, Sydney, 2020.

Stevenson, Clare, and Honor Darling, *The W.A.A.A.F. Book*, Hale & Iremonger, Sydney, 1984.

Thomson, Joyce, *The WAAAF in Wartime Australia*, Melbourne University Press, Melbourne, 1992.

Articles and chapters

'Ancillary Units', in *Units of the Royal Australian Air Force: A Concise History*, Australian Government Publishing Service, Canberra, 1995.

Clark, Chris, 'Women in the RAAF – Talking Points', Department of Defence, Canberra, unpublished.

Lax, Mark, 'Women in the RAAF' in *Taking the Lead: The Royal Australian Air Force 1972–1996*, Simon and Schuster, Cammeray, 2020.

McDonald, John, 'Introduction of the all seasons uniform and clothing and insignia developments during the 1970s, 1980s and 1990s' in *Shades of Blue*, Department of Defence, Canberra, unpublished.

McDonald, John, 'Women's services 1944–1977' in *Shades of Blue*, Department of Defence, Canberra, unpublished.

Mitchell, Lynette, 'A WRAAF's Story', in *In Our Spirit: Creative Works of Australian Defence Force Women from 1960s Onward*, Melanie Bird and Jennifer Crane, 2020.

'My Story!', *Radschool Association Magazine*, February 2012.

'Noting Brief for the Chief of the Defence Force', June 2019, Department of Defence, Canberra, unpublished.

Parry, Naomi, 'Tresillian Mothercraft Homes (1918 –)', *Royal Society for the Welfare of Mothers and Babies*, 2023.

Pregnancy, Maternity and Returning to Work Guide, Version 2, September 2022, Department of Defence, Canberra, unpublished.

'Sheila Van Emden', UNSW Canberra at the Australian Defence Force Academy, Canberra, 2003.

'Women in the Service' in *Customs and Traditions Manual*, Department of Defence, Canberra, unpublished.

Newspapers and periodicals

Army News

Defence News

Daily Advertiser

Daily Telegraph

Defence News

Lakes Post

Newcastle Morning Herald and Miners' Advocate

Newcastle Sun

RAAF News

Royal Australian Navy News

Sunday Sun and Guardian

Sydney Morning Herald

Temora Independent

The Advertiser

The Age

The Area News

The Argus

The Australian Financial Review

The Australian Quarterly

The Australian Women's Weekly

The Canberra Times

The Courier-Mail

The Herald

The Irrigator

The News

The Telegraph

The Western Mail

Weekly Times

Audio recording

'Clare Stevenson', *Wing and a Prayer*, Australian Broadcasting Corporation, n.d.

Interviews

Ball, Martin, *Martin Ball interviews Rena Pascoe* [unpublished interview transcript], Royal Australian Air Force, n.d.

Bolitho, Sharyn, *Sharyn Bolitho interviews Lynette Mitchell* [unpublished interview transcript], Royal Australian Air Force, 22 September 2023.

Brodie Stewart [question and answer transcript], 1 March 2023.

Dani Cornish [question and answer transcript], 6 July 2023.

Dearing, Kirrily, *Kirrily Dearing interviews Brodie Stewart* [unpublished interview transcript], Royal Australian Air Force, 16 May 2023.

Dearing, Kirrily, *Kirrily Dearing interviews Emma Gall* [unpublished interview transcript], Royal Australian Air Force, 16 May 2023.

Dearing, Kirrily, *Kirrily Dearing interviews Hannah Jude-Smith* [unpublished interview transcript], Royal Australian Air Force, 25 May 2023.

Dearing, Kirrily, *Kirrily Dearing interviews Ingrid Van der Vlist* [unpublished interview transcript], Royal Australian Air Force, 2 May 2023.

Dearing, Kirrily, *Kirrily Dearing interviews Jade Evans* [unpublished interview transcript], Royal Australian Air Force, 2 May 2023.

Dearing, Kirrily, *Kirrily Dearing interviews Jenny Fantini* [unpublished interview transcript], Royal Australian Air Force, 30 April 2023.

Dearing, Kirrily, *Kirrily Dearing interviews Kate Clarkson* [unpublished interview transcript], Royal Australian Air Force, 15 May 2023.

Dearing, Kirrily, *Kirrily Dearing interviews Kobey Misios* [unpublished interview transcript], Royal Australian Air Force, 15 July 2023.

Dearing, Kirrily, *Kirrily Dearing interviews Melinda Skinner* [unpublished interview transcript], Royal Australian Air Force, 31 May 2023.

Dearing, Kirrily, *Kirrily Dearing interviews Michelle Hardy* [unpublished interview transcript], Royal Australian Air Force, 16 May 2023.

Dearing, Kirrily, *Kirrily Dearing interviews Olivia Little* [unpublished interview transcript], Royal Australian Air Force, 2 May 2023.

Dearing, Kirrily, *Kirrily Dearing interviews Paige Boyd* [unpublished interview transcript], Royal Australian Air Force, 16 May 2023.

Emma Gall [question and answer transcript], 13 March 2023.

Garside, Michael, *Michael Garside interviews Margaret Clarke* [unpublished interview transcript], Royal Australian Air Force, 12 August 2019.

Garside, Michael, *Michael Garside interviews Shirley Brettle* [unpublished interview transcript], Royal Australian Air Force, 6 January 2016.

Garside, Michael, *Michael Garside interviews Shirley McLaren* [unpublished sound recording], Royal Australian Air Force, 27 February 2020.

Ingrid Van der Vlist [question and answer transcript], 7 March 2023.

Jade Evans [question and answer transcript], 2 May 2023.

Julie Hammer [question and answer transcript], 8 March 2023.

Kate Clarkson [question and answer transcript], 30 April 2023.

Kobey Misios [question and answer transcript], 18 May 2023.

Michelle Hardy [question and answer transcript], 28 April 2023.

'Olive Jardine – Transcript of Interview' [unpublished interview transcript], *Australians at War Film Archive*, 3 June 2003.

Morrall, Phil, *Phil Morrall interviews Julie Hammer* [unpublished interview transcript], Royal Australian Air Force, 6 March, 2013.

Morrall, Phil, *Phil Morrall interviews Tracy Smart* [unpublished interview transcript], Royal Australian Air Force, 4 August 2009.

Nelmes, Michael, *Michael Nelmes interviews Julie Hammer* [unpublished interview transcript], Australian War Memorial, 14 November 2005.

New, Linda, *Linda New interviews Yvonne Thompson* [unpublished sound recording], Royal Australian Air Force, 11 November 2022.

Paige Boyd [question and answer transcript], 22 March 2023.

'Sheila Van Emden – Transcript of Interview', *Australians at War Film Archive*, no. 369, 26 May 2003.

Turner, David, *David Turner interviews Sandra Perry* [unpublished interview transcript], Royal Australian Air Force, 2 June 2022.

Correspondence

Baird, Connie, 'RE: Audrey Jean Campbell Haughton-James (Nee Philp) DOB: 20 Jan 1916 [Sec=Official]', letter to Anna Williams, 15 May 2023.

Connie Dixon, personal correspondence, 2 May 2023.

Dani Cornish, personal correspondence, 13 July 2023.

Jess Stone, personal correspondence, 3 April 2023.

Lynette Mitchell, personal correspondence, 7 December 2023.

Tracy Smart, email to Kirrily Dearing, 10 July 2023.

Internet resources

'3. Women in Combat Duties - Reservation Withdrawal', *Parliament of Australia*, n.d., at https://www.aph.gov.au/Parliamentary_Business/Committees/Joint/Electoral_Matters/VotingAge/Advisory_report/Section?id=committees%2Freportjnt%2F024073%2F24681.

'A Life of Adventure and Faith: DHL Resident Olive Jardine Turns 100', *BaptistCare*, updated 2024, at https://baptistcare.org.au/blog/a-life-of-adventure-and-faith-dhl-resident-olive-jardine-turns-100.

'ABC Archives and Library Services', *Australian Broadcasting Corporation*, updated 2002, at https://www.abc.net.au/archives/timeline/1970s.htm.

'ABC Archives and Library Services', *Australian Broadcasting Corporation*, updated 2002, at https://www.abc.net.au/archives/timeline/1980s.htm.

'Acting Squadron Leader (Sqn Ldr) Edward Arthur Hudson DFC and Bar, pilot of Rockhampton, Qld', *Australian War Memorial*, updated 2024, at https://www.awm.gov.au/collection/C386807.

'Air Vice-Marshal Julie Hammer is UQ's 2003 alumni ace', *The University of Queensland*, 17 September 2003, at https://www.uq.edu.au/news/article/2003/09/air-vice-marshal-julie-hammer-uq%E2%80%99s-2003-alumni-ace.

'Air Vice-Marshal Tracy Smart', *Air Force 2021*, n.d., at https://airforce2021.airforce.gov.au/people/tracy-smart.

'Airwomen to be posted overseas', *Parliament of Australia*, n.d., at https://parlinfo.aph.gov.au/parlInfo/search/display/display.w3p;query=Id%3A%22media%2Fpressrel%2FHPR09008263%22;src1=sm1.

Allen, Lynda, 'Making medicine and peacekeeping her mission', *Flinders University*, 18 February 2020, at https://blogs.flinders.edu.au/alumni-stories/2020/02/18/tracysmart/.

'Alma Skeers', *Australians at War Film Archive*, updated 2020, at https://australiansatwarfilmarchive.unsw.edu.au/archive/826.

Armbruster, Stefan, 'Darwin marks the day Tracy blew Christmas away', updated 25 December 2014, at https://www.sbs.com.au/news/article/darwin-marks-the-day-tracy-blew-christmas-away/i12tf1bsg.

'Audrey Haughton-James (Jean)', *Australians at War Film Archive*, updated 2020, at https://australiansatwarfilmarchive.unsw.edu.au/archive/1535/archive/826.

'Audrey Haughton James Obituary', *Legacy*, n.d., at https://www.legacy.com/us/obituaries/legacyremembers/audrey-haughton-james-obituary?id=44978610.

'Australia in the 1960s', *My Place*, n.d., at https://myplace.edu.au/decades_timeline/decade/1960.

'Australia in the 1990s', *My Place*, n.d., at https://myplace.edu.au/decades_timeline/decade/1990.

'Australia in the 2000s', *My Place*, n.d., at https://myplace.edu.au/decades_timeline/decade/2000.

'Australia in the 2010s', *My Place*, n.d., at https://myplace.edu.au/decades_timeline/decade/2010.

'Australian Defence Medal', *Department of Defence*, n.d., at https://www.defence.gov.au/adf-members-families/honours-awards/medals/australian-awards/australian-defence-medal.

Aviation Safety Net, n.d., at https://aviation-safety.net/database/record.php?id=19420227-2.

'Bali Bombing', *Royal Australian Air Force*, n.d., at https://www.airforce.gov.au/about-us/history/our-journey/bali-bombing.

Banning, GL, 'Origins of uniforms, rank and insignia of the RAAF', *Department of Defence*, 23 September 2020, at http://drnet/raaf/AirForce/AirForceUniform/Pages/Uniform%20History.aspx.

Bardoe, Barrie, 'Women in the RAAF', *Australian Air Power Today*, n.d., at https://australianairpowertoday.com.au/women-in-the-raaf/.

Bremner, Dorothy, 'Ida Clare Marie Johnston', *Smythe Family*, 2001, at http://www.smythe.id.au/family/ida.htm.

'Carey Margaret Jones 105088', *RAAFA Aviation Heritage Museum*, updated 2022, at https://aviationmuseumwa.org.au/afcraaf-roll/carey-margaret-jones-105088/.

'Cold war nurses', *Australian War Memorial*, updated 6 May 2021, at https://www.awm.gov.au/visit/exhibitions/nurses/cold.

'Commonwealth War Graves', *Commonwealth War Graves Commission*, updated 2023 at: https://www.cwgc.org/.

'Cyclone Tracy's destruction of Darwin (25 December 1975)', *Royal Australian Air Force*, n.d., at https://www.airforce.gov.au/about-us/history/our-journey/cyclone-tracys-destruction-darwin.

Dahl, Maxine, 'Clare Grant Stevenson (1903–1988)', *Australian Dictionary of Biography*, updated 2012, at https://adb.anu.edu.au/biography/stevenson-clare-grant-15550/text26762.

'Diggles, Ray Silvester', *Virtual War Memorial Australia*, n.d., at https://vwma.org.au/explore/people/625942.

'"Doing a grand job!" Join the WAAAF', *Australian War Memorial*, updated 2023, at https://www.awm.gov.au/collection/C100622.

Gilchrist, Catie, 'Home and Away; Australian Nurses During The Vietnam War', *Anzac Memorial*, updated 2023, at https://www.anzacmemorial.nsw.gov.au/our-stories/our-stories/home-and-away-australian-nurses-during-vietnam-war.

'Grace Halstead (Gay (nee Bury))', *Australians at War Film Archive*, updated 2020, at http://australiansatwarfilmarchive.unsw.edu.au/archive/2593.

Groves, Derham, 'History of Australian television', *Only Melbourne*, n.d., at https://www.onlymelbourne.com.au/history-of-aus-television.

'Hammer, Julie Margaret (1955 –)', *Swinburne University of Technology*, 1 August 2007, at https://www.eoas.info/biogs/P004274b.htm.

'Hammer, Julie Margaret, (Air Vice Marshal, AM, CSC, FIEAust, CPEng, FRAeS, GAICD) (1955-)', *Trove*, n.d., at https://trove.nla.gov.au/people/769076?c=people.

Heywood, Anne, 'Women's Auxiliary Australian Air Force (WAAAF)', *The Australian Women's Register*, 5 June 2009, at https://www.womenaustralia.info/entries/womens-auxiliary-australian-air-force-waaaf/.

'Indonesian Tsunami', *Royal Australian Air Force*, n.d., at https://www.airforce.gov.au/about-us/history/our-journey/indonesian-tsunami.

'Keep them flying!', *Australian War Memorial*, updated 2023, at https://www.awm.gov.au/collection/C103197.

'Julie Hammer', *Radschool Association Magazine*, n.d., at https://www.radschool.org.au/magazines/Vol68/Page7.htm.

'Last Combat Mission of Iraq War', *Royal Australian Air Force*, n.d., at https://www.airforce.gov.au/about-us/history/our-journey/last-combat-mission-iraq-war.

'Lockheed C-141 Starlifter', *The AMARC Experience*, updated 2024, at http://www.amarcexperience.com/ui/index.php?option=com_content&view=article&id=189&catid=8&Itemid=496.

'Lucy Lane', *Australians at War Film Archive*, updated 2020, at http://australiansatwarfilmarchive.unsw.edu.au/archive/417.

Maguire, Sarah, 'The 2010s: A decade of disrupters', *Macquarie University*, updated 27 December 2019, at https://lighthouse.mq.edu.au/article/december-2019/The-2010s-A-decade-of-disrupters.

'Margaret Helen (Mardi) Gething (1920–2005)', *Obituaries Australia*, at https://oa.anu.edu.au/obituary/gething-margarethelen- mardi-18717/text30317.

'Margaret McIntosh Clarke', *Pettigrew*, updated 2024, at https://www.pettigrew.com.au/upcoming-services/clarke-margaret.

'Marie Eileen Craig', *Australian War Memorial*, updated 2023, at https://www.awm.gov.au/collection/R1702456.

'Marjorie Boyling WAAAF uniform', *Australian Dress Register*, n.d., at https://australiandressregister.org/garment/275/.

'Melbourne, Vic. 1943-06-04. The trend of communal life alters during wartime. This Melbourne ...', *Australian War Memorial*, updated 2023, at https://www.awm.gov.au/collection/052228.

'NAA: J1113, 3-259-AIR PART 1', *National Archives of Australia*, 2024 at: https://recordsearch.naa.gov.au/SearchNRetrieve/Interface/ViewImage.aspx?B=21039223

'Our journey', *Royal Australian Air Force*, n.d., at https://airforce2021.airforce.gov.au/journey.

'Pamela Penglase', *Australians at War Film Archive*, updated 2020, at http://australiansatwarfilmarchive.unsw.edu.au/archive/1737.

'Pantyhose : Section Officer (Sister) P A Furbank, No 4 Hospital Butterworth Malaya', *Australian War Memorial*, updated 2024, at https://www.awm.gov.au/collection/C1203642?image=1.

'Patricia Furbank (Pat or Furby) – Transcript of interview', *Australians at War Film Archive*, updated 25 March 2004, at https://australiansatwarfilmarchive.unsw.edu.au/archive/htmlTranscript/1656.

'Presentation of the United States Air Medal', *Journal of Military and Veterans' Health*, updated 2024, at https://jmvh.org/article/presentation-of-the-united-states-air-medal/.

'RAAF personnel deployed to international coalition based in Kyrgyzstan', *Royal Australian Air Force*, n.d., at https://www.airforce.gov.au/about-us/history/our-journey/raaf-personnel-deployed-international-coalition-based-kyrgyzstan.

Robertson, Sophie, 'Tribute to the 1950s', *News Corps Australia*, updated 6 April 2021, at https://www.mytributes.com.au/article/australian-stories/tribute-1950s/4229908/.

'Robyn Clay-Williams', *Royal Australian Air Force*, n.d., at https://airforce2021.airforce.gov.au/people/robyn-clay-williams.

'Roll of Honour', *Australian War Memorial*, updated 2023. at https://www.awm.gov.au/advanced-search/people?roll=Roll%20of%20Honour.

Simpson, Margaret, 'The 1950s Australian Dream – Holdens, Victas and Mixmasters', *Museum of Applied Arts and Sciences*, updated 22 August 2018, at https://www.maas.museum/inside-the-collection/2018/08/22/the-1950s-australian-dream-holdens-victas-and-mixmasters/.

Street, Jacqui, 'Women Forced to Quit the Military Are Tracking down Their Australian Defence Medals', *ABC News*, updated 2 January 2019, at https://www.abc.net.au/news/2019-01-02/women-forced-to-quit-military-tracking-down-their-defence-medals/10672670.

'The Corporal Margaret Clarke Award', *Air and Space Power Centre*, n.d., at https://airpower.airforce.gov.au/corporal-margaret-clarke-award.

'The Defence of Australia (1994 Defence White Paper)', *Parliament of Australia*, n.d., at https://www.aph.gov.au/About_Parliament/Parliamentary_departments/Parliamentary_Library/pubs/rp/rp1516/DefendAust/1994.

'The pill', *The National Museum of Australia*, updated 6 March 2023, at https://www.nma.gov.au/defining-moments/resources/the-pill.

'The RAAF in art: Women's Auxiliary Australian Air Force', *Australian War Memorial*, updated 10 March 2021, at https://www.awm.gov.au/raaf-in-art/second-world-war/waaaf.

Tikkanen, Amy, 'Timeline of the 1980s', *Britannica*, n.d., at http://www.britannica.com/story/timeline-of-the-1980s.

'United Nations Transitional Administration In East Timor: UNTAET', *United Nations*, updated 2001, at https://peacekeeping.un.org/sites/default/files/past/etimor/etimor.htm.

'Verdun Bernice Sheah', *Australian War Memorial*, updated 2023, at https://www.awm.gov.au/collection/R1717900.

Williamson, Brett, 'Air Vice Marshal Tracy Smart: From country girl to Australian Defence Force Surgeon General', *ABC News*, 18 July 2016, at https://www.abc.net.au/news/2016-07-18/from-country-girl-to-adf-surgeon-general-tracy-smart/7637582.

Wilson, Caroline, 'AFL's quarantine hub a "template for future confinements"', *The Age*, 31 July 2020, at https://www.theage.com.au/sport/afl/afl-s-quarantine-hub-a-template-for-future-confinements-20200730-p55h2q.html.

'Women's Auxiliary Australian Air Force', *Smythe Family*, 2001, at www.smythe.id.au/waaaf/index.htm.

'Women's Auxiliary Australian Air Force (WAAAF) Uniform worn by Ena Wilson', *Australian Dress Register*, n.d., at https://australiandressregister.org/garment/538/.

'Women's Royal Australian Air Force (1951–1977)', *WRAAF Branch Qld*, updated 2009, at http://www.wraaf.org.au/History.html.

'WRAAF's Greatest Champion Honoured with an OAM', *Department of Veterans' Affairs*, n.d., at https://www.dva.gov.au/newsroom/latest-news-veterans/wraafs-greatest-champion-honoured-oam.

'WRAAF uniforms', *Radschool Association Inc.*, n.d., at https://www.radschool.org.au/magazines/Vol73/Page15.htm#WRAAF%20Uniforms.

Thesis

Williams, Anna, 'Heritage of the Empire Air Armada: The Museological Inheritance of the Empire Air Training Scheme in Australia', The University of Sydney, 2022.

ENDNOTES

Front cover image

1 'Aerial Photography: Unique Job for a WAAAF', *The Western Mail*, 30 December 1943; 'Benn Hilary Josephine : Service Number - 90664 : Date of Birth - 22 May 1923 : Place of Birth - Carlton VIC : Place of Enlistment - Melbourne : Next of Kin - Turner A', n.d. A9301, National Archives of Australia.

2 Margaret Beveridge, 'WAAAF Cinema Photographers', *Weekly Times*, 28 July 1943.

3 Ibid.

4 'Aerial Photography: Unique Job for a WAAAF', *The Western Mail*, 30 December 1943.

Timeline of key events for Air Force servicewomen

1 'Women in the Service' in *Customs and Traditions Manual*, Department of Defence, Canberra, unpublished; John McDonald, 'Women's services 1944–1977' in *Shades of Blue*, Department of Defence, Canberra, unpublished; Christine Reghenzani, 'Women in the ADF: six decades of policy change (1950 to 2011)', Department of Parliamentary Services, Parliament of Australia, November 2015; Mark Lax, 'Women in the RAAF' in *Taking the Lead: The Royal Australian Air Force 1972–1996*, Simon and Schuster, Cammeray, 2020.

2 McDonald, 'Women's services 1944–1977'; Lax, 'Women in the RAAF'; Chris Clark, 'Women in the RAAF – Talking Points', *Department of Defence*, Canberra, unpublished; 'Women in the Service'; Reghenzani, 'Women in the ADF'.

3 Lax, 'Women in the RAAF'; McDonald, 'Women's services 1944–1977'; 'Women in the Service'.

4 Reghenzani, 'Women in the ADF'; Lax, 'Women in the RAAF'; 'Women in the Service'.

THE 1940s

Introduction

1 Anna Williams, 'Heritage of the Empire Air Armada: The Museological Inheritance of the Empire Air Training Scheme in Australia', The University of Sydney, 2022, p. 7.

2 Roland Wilson (Ed.), 'Commonwealth Bureau of Census and Statistics. Official Year Book of the Commonwealth of Australia. No. 36: 1944 and 1945', Canberra, 1947; Williams, 'Heritage of the Empire Air Armada', p. 4.

3 Tony Brady, *The Empire Has An Answer: The Empire Air Training Scheme As Reported in the Australian Press 1939–1945*, Big Sky Publishing, Newport, 2019, p. 41; 'Bell Mary Teston Luis : Service Number - 350307 : Date of Birth - 03 Dec 1903 : Place of Birth - Unknown : Place of Enlistment - Unknown : Next of Kin - Bell J', n.d. A9300, National Archives of Australia.

4 Douglas Gillison, *Royal Australian Air Force, 1939–1942*, Australian War Memorial, Canberra, 1962, p. 99.

5 Ibid.; 'Air Board Agenda 3341 (RAAF) - Proposed Expansion of Women's Auxiliary Australian Air Force', n.d. A14487, National Archives of Australia; 'Royal Australian Air Force', *Australian Air War Effort*, 10th Ed., 31 Aug 1945.

6 Gillison, *Royal Australian Air Force, 1939–1942*, pp. 99–100; 'Bell Mary Teston Luis', National Archives of Australia.

7 Clare Stevenson and Honor Darling, *The W.A.A.A.F. Book*, Hale & Iremonger, Sydney, 1984, pp. 13–15; 'Big Air Post For Sydney Woman', *The News*, 21 May 1941; 'Women's Auxiliary Air Force', *Daily Advertiser*, 22 May 1941; 'Women's Air Job Surprise', *Daily Telegraph*, 22 May 1941.

8 Ibid.

9 'Stevenson Clare Grant : Service Number - 351001 : Date of Birth - 18 Jul 1903 : Place of Birth - Unknown : Place of Enlistment - Unknown : Next of Kin - Stevenson A', n.d. A9300, National Archives of Australia.

10 Gillison, *Royal Australian Air Force, 1939–1942*, p. 2.

11 *Australian Air War Effort*, p. 80.

12 'Pamela Penglase', *Australians at War Film Archive*, updated 2020, at http://australiansatwarfilmarchive.unsw.edu.au/archive/1737.

13 Ibid.

14 *Australian Air War Effort*, p. 79.

15 'Clare Stevenson', *Wing and a Prayer*, Australian Broadcasting Corporation (n.d).

16 Stevenson and Darling, *The W.A.A.A.F. Book*, p. 10.

17 *Australian Air War Effort*, p. 80.

18 Wilson, 'Commonwealth Bureau of Census and Statistics', p. 1034.

19 *Australian Air War Effort*, p.79.

20 'Director of W.A.A.F. Appointed: Squadron Officer Clare Stevenson Of Sydney', *The Advertiser*, 22 May 1941.

21 Ibid.

22 'Organisation & Administration WAAAF', n.d. A705, National Archives of Australia.

23 Maxine Dahl, 'Clare Grant Stevenson (1903–1988)', *Australian Dictionary of Biography*, updated 2012, at https://adb.anu.edu.au/biography/stevenson-clare-grant-15550/text26762.

24 Stevenson and Darling, *The W.A.A.A.F. Book*, p. 37.

25 Dahl, 'Clare Grant Stevenson (1903–1988)'.

26 'Pamela Penglase', *Australians at War Film Archive.*

27 'Girl Pilots Have the Last Laugh', *Sunday Sun and Guardian*, 11 April 1943; 'WAAAFs with Wings', *Army News* (13 April 1943).

28 'Gorey Leila Isabelle : Service Number - 93581 : Date of Birth - 29 Jan 1921 : Place of Birth - Leeton NSW : Place of Enlistment - Sydney : Next of Kin - Gorey Herbert', n.d. A9301, National Archives of Australia; Joyce Thomson, *The WAAAF in Wartime Australia*, Melbourne University Press, Melbourne, 1992, p. 342.

29 'Australian Woman to Ferry Planes', *Newcastle Sun*, 8 April 1942; 'Congratulated Over Long Distance: Gething – Gepp', *The Argus*, 13 May 1940; Kathy Mexted, *Australian Women Pilots: Amazing True Stories of Women in the Air*, New South Publishing, Sydney, 2020.

30 'Margaret Helen (Mardi) Gething (1920–2005)', *Obituaries Australia*, at https://oa.anu.edu.au/obituary/gething-margarethelen- mardi-18717/text30317; 'Lancaster Bomber's Visit', *Temora Independent*, 23 March 1945; Williams, 'Heritage of the Empire Air Armada'.

31 'Acting Squadron Leader (Sqn Ldr) Edward Arthur Hudson DFC and Bar, pilot of Rockhampton, Qld', *Australian War Memorial*, updated 2024, at https://www.awm.gov.au/collection/C386807.

32 'Alma Skeers', *Australians at War Film Archive*, updated 2020, athttps://australiansatwarfilmarchive.unsw.edu.au/archive/826.

33 *Australian Air War Effort*, p. 72; Gay Halstead, *Story of the RAAF Nursing Service 1940–1990*, Nungurner Press, Metung, 1994, p. 3.

34 'Air Board Agenda 2878 (RAAF) - Establishment of a Royal Australian Air Force Nursing Service', n.d. A14487, National Archives of Australia.

35 Halstead, p. 6.

36 'Air Board Agenda 2953 (RAAF) - Royal Australian Air Force Nursing Service', n.d. A14487, National Archives of Australia.

37 Halstead, *Story of the RAAF Nursing Service 1940–1990*, pp. 6–7.

38 Ibid., p. 7.

39 *Australian Air War Effort*, p. 75.

40 Ibid., pp. 16, 110.

41 'Lang Margaret Irene : Service Number - 500001 : Date of Birth - 23 May 1893 : Place of Birth - Unknown : Place of Enlistment - Unknown : Next of Kin - Kearney J', n.d. A9300, National Archives of Australia; 'Lang Margaret Irene : Service Number - Sister : Place of Birth - Oxley VIC : Place of Enlistment - 3MD [Third Military District] : Next of Kin - (Mother) Lang A', n.d. B2455, National Archives of Australia.

42 'Lang Margaret Irene', National Archives of Australia.

43 Halstead, *Story of the RAAF Nursing Service 1940–1990*, p. 23.

44 'Nursing Service of RAAF Five Years Old', *The Herald*, 26 July 1945.

45 'Lang Margaret Irene', National Archives of Australia.

46 'Death of Matron Lang: Founder of RAAF Nursing Service', *RAAF News*, 1 March 1983.

Sister Alma Skeers

1 'Pearse Alma Sarah Jane : Service Number - 501101 : Date of Birth - 08 Jan 1911 : Place of Birth - Unknown : Place of Enlistment - Unknown : Next of Kin - Pearse G Copies', n.d. A9300, National Archives of Australia; 'Alma Skeers', *Australians at War Film Archive*, updated 2020, at:https://australiansatwarfilmarchive.unsw.edu.au/archive/826.

2 'Alma Skeers', *Australians at War Film Archive.*

3 Ibid.

4 Ibid.

5 Ken Grimson, 'A Service of Thanksgiving Will Be Held Today', *The Daily Advertiser*, 4 January 2011, p. 5.

6 *Australians at War Film Archive.*

7 Ibid.

8 Ibid.

9 National Archives of Australia.

10 'Alma Skeers', *Australians at War Film Archive.*

11 Ibid.

12 Ibid.

13 Ibid.

14 Ibid.

15 Ibid.

16 'Ancillary Units' in *Units of the Royal Australian Air Force: A Concise History*, Australian Government Publishing Service, Canberra, 1995, p. 69.

17 'Alma Skeers', *Australians at War Film Archive.*

18 Ibid.

19 Grimson, 'A Service of Thanksgiving Will Be Held Today'.

20 'Alma Skeers', *Australians at War Film Archive.*

21 Grimson, 'A Service of Thanksgiving Will Be Held Today'; Rebekah Holliday, 'Celebrations over RAAF Win', *The Daily Advertiser*, updated 7 November 2012, at https://www.dailyadvertiser.com.au/story/726148/celebrations-over-raaf-win/.

Flight Officer Norah Penglase

1 'Cooke Norah Pamela : Service Number - 91544 : Date of Birth - 22 Jul 1920 : Place of Birth - Prospect SA : Place of Enlistment - Adelaide SA : Next of Kin - Cooke Percival', n.d. A9300., National Archives of Australia.

2 'Pamela Penglase', *Australians at War Film Archive*, updated 2020, at http://australiansatwarfilmarchive.unsw.edu.au/archive/1737; 'Cooke Percy Bennett : Service Number - S42881 : Date of Birth - 26 Oct 1885 : Place of Birth - Hampshire England : Place of Enlistment - Unley SA : Next of Kin - Cooke Freda', n.d. B884, National Archives of Australia.

3 'Pamela Penglase', *Australians at War Film Archive.*

4 Ibid.

5 Ibid.

6 Ibid.

7 'Cooke Percy Bennett', National Archives of Australia.

8 'Pamela Penglase', *Australians at War Film Archive.*

9 'Cooke Gordon Oliver : Service Number - 28709 : Date of Birth - 06 Jan 1922 : Place of Birth - Rose Park SA : Place of Enlistment - Adelaide : Next of Kin - Cooke Joyce', n.d. A9301, National Archives of Australia; 'Volume 1 - RAAF Station, Parafield, South Australia - Personnel Occurrence Reports - 1/1945 - 25/1945, 1/1946 - 6/1946', n.d. A10605, National Archives of Australia.

10 'Pamela Penglase', *Australians at War Film Archive.*

11 Ibid.

12 Ibid.

13 Ibid.

14 'Ibid.

15 Ibid.

16 Ibid.

17 Ibid.

18 Clare Stevenson and Honor Darling, *The W.A.A.A.F. Book*, Hale & Iremonger, Sydney, 1984, pp. 35–6.

19 Ibid., p. 36.

20 'Pamela Penglase', *Australians at War Film Archive.*

21 Stevenson and Darling, *The W.A.A.A.F. Book*, p. 43.

22 'Pamela Penglase', *Australians at War Film Archive.*

23 Ibid.

24 'Cooke Norah Pamela', National Archives of Australia.

25 'Pamela Penglase', *Australians at War Film Archive.*

26 Ibid.

27 Ibid.

28 Ibid.

29 Ibid.

30 Ibid.

31 Ibid.

32 'Cooke Norah Pamela', National Archives of Australia.

33 'Pamela Penglase', *Australians at War Film Archive.*

34 Ibid.

35 Ibid.

36 'Cooke Norah Pamela', National Archives of Australia.

37 'Pamela Penglase', *Australians at War Film Archive.*

38 'Bride's Gown Was Sari: Navy Ceremony', *The News*, February 1946.

39 'Pamela Penglase', *Australians at War Film Archive.*

40 Ibid.

41 Ibid.

Corporal Audrey Haughton-James

1 'Audrey Haughton-James (Jean)', *Australians at War Film Archive*, updated 2020, at https://australiansatwarfilmarchive.unsw.edu.au/archive/1535/archive/826; 'Wyaralong Dam – Environmental Impact Statement.' Queensland Water Infrastructure Pty Ltd (2007).

2 Connie Baird, 'Re: Audrey Jean Campbell Haughton-James (Nee Philp) DOB: 20 Jan 1916 [Sec=Official]' [letter to Anna Williams], 15 May 2023.

3 'Audrey Haughton-James (Jean)', *Australians at War Film Archive.*

4 Ibid.

5 Ibid.

6 Naomi Parry, 'Tresillian Mothercraft Homes (1918 –)', *Royal Society for the Welfare of Mothers and Babies*, 2023.

7 'Audrey Haughton-James (Jean)', *Australians at War Film Archive.*

8 Ibid.

9 Ibid.

10 'Jackson Leslie Douglas : Service Number - 270520 : Date of Birth - 24 Feb 1917 : Place of Birth - Brisbane QLD : Place of Enlistment – Point Cook VIC : Next of Kin - Jackson William', n.d. A9300, National Archives of Australia; 'Big Air Race Plans: 'Planes Flock to Brisbane', *The Courier-Mail*, 14 December 1936.

11 'Audrey Haughton-James (Jean)', *Australians at War Film Archive*.

12 'Haughton-James Audrey Jean Campbell : Service Number - 94177 : Date of Birth - 20 Jan 1916 : Place of Birth - Beaudesert QLD : Place of Enlistment - Brisbane : Next of Kin - HaughtonJames Douglas', n.d., National Archives of Australia.

13 'Audrey Haughton-James (Jean)', *Australians at War Film Archive*.

14 Ibid.

15 Ibid.

16 Ibid.

17 Ibid.

18 Ibid.

19 Ibid.

20 Ibid.

21 Jean Haughton-James and Sheila Manley, *Wings at War: RAAF at Evans Head, 1939–1945*. Published by the authors, St Lucia, 1995, p. 77.

22 'Audrey Haughton-James (Jean)', *Australians at War Film Archive*.

23 Ibid.

24 Ibid.

25 Ibid.

26 Ibid.

27 Ibid.

28 Ibid.

29 Ibid.

30 Ibid.

31 Ibid.

32 Ibid.

33 Ibid.

34 Ibid.

35 Ibid.

36 'Haughton-James Audrey Jean Campbell', National Archives of Australia.

37 'Connelly Dermott Anthony : Service Number - 45 : Date of Birth - 02 Apr 1903 : Place of Birth - Melbourne VIC : Place of Enlistment – Point Cook : Next of Kin - Connelly B', n.d., National Archives of Australia.

38 'Audrey Haughton-James (Jean)', *Australians at War Film Archive*.

39 'Haughton-James Audrey Jean Campbell', National Archives of Australia.

40 'Connelly Dermott Anthony (Wing Commander) : Service Number - 45 : Unit - Royal Australian Air Force Station Sandgate, Royal Australian Air Force : Date of Court Martial - 22 September 1944', n.d., National Archives of Australia.

41 'Audrey Haughton-James (Jean)', *Australians at War Film Archive*.

42 'Connelly Dermott Anthony (Wing Commander)', National Archives of Australia.

43 'Audrey Haughton-James (Jean)', *Australians at War Film Archive*.

44 Ibid.

45 'Audrey Haughton James Obituary', *Legacy*, n.d., at https://www.legacy.com/us/obituaries/legacyremembers/audrey-haughton-james-obituary?id=44978610.

46 'Audrey Haughton-James (Jean)', *Australians at War Film Archive*.

47 'Audrey Haughton-James (Jean)', *Australians at War Film Archive*, updated 2020, at https://australiansatwarfilmarchive.unsw.edu.au/archive/1535/archive/826.

48 Ibid.

49 Ibid.

Aircraftwoman Rena Pascoe

1 Martin Ball, *Martin Ball interviews Rena Pascoe* [unpublished interview transcript], Royal Australian Air Force, n.d.

2 Ibid.

3 Ibid.

4 Ibid.

5 Ibid.

6 Ibid.

7 Ibid.

8 Ibid.

9 Ibid.

10 Ibid.

11 Ibid.

12 Ibid.

13 'Porter Rena June : Service Number - 91859 : Date of Birth - 12 May 1921 : Place of Birth – Yorketown SA : Place of Enlistment - Adelaide : Next of Kin – Unknown', n.d. A9301, National Archives of Australia.

14 Ball, *Martin Ball interviews Rena Pascoe.*

15 National Archives of Australia.

16 Ball, *Martin Ball interviews Rena Pascoe.*

17 Ibid.

18 National Archives of Australia.

19 Ball, *Martin Ball interviews Rena Pascoe.*

20 Ibid.

Corporal Olive Jardine

1 'McNeil Olive Winifred : Service Number - 93766 : Date of Birth - 23 Jan 1921 : Place of Birth - Gladesville NSW : Place of Enlistment - Sydney : Next of Kin – McNeil Hector', n.d. A9301, National Archives of Australia.

2 Ibid.

3 'Olive Jardine – Transcript of Interview' [unpublished interview transcript], *Australians at War Film Archive*, 3 June 2003.

4 'McNeil Olive Winifred', National Archives of Australia.

5 Ibid.

6 Anna Williams, 'Heritage of the Empire Air Armada: The Museological Inheritance of the Empire Air Training Scheme in Australia', The University of Sydney (2022), p. 200.

7 'Curnow Thomas Charles: Service Number - 59: Date of Birth - 07 Aug 1911: Place of Birth - Ballarat VIC: Place of Enlistment – Point Cook: Next of Kin - Curnow Claire', n.d., National Archives of Australia.

8 'Olive Jardine – Transcript of Interview' *Australians at War Film Archive.*

9 Ibid.

10 'McNeil Olive Winifred', National Archives of Australia.

11 Ibid.

12 'Olive Jardine – Transcript of Interview' *Australians at War Film Archive.*

13 Peter Ilbery, *Empire Airmen Strike Back: The Empire Air Training Scheme and 5 SFTS, Uranquinty*, Banner Books, Maryborough, 1999, p. 161.

14 'Olive Jardine – Transcript of Interview' *Australians at War Film Archive.*

15 Ibid.; 'McNeil Olive Winifred', National Archives of Australia.

16 'McNeil Olive Winifred', National Archives of Australia.

17 'Olive Winifred Jardine', *Sydney Morning Herald*, updated 12 October 2022, at https://tributes.smh.com.au/obituaries/460279/olive-winifred-jardine/?r=https://tributes.smh.com.au/obituaries/smh-au/; 'A Life of Adventure and Faith: DHL Resident Olive Jardine Turns 100', *BaptistCare*, updated 2024, at https://baptistcare.org.au/blog/a-life-of-adventure-and-faith-dhl-resident-olive-jardine-turns-100.

Corporal Shirley Brettle

1 Michael Garside, *Michael Garside interviews Shirley Brettle* [unpublished interview transcript], Royal Australian Air Force, 6 January 2016.

2 Ibid.

3 'Brettle Shirley Joan : Service Number - 98395 : Date of Birth - 03 Jun 1921 : Place of Birth - Randwick NSW : Place of Enlistment - Sydney : Next of Kin - Brettle Horace', n.d. A9301, National Archives of Australia.

4 Ibid.

5 Garside, *Michael Garside interviews Shirley Brettle.*

6 Clare Stevenson and Honor Darling, *The W.A.A.A.F. Book*, Hale & Iremonger, Sydney, 1984, p. 114.

7 Morrie Fenton, *The History and Stories of 131 Radar Ash Island 1942–46*, Fenton, Lockleys, 1995, p. 1.

8 Stevenson and Darling, *The W.A.A.A.F. Book*, p. 114.

9 Ibid., p. 115.

10 Garside, *Michael Garside interviews Shirley Brettle.*

11 Fenton, *The History and Stories of 131 Radar Ash Island 1942–46*, pp. 1–4.

12 Garside, *Michael Garside interviews Shirley Brettle.*

13 Fenton, *The History and Stories of 131 Radar Ash Island 1942–46*, p. 111.

14 Garside, *Michael Garside interviews Shirley Brettle.*

15 Ibid.

16 Ibid.

17 Ibid.

18 Ibid.

Corporal Margaret Clarke

1 'Women's Auxiliary Australian Air Force', *Smythe Family*, 2001, at www.smythe.id.au/waaaf/index.htm.

2 Michael Garside, *Michael Garside interviews Margaret Clarke* [unpublished interview transcript], Royal Australian Air Force, 12 August 2019.

3 Dorothy Bremner, 'Ida Clare Marie Johnston', *Smythe Family*, 2001, at http://www.smythe.id.au/family/ida.htm.

4 Garside, *Michael Garside interviews Margaret Clarke*; Bremner, 'Ida Clare Marie Johnston'.

5 Bremner, 'Ida Clare Marie Johnston'.

6 'Clarke Margaret McIntosh : Service Number - 105705 : Date of Birth - 19 May 1924 : Place of Birth - Rockdale NSW : Place of Enlistment - Sydney : Next of Kin – Clarke Leo', n.d. A9301, National Archives of Australia.

7 228 *Smythe Family.*

8 Ibid.

9 National Archives of Australia.

10 Garside.

11 Ibid.

12 Ibid.

13 Ibid.

14 Ibid.

15 Ibid.

16 Ibid.

17 *Smythe Family.*

18 Garside.

19 Ibid.

20 Bremner.

21 Garside.

22 Ibid.

23 National Archives of Australia.

24 Garside.

25 'The Corporal Margaret Clarke Award', *Air and Space Power Centre*, n.d. at: https://airpower.airforce.gov.au/corporal-margaret-clarke-award

26 Ibid.

Sister Lucy Lane

1 'Lucy Lane', *Australians at War Film Archive*, updated 2020 at: http://australiansatwarfilmarchive.unsw.edu.au/archive/417

2 Ibid.

3 'Mackenzie Lucy Georgia : Service Number - 500358 : Date of Birth - 11 Oct 1918 : Place of Birth - Unknown : Place of Enlistment - Unknown : Next of Kin - Mackenzie James', n.d. A9300, National Archives of Australia.

4 'Lucy Lane', *The Age*, updated 2022 at: https://tributes.theage.com.au/obituaries/93800/lucy-lane/

Aircraftwoman Sheila Van Emden

1 'Sheila Van Emden - Transcript of Interview', *Australians at War Film Archive*, no. 369, 26 May 2003.

2 'Ferguson, Sheila Catherine [Australian Women's Land Army History Card]', n.d., National Archives of Australia.

3 'Sheila Van Emden - Transcript of Interview', *Australians at War Film Archive.*

4 'Ferguson William Henry : Service Number - N102710 : Date of Birth - 05 Nov 1894 : Place of Birth - Nth Botany Nsw : Place of Enlistment - Marrickville Nsw : Next of Kin - Ferguson Olivia', n.d., National Archives of Australia.

5 'Ferguson Sheila Catherine: Service Number - 177348: Date of Birth - 07 May 1926: Place of Birth - Paddington Nsw: Place of Enlistment - Sydney: Next of Kin - Ferguson William', n.d., National Archives of Australia; 'Ferguson Eric Robert : Sern 5079 : Pob Repton Nsw : Poe Holsworthy Nsw : Nok F Ferguson George Ross', n.d., National Archives of Australia.

6 'Dalzell George : Sern 4763 : Pob Newcastle Nsw : Poe Warwick Farm Nsw : Nok F Dalzell Thomas', n.d., National Archives of Australia.

7 'Ferguson William Henry', National Archives of Australia.

8 'Ferguson, Joan [Australian Women's Land Army Medical and Hospital Card]', n.d., National Archives of Australia.

9 'Ferguson, Sheila [Australian Women's Land Army Medical and Hospital Card]', n.d., National Archives of Australia; 'Sheila Van Emden - Transcript of Interview', *Australians at War Film Archive.*

10 'Sheila Van Emden - Transcript of Interview', *Australians at War Film Archive.*

11 Ibid.

12 Ibid.

13 Ibid.

14 Ibid.

15 'Ferguson Sheila Catherine', National Archives of Australia.

16 Ibid.

17 'Sheila Van Emden - Transcript of Interview', *Australians at War Film Archive.*

18 Ibid.

19 'Ferguson Sheila Catherine', National Archives of Australia.

20 'Sheila Van Emden - Transcript of Interview', *Australians at War Film Archive.*

21 Ibid.

22 'Ferguson Sheila Catherine', National Archives of Australia.

23 'Sheila Van Emden - Transcript of Interview', *Australians at War Film Archive.*

24 Ibid.

25 Frank Smyth, 'Pigs of the R.A.A.F.', *Sydney Morning Herald*, 27 March 1943.

26 'Sheila Van Emden - Transcript of Interview', *Australians at War Film Archive.*

27 Ibid.

28 'Ferguson Sheila Catherine', National Archives of Australia.

29 Ibid.

30 'Anzac Day Spirit a Legacy We Must Preserve', *The Irrigator*, 27 April 2018; Tim Barlass, 'Battler Who Has Helped Put Women on the Front Line of Anzac Day March', *The Area News*, 25 April 2018.

31 Catherine Kenny, 'Making Hay for War', *Sydney Morning Herald*, 21 February 1987; John Stapelton, 'Silent Battlers Get a Great Hearing', *Sydney Morning Herald*, 14 November 1988.

32 'Sheila Vanemden', *Sydney Morning Herald*, n.d., at https://tributes.smh.com.au/obituaries/22201/sheila-vanemden/.

Second World War recruitment language and imagery

1 'W.A.A.A.F's do vital war jobs', *PIX*, vol. 9, no. 18, 2 May 1942, pp. 3–5.

2 Ibid.

3 Ibid.

4 'Keep them flying!', *Australian War Memorial*, updated 2023, at https://www.awm.gov.au/collection/C103197.

5 Ibid.

6 'Melbourne, Vic. 1943-06-04. The trend of communal life alters during wartime. This Melbourne ...' *Australian War Memorial*, updated 2023. at https://www.awm.gov.au/collection/052228.

7 'Airwoman we thank you,' *Department of Defence*, 1943.

8 Ibid.

9 'A tribute to the W.A.A.A.F.', *Department of Defence*, 1943.

10 'W.A.A.A.F's do vital war jobs', *PIX*.

11 'Girls with sports ability volunteer for W.A.A.A.F.', *The Telegraph*, 5 Jan 1942, p. 7.

12 '"Doing a grand job!" Join the WAAAF', *Australian War Memorial*, updated 2023, at https://www.awm.gov.au/collection/C100622.

13 'I wouldn't be out of it for anything, Dad!', *The Australian Women's Weekly*, 28 October 1944, p. 6.

14 'A tribute to the W.A.A.A.F.', *Department of Defence*.

15 *The Australian Women's Weekly*.

16 Ibid.

17 Ibid.

18 'Girls with sports ability volunteer for W.A.A.A.F.', *The Telegraph*; 'W.A.A.A.F's do vital war jobs', *PIX*.

THE 1950s

Introduction

1 Andrew Clark, 'How the 1950s paved the way for modern Australia', *The Australian Financial Review*, updated 30 September 2021, at https://www.afr.com/policy/economy/how-the-1950s-paved-the-way-for-modern-australia-20210809-p58hcg.

2 Margaret Simpson, 'The 1950s Australian Dream – Holdens, Victas and Mixmasters', *Museum of Applied Arts and Sciences*, updated 22 August 2018, at https://www.maas.museum/inside-the-collection/2018/08/22/the-1950s-australian-dream-holdens-victas-and-mixmasters/; Sophie Robertson, 'Tribute to the 1950s', *News Corps Australia*, updated 6 April 2021, at https://www.mytributes.com.au/article/australian-stories/tribute-1950s/4229908/; Clark, 'How the 1950s paved the way for modern Australia'.

3 Clark, 'How the 1950s paved the way for modern Australia'; Robertson, 'Tribute to the 1950s'.

4 'Women in the Service' in *Customs and Traditions Manual*, Department of Defence, Canberra, unpublished; John McDonald, 'Women's services 1944–1977' in *Shades of Blue*, Department of Defence, Canberra, unpublished; Christine Reghenzani, 'Women in the ADF: six decades of policy change (1950 to 2011)', Department of Parliamentary Services, Parliament of Australia (November 2015); Mark Lax, 'Women in the RAAF' in *Taking the Lead: The Royal Australian Air Force 1972–1996*, Simon and Schuster, Cammeray, 2020.

5 Lax, 'Women in the RAAF'; McDonald, 'Women's services 1944–1977'; 'Women's Royal Australian Air Force (1951–1977)', *WRAAF Branch Qld*, updated 2009, at http://www.wraaf.org.au/History.html.

Sergeant Shirley McLaren

1 Michael Garside, *Michael Garside interviews Shirley McLaren* [unpublished sound recording], Royal Australian Air Force, 27 February 2020.

2 Ibid.

3 Ibid.

4 Ibid.

5 Ibid.

6 Ibid.

7 Ibid.

8 Ibid.

9 'WRAAF's Greatest Champion Honoured with an OAM', *Department of Veterans' Affairs*, n.d., at https://www.dva.gov.au/newsroom/latest-news-veterans/wraafs-greatest-champion-honoured-oam.

10 Garside, *Michael Garside interviews Shirley McLaren.*

11 'New Medal for Defence Service Approved', *Royal Australian Navy News*, 15 July 2004; 'Medal Reflects on Volunteers', *Royal Australian Navy News*, 15 July 2004; 'Medal Struck for Military Service. Recognition of Volunteer Service for ADF Members', *Royal Australian Navy News*, 4 November 2004.

12 Michael Garside, 'Gold Commendation for Veteran', *Defence News*, updated 17 September 2020, at https://www.defence.gov.au/news-events/news/2020-09-17/gold-commendation-veteran.

13 'Australian Defence Medal', *Department of Defence*, n.d., at https://www.defence.gov.au/adf-members-families/honours-awards/medals/australian-awards/australian-defence-medal; 'More Eligible for Medal', *Royal Australian Navy News*, 20 April 2006.

14 'Australian Defence Medal', *Department of Defence*; 'More Eligible for Medal', *Royal Australian Navy News.*

15 Jacqui Street, 'Women Forced to Quit the Military Are Tracking down Their Australian Defence Medals', *ABC News*, updated 2 January 2019, at https://www.abc.net.au/news/2019-01-02/women-forced-to-quit-military-tracking-down-their-defence-medals/10672670.

Sister Grace Halstead

1 'Bury Grace Elizabeth : Service Number - N35304 : Date of Birth - 21/03/1929 : Place of Birth - Bairnsdale, VIC : Conflict – Korea', n.d. A12372, National Archives of Australia.

2 'Gay Loving Life Nine Decades On', *Lakes Post*, 30 March 2019.

3 Ibid.

4 'Bury Grace Elizabeth', National Archives of Australia.

5 Ibid.

6 Gay Halstead, *Story of the RAAF Nursing Service 1940–1990*, Nungurner Press, Metung, 1994, pp. 270–73.

7 Ibid., p. 279.

8 'Grace Halstead (Gay (nee Bury))', *Australians at War Film Archive*, updated 2020, at http://australiansatwarfilmarchive.unsw.edu.au/archive/2593.

9 Halstead, *Story of the RAAF Nursing Service 1940*–1990, p. 295.

10 Grace Halstead (Gay (nee Bury))', *Australians at War Film Archive.*

11 Ibid.

12 Ibid.

13 Ibid.

14 Ibid.

15 Ibid.

16 Ibid.

17 Halstead, *Story of the RAAF Nursing Service 1940*–1990, p. 342.

18 'Grace Halstead (Gay (nee Bury))', *Australians at War Film Archive.*

19 'A Girl from the Backblocks, She Will Be Hostess to the Queen', *The Courier-Mail*, 30 December 1953; Halstead, *Story of the RAAF Nursing Service 1940*–1990, p. 339.

20 Halstead, *Story of the RAAF Nursing Service 1940*–1990, p. 342.
21 'Bury Grace Elizabeth', National Archives of Australia.
22 Halstead, *Story of the RAAF Nursing Service 1940*–1990, p. 339.
23 Ibid., p. 343.
24 'Grace Halstead (Gay (nee Bury))', *Australians at War Film Archive.*
25 Halstead, *Story of the RAAF Nursing Service 1940*–1990, pp. 344–46.
26 'Grace Halstead (Gay (nee Bury))', *Australians at War Film Archive.*
27 'She Was Queen's Flight Hostess', *The Argus*, 4 May 1954.
28 'Bury Grace Elizabeth', National Archives of Australia.
29 'Gay Loving Life Nine Decades On', *Lakes Post.*

Sergeant Yvonne Thompson

1 Linda New, *Linda New interviews Yvonne Thompson* [unpublished sound recording], Royal Australian Air Force, 11 November 2022.
2 Ibid.
3 Ibid.
4 Ibid.
5 Ibid.
6 Ibid.
7 Ibid.
8 Ibid.
9 Ibid.
10 Ibid.
11 Ibid.
12 Ibid.
13 Ibid.
14 Ibid.
15 Ibid.
16 Ibid.
17 Ibid.
18 Ibid.
19 Ibid.

THE 1960s

Introduction

1 'The dream decade that produced modern Australia', *The Australian Financial Review*, updated 21 October 2021, at https://www.afr.com/policy/economy/the-dream-decade-that-produced-modern-australia-20211021-p591ul; 'Australia in the 1960s', *My Place*, undated, at https://myplace.edu.au/decades_timeline/decade/1960.
2 'The pill', *The National Museum of Australia*, updated 6 March 2023, at https://www.nma.gov.au/defining-moments/resources/the-pill.
3 'Australia in the 1960s', *My Place*; Derham Groves, 'History of Australian television', *Only Melbourne*, undated, at https://www.onlymelbourne.com.au/history-of-aus-television.
4 Groves, 'History of Australian television'.
5 Catie Gilchrist, 'Home and Away; Australian Nurses During the Vietnam War', *Anzac Memorial*, 2022, at https://www.anzacmemorial.nsw.gov.au/our-stories/our-stories/home-and-away-australian-nurses-during-vietnam-war.
6 Christine Reghenzani, 'Women in the ADF: six decades of policy change (1950 to 2011)', Department of Parliamentary Services, Parliament of Australia, November 2015; Chris Clark, 'Women in the RAAF – Talking Points', *Department of Defence*, Canberra, unpublished.

Leading Aircraftwoman Lynette Mitchell

1 Sharyn Bolitho, *Sharyn Bolitho interviews Lynette Mitchell* [unpublished interview transcript], Royal Australian Air Force, 22 September 2023.

2 Lynette Mitchell, 'A WRAAF's Story', in *In Our Spirit: Creative Works of Australian Defence Force Women from 1960s Onward*, Melanie Bird and Jennifer Crane, 2020, pp. 106–10.

3 Ibid., p. 106.

4 Ibid., p. 107.

5 Ibid., p. 109.

6 Ibid., p. 108.

7 Ibid.

8 Ibid.

9 Bolitho, *Sharyn Bolitho interviews Lynette Mitchell.*

10 'My Story!', *Radschool Association Magazine*, February 2012.

11 Bolitho, *Sharyn Bolitho interviews Lynette Mitchell.*

12 Ibid.

13 'My Story!', *Radschool Association Magazine.*

14 Bolitho, *Sharyn Bolitho interviews Lynette Mitchell.*

15 Ibid.

16 Ibid.

17 Mitchell, 'A WRAAF's Story', p. 106.

18 Lynette Mitchell [personnel correspondence], 7 December 2023.

19 Bolitho, *Sharyn Bolitho interviews Lynette Mitchell.*

20 Mitchell, 'A WRAAF's Story', p. 106.

21 Ibid., p. 110.

Leading Aircraftwoman Sandra Perry

1 David Turner, *David Turner interviews Sandra Perry* [unpublished interview transcript], Royal Australian Air Force, 2 June 2022.

2 Ibid.

3 Ibid.

4 Ibid.

5 Ibid.

6 Ibid.

7 Ibid.

8 Ibid.

9 Ibid.

10 Ibid.

11 Ibid.

12 Ibid.

13 Ibid.

Squadron Leader Patricia Furbank

1 'Patricia Furbank (Pat or Furby) - Transcript of interview', *Australians at War Film Archive*, updated 25 March 2004, at https://australiansatwarfilmarchive.unsw.edu.au/archive/htmlTranscript/1656.

2 Ibid.

3 Ibid.

4 Ibid.

5 Ibid.

6 Ibid.
7 Ibid.
8 Ibid.
9 Ibid.
10 Ibid.
11 Ibid.
12 Ibid.
13 Ibid.
14 Ibid.
15 Ibid.
16 Ibid.
17 Ibid.
18 Ibid.
19 Ibid.
20 Ibid.
21 Ibid.
22 'Lockheed C-141 Starlifter', *The AMARC Experience*, updated 2024, at http://www.amarcexperience.com/ui/index.php?option=com_content&view=article&id=189&catid=8&Itemid=496.
23 'Patricia Furbank (Pat or Furby) - Transcript of interview', *Australians at War Film Archive.*
24 'Pantyhose : Section Officer (Sister) P A Furbank, No 4 Hospital Butterworth Malaya', *Australian War Memorial*, updated 2024 at: https://www.awm.gov.au/collection/C1203642?image=1
25 Annabelle Brayley, *Our Vietnam Nurses*, Penguin Random House Australia, Southbank, 2016, p. 95.

The Vietnam War: the silent contributors

1 Gay Halstead, *Story of the RAAF Nursing Service 1940–1990*, Nungurner Press, Metung, 1994, p. 327.
2 Ibid., pp. 329–30.
3 Gaynor Tilley [submission to Royal Australian Air Force historical records], Department of Defence, 19 July 1994.
4 Ibid.
5 *Report of the Committee of Inquiry into Defence Awards*, 1993, Department of Defence, Canberra, pp. 52–3.
6 'Presentation of the United States Air Medal', *Journal of Military and Veterans' Health*, updated 2024 at: https://jmvh.org/article/presentation-of-the-united-states-air-medal/
7 Annabelle Brayley, *Our Vietnam Nurses*, Penguin Random House Australia, Southbank, 2016, p. 261.
8 Ibid., p. 262.

THE 1970s

Introduction

1 'ABC Archives and Library Services', *Australian Broadcasting Corporation*, updated 2002, at https://www.abc.net.au/archives/timeline/1970s.htm; Andrew Clark, 'The 1970s: Why the 1970s was the decade of living dangerously', *The Australian Financial Review*, updated 30 September 2021, at https://www.afr.com/policy/economy/why-the-1970s-was-the-decade-of-living-dangerously-20210916-p58s6r.
2 Christine Reghenzani, 'Women in the ADF: six decades of policy change (1950 to 2011)', Department of Parliamentary Services, Parliament of Australia, November 2015.
3 'Cyclone Tracy's destruction of Darwin (25 December 1975)', *Royal Australian Air Force*, n.d., at https://www.airforce.gov.au/about-us/history/our-journey/cyclone-tracys-destruction-darwin; Stefan Armbruster, 'Darwin marks the day Tracy blew Christmas away', updated 25 December 2014, at https://www.sbs.com.au/news/article/darwin-marks-the-day-tracy-blew-christmas-away/i12tf1bsg.
4 'Royal Tributes to the RAAF (1 March 1971)', *RAAF News*, 1 March 1971, at https://trove.nla.gov.au/newspaper/article/259477549?searchTerm=RAAF%20women%201970s.

Air Vice-Marshal Julie Hammer

1 Phil Morrall, *Phil Morrall interviews Julie Hammer* [unpublished interview transcript], Royal Australian Air Force, 6 March, 2013, p. 2.

2 'Air Vice-Marshal Julie Hammer is UQ's 2003 alumni ace', *The University of Queensland*, 17 September 2003, at https://www.uq.edu.au/news/article/2003/09/air-vice-marshal-julie-hammer-uq%E2%80%99s-2003-alumni-ace.

3 Michael Nelmes, *Michael Nelmes interviews Julie Hammer* [unpublished interview transcript], Australian War Memorial, 14 November 2005, p. 4.

4 Julie Hammer [question and answer transcript], 8 March 2023.

5 'Julie Hammer', *Radschool Association Magazine*, n.d., at: https://www.radschool.org.au/magazines/Vol68/Page7.htm; Christine Reghenzani, 'Women in the ADF: six decades of policy change (1950 to 2011)', Department of Parliamentary Services, Parliament of Australia (November 2015), p. 14.

6 Nelmes, p. 7.

7 Morrall, *Phil Morrall interviews Julie Hammer*, p. 2.

8 Ibid.

9 Nelmes, p. 10.

10 Hammer, 8 March 2023.

11 Morrall, *Phil Morrall interviews Julie Hammer*, p. 3.

12 Nelmes, p. 14.

13 Morrall, *Phil Morrall interviews Julie Hammer*, p. 9.

14 Ibid, p. 4.

15 Nelmes, p. 19.

16 Ibid, p. 20.

17 Morrall, *Phil Morrall interviews Julie Hammer*, p. 5.

18 Ibid, p. 6.

19 Ibid, p. 8.

20 Ibid, p. 10.

21 Hammer, 8 March 2023.

Group Captain Jenny Fantini

1 Kirrily Dearing, *Kirrily Dearing interviews Jenny Fantini* [unpublished interview transcript], Royal Australian Air Force, 30 April 2023.

2 Ibid.

3 Ibid.

4 Ibid.

5 Ibid.

6 Ibid.

7 Ibid.

8 Ibid.

9 Ibid.

10 Ibid.

11 Ibid.

12 Ibid.

13 Ibid.

14 Ibid.

15 Ibid.

16 Ibid.

17 Ibid.

Society's attitudes and national policies: the impact on women in the Air Force

1 Christine Reghenzani, 'Women in the ADF: six decades of policy change (1950 to 2011)', Department of Parliamentary Services, Parliament of Australia (November 2015), p. 5.

2 Anne Heywood, 'Women's Auxiliary Australian Air Force (WAAAF)', *The Australian Women's Register*, 5 June 2009, at https://www.womenaustralia.info/entries/womens-auxiliary-australian-air-force-waaaf/.

3 Reghenzani, 'Women in the ADF', p. 7.

4 Ibid., p. 12.

5 Mark Lax, 'Women in the RAAF' in *Taking the Lead: The Royal Australian Air Force 1972–1996*, Simon and Schuster, Cammeray, 2020, p. 193.

6 Ibid., pp. 192–93.

7 Ibid., p. 199.

8 Reghenzani, 'Women in the ADF', p. 9.

9 Finance Circular No. 1965/10, 19 March 1965, Commonwealth of Australia, Canberra.

10 Lax, 'Women in the RAAF', p. 199.

11 Ibid.

12 Ibid., p. 195.

13 Reghenzani, 'Women in the ADF', p. 13.

14 Lax, 'Women in the RAAF', p. 202.

15 '3. Women in Combat Duties - Reservation Withdrawal', *Parliament of Australia*, n.d., at https://www.aph.gov.au/Parliamentary_Business/Committees/Joint/Electoral_Matters/VotingAge/Advisory_report/Section?id=committees%2Freportjnt%2F024073%2F24681.

THE 1980s

Introduction

1 Amy Tikkanen, 'Timeline of the 1980s', *Britannica*, n.d., at http://www.britannica.com/story/timeline-of-the-1980s.

2 Andrew Clark, 'The 1980s: When things actually happened', *The Australian Financial Review*, updated 30 September 2021, at https://www.afr.com/politics/federal/the-1980s-when-things-actually-happened-20220118-p59p9k.

3 Hugh Smith, 'Women in the Australian Defence Force: In Line for the Front Line?', *The Australian Quarterly*, vol. 62, no. 2, p. 129.

4 'ABC Archives and Library Services', *Australian Broadcasting Corporation*, updated 2002, athttps://www.abc.net.au/archives/timeline/1980s.htm; Clark, 'The 1980s'.

5 Smith, 'Women in the Australian Defence Force', p. 132.

Air Vice-Marshal Tracy Smart

1 'Air Vice-Marshal Tracy Smart', *Air Force 2021*, n.d., at https://airforce2021.airforce.gov.au/people/tracy-smart.

2 Brett Williamson, 'Air Vice Marshal Tracy Smart: From country girl to Australian Defence Force Surgeon General', *ABC News*, 18 July 2016, at https://www.abc.net.au/news/2016-07-18/from-country-girl-to-adf-surgeon-general-tracy-smart/7637582.

3 'Air Vice-Marshal Tracy Smart', *Air Force 2021*.

4 Ibid.

5 Phil Morrall, *Phil Morrall interviews Tracy Smart* [unpublished interview transcript], Royal Australian Air Force, 4 August 2009, p. 2.

6 Ibid., p. 3.

7 Ibid., p. 4.

8 Ibid., p. 2.

9 'United Nations Transitional Administration In East Timor: UNTAET', *United Nations*, updated 2001 at: https://peacekeeping.un.org/sites/default/files/past/etimor/etimor.htm

10 Morrall, *Phil Morrall interviews Tracy Smart*, p. 6.

11 Ibid., p. 7.

12 Ibid., p. 9.

13 Ibid., p. 13.

14 Tracy Smart, email to Kirrily Dearing, 10 July 2023.

15 Megan Doherty, 'Defence surgeon Tracy Smart to tackle next challenge after decades in the job', *The Canberra Times*, 13 September 2019 at: https://www.canberratimes.com.au/story/6291346/defence-surgeon-to-tackle-next-challenge-after-decades-in-the-job/

16 Ibid.

17 Ibid.

18 Ibid.

Warrant Officer Melinda Skinner

1 Kirrily Dearing, *Kirrily Dearing interviews Melinda Skinner* [unpublished interview transcript], Royal Australian Air Force, 31 May 2023, p. 6.

2 Ibid.

3 Ibid., pp. 7–8.

4 Ibid., pp. 10–11.

5 Ibid., pp. 14–15.

6 Ibid., p. 16.

7 Ibid., pp. 17–18.

8 Ibid., p. 19.

9 Ibid., pp. 20–1.

10 Ibid., p. 24.

11 Ibid., pp. 29–30.

12 Ibid., p. 31.

13 Ibid., pp. 33–4.

14 Ibid., p. 39.

15 Ibid., p. 43.

16 Ibid., p. 50.

Warrant Officer Michelle Hardy

1 Michelle Hardy [question and answer transcript], 28 April 2023.

2 Kirrily Dearing, *Kirrily Dearing interviews Michelle Hardy* [unpublished interview transcript], Royal Australian Air Force, 16 May 2023, pp. 4–5.

3 Ibid., p. 11.

4 Hardy, 28 April 2023.

5 Dearing, *Kirrily Dearing interviews Michelle Hardy*, pp. 19–20.

6 Ibid., p. 26.

7 Ibid., pp. 27–9.

8 Ibid., pp. 31–2.

9 Hardy, 28 April 2023.

10 Dearing, *Kirrily Dearing interviews Michelle Hardy*, pp. 40–1.

11 Ibid., p. 46.

12 Ibid., pp. 53–4

13 Ibid., pp. 54–5.

14 Ibid., p. 55.

15 Ibid., pp. 56–7.

THE 1990s

Introduction

1 'Australia in the 1990s', *My Place*, n.d., at https://myplace.edu.au/decades_timeline/decade/1990; Andrew Clark, 'Aspirational 1990s marked the start of Australia's modern prosperity', *The Australian Financial Review*, updated 24 February 2022, at https://www.afr.com/policy/economy/aspirational-1990s-marked-the-start-of-australia-s-modern-prosperity-20220223-p59z43.

2 'Australia in the 1990s', *My Place*; Clark, 'Aspirational 1990s marked the start of Australia's modern prosperity'.

3 'Australia in the 1990s', *My Place*.

4 'The Defence of Australia (1994 Defence White Paper)', *Parliament of Australia*, undated, at https://www.aph.gov.au/About_Parliament/Parliamentary_departments/Parliamentary_Library/pubs/rp/rp1516/DefendAust/1994.

5 Mark Lax, 'Women in the RAAF' in *Taking the Lead: The Royal Australian Air Force 1972–1996*, Simon and Schuster, Cammeray, 2020; 'Women in the Service' in *Customs and Traditions Manual*, Department of Defence, Canberra, unpublished; Christine Reghenzani, 'Women in the ADF: six decades of policy change (1950 to 2011)', Department of Parliamentary Services, Parliament of Australia (November 2015); Chris Clark, 'Women in the RAAF – Talking Points', *Department of Defence*, Canberra, unpublished.

Group Captain Hannah Jude-Smith

1 Kirrily Dearing, *Kirrily Dearing interviews Hannah Jude-Smith* [unpublished interview transcript], Royal Australian Air Force, 25 May 2023, pp. 3–4.

2 Ibid.

3 Ibid., p. 5.

4 Ibid., p. 12.

5 Ibid., p. 14.

6 Ibid., p. 18.

7 Ibid., p. 19.

8 Ibid., p. 23.

9 Ibid., p. 20.

10 Ibid., p. 27.

11 Ibid., p. 30.

12 Ibid., pp. 30–1.

13 Ibid., pp. 33–4.

14 Ibid., p. 47.

15 Ibid., p. 66.

16 Ibid., p. 44.

17 Ibid., p. 50.

18 Ibid., p. 63.

The evolution of women's uniforms

1 John McDonald, 'Women's services 1944–1977' in *Shades of Blue*, Department of Defence, Canberra, unpublished.

2 Ibid.

3 Ibid.

4 Ibid.

5 Ibid.

6 'Women's Auxiliary Australian Air Force (WAAAF) Uniform worn by Ena Wilson', *Australian Dress Register*, undated, at https://australiandressregister.org/garment/538/.

7 GL Banning, 'Origins of uniforms, rank and insignia of the RAAF', *Department of Defence*, 23 September 2020, at http://drnet/raaf/AirForce/AirForceUniform/Pages/Uniform%20History.aspx.

8 'Marjorie Boyling WAAAF uniform', *Australian Dress Register*, undated, at https://australiandressregister.org/garment/275/; 'Women's Royal Australian Air Force (1951–1977)', *WRAAF Branch Qld*, updated 2009, at http://www.wraaf.org.au/History.html.

9 McDonald, 'Women's services 1944–1977'.

10 Ibid.

11 'Women's Royal Australian Air Force (1951–1977)', *WRAAF Branch Qld.*

12 Ibid; McDonald, 'Women's services 1944–1977'.

13 'WRAAF uniforms', *Radschool Association Inc.*, undated, at https://www.radschool.org.au/magazines/Vol73/Page15.htm#WRAAF%20Uniforms; 'Women's Royal Australian Air Force (1951–1977)', *WRAAF Branch Qld*; McDonald, 'Women's services 1944–77'.

14 McDonald, 'Women's services 1944–77'.

15 Banning, 'Origins of uniforms, rank and insignia of the RAAF'; John McDonald, 'Introduction of the all seasons uniform and clothing and insignia developments during the 1970s, 1980s and 1990s' in *Shades of Blue*, Department of Defence, Canberra, unpublished.

16 Banning, 'Origins of uniforms, rank and insignia of the RAAF'; McDonald, 'Introduction of the all seasons uniform and clothing and insignia developments during the 1970s, 1980s and 1990s'.

17 Banning, 'Origins of uniforms, rank and insignia of the RAAF'.

18 Ibid; McDonald, 'Introduction of the all seasons uniform and clothing and insignia developments during the 1970s, 1980s and 1990s'.

19 *Pregnancy, Maternity and Returning to Work Guide*, Version 2, September 2022, Department of Defence, Canberra, unpublished, p. 11.

THE 2000s

Introduction

1 'Australia in the 2000s', *My Place*, undated, at https://myplace.edu.au/decades_timeline/decade/2000.

2 Andrew Clark, '70 years in Australian business as told through the archives', *The Australian Financial Review*, undated, at https://www.afr.com/about-us/timeline; 'Australia in the 2000s', *My Place.*

3 Clark, '70 years in Australian business as told through the archives'; 'RAAF personnel deployed to international coalition based in Kyrgyzstan', *Royal Australian Air Force*, undated, at https://www.airforce.gov.au/about-us/history/our-journey/raaf-personnel-deployed-international-coalition-based-kyrgyzstan; 'Last Combat Mission of Iraq War', *Royal Australian Air Force*, undated, at https://www.airforce.gov.au/about-us/history/our-journey/last-combat-mission-iraq-war; 'Bali Bombing', *Royal Australian Air Force*, undated, at https://www.airforce.gov.au/about-us/history/our-journey/bali-bombing; 'Indonesian Tsunami', *Royal Australian Air Force*, undated, at https://www.airforce.gov.au/about-us/history/our-journey/indonesian-tsunami.

4 Christine Reghenzani, 'Women in the ADF: six decades of policy change (1950 to 2011)', Department of Parliamentary Services, Parliament of Australia, November 2015; Mark Lax, 'Women in the RAAF' in *Taking the Lead: The Royal Australian Air Force 1972–1996*, Simon and Schuster, Cammeray, 2020; 'Women in the Service' in *Customs and Traditions Manual*, Department of Defence, Canberra, unpublished.

Sergeant Jade Evans

1 Jade Evans [question and answer transcript], 2 May 2023.

2 Kirrily Dearing, *Kirrily Dearing interviews Jade Evans* [unpublished interview transcript], Royal Australian Air Force, 2 May 2023, p. 2.

3 Ibid.

4 Ibid., p. 5.

5 Ibid., p. 6.

6 Ibid., pp. 8–9.

7 Evans, 2 May 2023.

8 Dearing, *Kirrily Dearing interviews Jade Evans*, pp. 12–13.

9 Evans, 2 May 2023.

10 Dearing, *Kirrily Dearing interviews Jade Evans*, p. 13.

11 Ibid., p. 19.

12 Evans, 2 May 2023.

13 Dearing, *Kirrily Dearing interviews Jade Evans*, p. 26.
14 Ibid., p. 30.
15 Ibid., pp. 34–5.
16 Ibid., p. 32.
17 Ibid., p. 33.
18 Evans, 2 May 2023.

Flight Lieutenant Ingrid Van der Vlist

1 Ingrid Van der Vlist [question and answer transcript], 7 March 2023.
2 Ibid.
3 Kirrily Dearing, *Kirrily Dearing interviews Ingrid Van der Vlist* [unpublished interview transcript], Royal Australian Air Force, 2 May 2023, p. 5.
4 Ibid., p. 5.
5 Ibid., p. 10.
6 Ibid., pp. 13–14.
7 Ibid., pp. 20–2.
8 Ibid., p. 22–4.
9 Ibid., pp. 27–9.
10 Ibid., p. 30.
11 Ibid., p. 35.
12 Ibid., pp. 38–9.
13 Ibid., p. 44.
14 Ibid., p. 51.
15 Ibid., p. 53.
16 Ibid., pp. 57–8.
17 Ibid., pp. 60–1.
18 Ibid., p. 62.

Air Force women killed in service

1 'Commonwealth War Graves', *Commonwealth War Graves Commission*, updated 2023, at https://www.cwgc.org/; 'Roll of Honour', *Australian War Memorial*, updated 2023 at: https://www.awm.gov.au/advanced-search/people?roll=Roll%20of%20Honour.
2 'Diggles, Ray Silvester', *Virtual War Memorial Australia*, undated, at https://vwma.org.au/explore/people/625942; *Aviation Safety Net*, undated, at https://aviation-safety.net/database/record.php?id=19420227-2; Carey Margaret Jones 105088', *RAAFA Aviation Heritage Museum*, updated 2022, at https://aviationmuseumwa.org.au/afcraaf-roll/carey-margaret-jones-105088/.
3 'Marie Eileen Craig', *Australian War Memorial*, updated 2023, at https://www.awm.gov.au/collection/R1702456; Verdun Bernice Sheah', *Australian War Memorial*, updated 2023, at https://www.awm.gov.au/collection/R1717900.
4 Noting Brief for the Chief of the Defence Force, June 2019, *Department of Defence*, Canberra, unpublished.
5 Ibid; 'Marie Eileen Craig', *Australian War Memorial*; 'Verdun Bernice Sheah', *Australian War Memorial*.
6 Noting Brief for the Chief of the Defence Force, *Department of Defence*.

THE 2010s AND 2020s

Introduction

1 Sarah Maguire, 'The 2010s: A decade of disrupters', *Macquarie University*, updated 27 December 2019, at https://lighthouse.mq.edu.au/article/december-2019/The-2010s-A-decade-of-disrupters; Andrew Clark, 'How Australia became the "coup capital" of the world in the 2010s', *Australian Financial Review*, updated 22 April 22, at https://www.afr.com/policy/economy/how-australia-became-the-coup-capital-of-the-world-in-the-2010s-20220415-p5adqb; 'Australia in the 2010s', *My Place*, undated, at https://myplace.edu.au/decades_timeline/decade/2010.

2 Maguire, 'The 2010s'; Clark, 'How Australia became the "coup capital" of the world in the 2010s'; 'Australia in the 2010s', *My Place*.

3 'Our journey', *Royal Australian Air Force*, undated, at https://airforce2021.airforce.gov.au/journey.

4 Ibid.

5 Connie Dixon [personal correspondence], 2 May 2023.

6 Jess Stone [personal correspondence], 3 April 2023.

7 Dixon, 2 May 2023.

8 Ibid.

9 Stone, 3 April 2023.

10 Ibid.

11 Dixon, 2 May 2023.

12 Stone, 3 April 2023.

13 Dixon, 2 May 2023.

14 Ibid.

15 Stone, 3 April 2023.

Flight Lieutenant Olivia Little

1 Kirrily Dearing, *Kirrily Dearing interviews Olivia Little* [unpublished interview transcript], Royal Australian Air Force, 2 May 2023.

2 Ibid.

3 Ibid.

4 Ibid.

5 Ibid.

6 Ibid.

7 Ibid.

8 Ibid.

9 Ibid.

10 Ibid.

11 Ibid.

12 Ibid.

13 Ibid.

Sergeant Brodie Stewart

1 Kirrily Dearing, *Kirrily Dearing interviews Brodie Stewart* [unpublished interview transcript], Royal Australian Air Force, 16 May 2023, pp. 2–4.

2 Ibid.

3 Ibid., pp. 6–7.

4 Ibid., p. 4.

5 Ibid., p. 9.

6 Ibid., p. 13.

7 Brodie Stewart [question and answer transcript], 1 March 2023.

8 Dearing, *Kirrily Dearing interviews Brodie Stewart*, p. 14.

9 Ibid., pp. 17–18.

10 Ibid., p. 26.

11 Ibid., pp. 28–30.

12 Ibid., p. 46.

13 Stewart, 1 March 2023.

14 Dearing, *Kirrily Dearing interviews Brodie Stewart*, p. 58.

15 Ibid., pp. 69–70.

16 Ibid., p. 82.

17 Ibid., p. 89.

18 Ibid., pp. 96–7.

19 Ibid., p. 98–9.

20 Ibid., p. 111.

21 Stewart, 1 March 2023.

Flight Lieutenant Dani Cornish

1 Dani Cornish [question and answer transcript], 6 July 2023.

2 Ibid.

3 Ibid.

4 Ibid.

5 Ibid.

6 Ibid.

7 Ibid.

8 Ibid.

9 Ibid.

10 Ibid.

11 Dani Cornish [personal correspondence], 13 July 2023.

12 Cornish, 6 July 2023.

13 Ibid.

Leading Aircraftwoman Kate Clarkson

1 Kate Clarkson [question and answer transcript], 30 April 2023.

2 Ibid.

3 Ibid.

4 Kirrily Dearing, *Kirrily Dearing interviews Kate Clarkson* [unpublished interview transcript], Royal Australian Air Force, 15 May 2023, p. 12.

5 Ibid., p. 15.

6 Ibid., p. 18.

7 Ibid., p. 23.

8 Ibid.

9 Ibid., p. 27.

10 Ibid., p. 29.

11 Ibid., p. 35.

12 Clarkson, 30 April 2023.

13 Ibid.

14 Ibid.

15 Ibid.

16 Dearing, *Kirrily Dearing interviews Kate Clarkson*, p. 48.

17 Ibid., p. 54.

Leading Aircraftwoman Emma Gall

1 Emma Gall [question and answer transcript], 13 March 2023.

2 Ibid.

3 Kirrily Dearing, *Kirrily Dearing interviews Emma Gall* [unpublished interview transcript], Royal Australian Air Force, 16 May 2023, p. 13.

4 Ibid., pp. 13–14.

5 Ibid., p. 14.

6 Ibid., p. 19.

7 Ibid., p. 25.

8 Ibid., p. 30.

9 Ibid., p. 42.

10 Gall, 13 March 2023.

11 Dearing, *Kirrily Dearing interviews Emma Gall*, p. 51.

12 Gall, 13 March 2023.

13 Dearing, *Kirrily Dearing interviews Emma Gall*, p. 55.

14 Ibid., p. 56.

15 Ibid., p. 58.

16 Ibid., pp. 61–2.

17 Gall, 13 March 2023.

18 Ibid.

Leading Aircraftwoman Paige Boyd

1 Kirrily Dearing, *Kirrily Dearing interviews Paige Boyd* [unpublished interview transcript], Royal Australian Air Force, 16 May 2023, pp. 10–1.

2 Ibid., p. 2.

3 Ibid., p. 5.

4 Ibid., p. 10

5 Ibid., pp. 10–1.

6 Ibid., p. 11.

7 Ibid., p. 13.

8 Ibid., p. 15.

9 Ibid., p. 20.

10 Paige Boyd [question and answer transcript], 22 March 2023.

11 Dearing, *Kirrily Dearing interviews Paige Boyd*, pp. 26–7.

12 Boyd, 22 March 2023.

Leading Aircraftwoman Kobey Misios

1 Kirrily Dearing, *Kirrily Dearing interviews Kobey Misios* [unpublished interview transcript], Royal Australian Air Force, 15 July 2023, pp. 7–8.

2 Kobey Misios [question and answer transcript], 18 May 2023.

3 Dearing, *Kirrily Dearing interviews Kobey Misios*, pp. 7–8.

4 Ibid., p. 3.

5 Ibid.

6 Ibid., p. 5.

7 Misios, 18 May 2023.

8 Ibid.

9 Dearing, *Kirrily Dearing interviews Kobey Misios*, p. 13.

10 Misios, 18 May 2023.

11 Dearing, *Kirrily Dearing interviews Kobey Misios*, pp. 14–15.

12 Ibid., p. 22.

13 Ibid., p. 9.

14 Ibid., p. 32.

15 Ibid., p. 24.

16 Ibid., pp. 28–9.

17 Ibid., pp. 34–5.

Sport and service

1 'W.A.A.A.F. Sports Held At Wagga', *Daily Advertiser*, 28 August 1944, at https://trove.nla.gov.au/newspaper/article/144857398/15781771.

2 'City Parade And Sports W.A.A.A.F. Anniversary', *Newcastle Morning Herald and Miners' Advocate*, 22 March 1943, at https://trove.nla.gov.au/newspaper/article/140443602?searchTerm=waaaf%20sports.

3 'Girls with sports ability volunteer for W.A.A.A.F.', *The Telegraph*, 5 Jan 1942, p. 7.

4 Robert Hodgson, 'Air Force Olympian achieves several firsts', *Defence News*, 4 August 2021, at https://www.defence.gov.au/news-events/news/2021-08-04/air-force-olympian-achieves-several-firsts.

5 Ibid.